GLAST⦵50⦵NBURY

GLAST⦵NBURY 50

MICHAEL EAVIS & EMILY EAVIS

TRAPEZE

'Love to faults is always blind;
Always is to joy inclin'd,
Lawless, wing'd and unconfin'd,
And breaks all chains from every mind.'

WILLIAM BLAKE

TICKETS ARE SOLD SUBJECT TO THE FOLLOWING CONDITIONS.

1) The organisers reserve the right to refuse admission. (ticket money paid may be refunded to anyone refused admission)

2) Tickets will not be exchanged or money refunded (except as above)

3) The organisers reserve the right to alter any announced billing of bands or other events.

4) The organisers reserve the right to make changes, if necessary due to unavoidable circumstances, to any of the Fayre arrangements.

Worthy Farm
POP FESTIVAL
Pilton, Shepton Mallet, Som.
Saturday, 19th September, 1970
Commencing 10 a.m.
Week-end Camp
★ THE KINKS ★
WAYNE FONTANA and at least
SIX OTHER GROUPS ! !
Ticket £1
Compere : D.J. MAD MICK

Midsummer 21st–23rd June 1979

3 DAYS GREEN £5
2 DAYS BLUE £4
1 DAY RED £3
INC____VAT

№ 01041   № 01041

I have received full payment for the security of the 1979 Pilton Festival

25-6-81

Stop Press !
THESE ADDITIONAL GROUPS HAVE NOW BEEN BOOKED
★ Steamhammer   ★ Alan Bown
          ★ Marsupilami
★ Duster Bennett, Ian Anderson & Ian Hunt
★ Stackeridge   ★ Amazing Blondel

Dependent upon size of audience, possibility of "unadvertised" session; if audience is large enough to warrant it, some bands asked to perform again on the Sunday.

This Festival is organised by Michael Eavis on his own property, which comprises 110 acres of pasture land and provides a superb setting for this occasion. All the farm's milk supply is being given free to campers and adequate catering facilities are available.

Walton Press, Benedict Street, Glastonbury   Tel. 3511

Glastonbury Fayre
1979

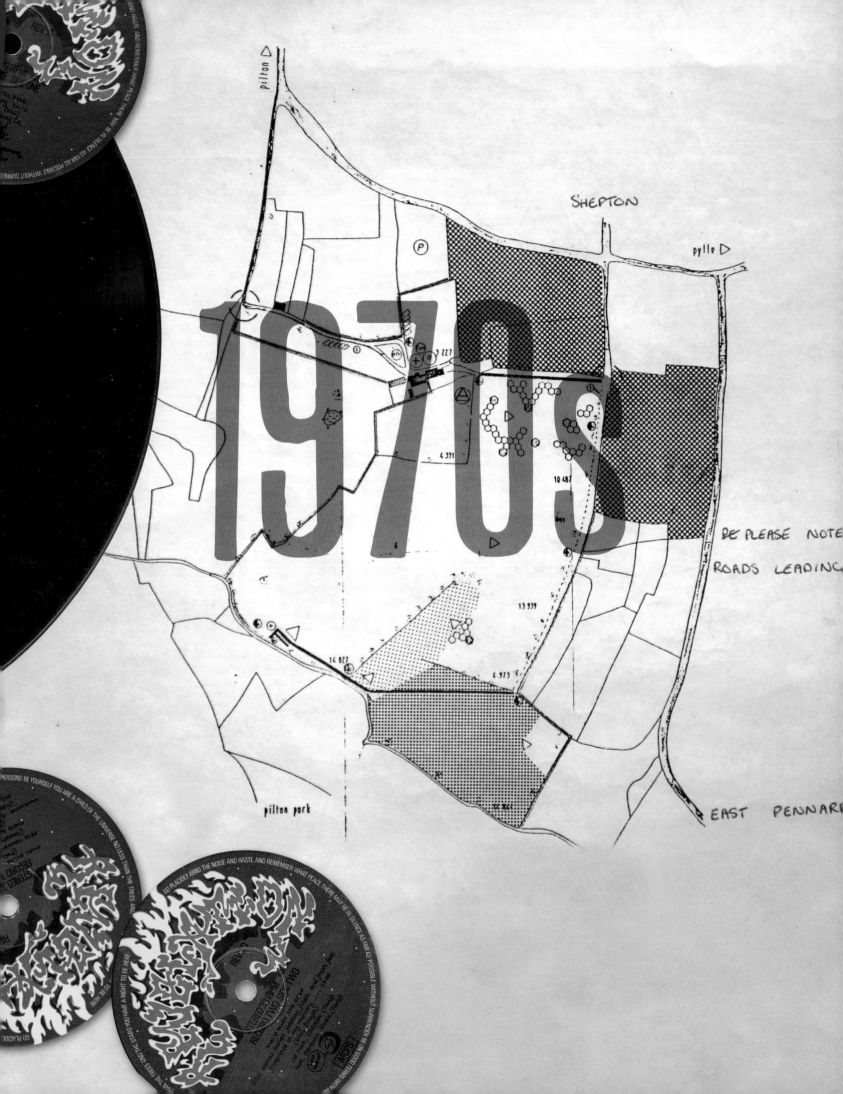

Michael

I was born in 1935 in Pilton, where the Festival is still held. Not at Worthy Farm, though; just down the road, in a house that is still there. My mother and father met playing tennis at Cranmore in 1934. My mother came from Penge, on the outskirts of London, and my father was a Somerset farmer who also happened to be a preacher. My mother was a city girl at heart, but that didn't stop them falling in love, and they actually ended up conceiving me before they were married. That was a hell of a thing, not least because of my father being a preacher. He had to swear on the Bible to the superintendent minister that they hadn't had me out of wedlock. Luckily he didn't mind telling a few fibs, my old man.

We moved to Worthy Farm in 1944, which my father shared with his brother. My father would milk the cows by hand and our only transport was horse and cart. My childhood was a very happy one, and I had a secure life, though I think I was quite a shy child, possibly because I stammered quite a lot.

Methodism was a big part of our family life. There was no questioning whether there was a God; it was accepted that that was the truth, and it had quite a big impact on me. John Wesley, who founded Methodism, essentially said that without social responsibility there is no religion, and that has certainly been a driving force of Glastonbury. The truth is, I could have been driving around in a Ferrari by now from the proceeds of the Festival, but I'd feel so guilty if we didn't use our money to do some good. That's Methodism for you.

I had quite a lofty education, boarding at Wells Cathedral School, which was paid for by my mother's inheritance from her father. My dad would have preferred to send me to school in Shepton, but my mother was adamant. It would be fair to say that my classmates at the Cathedral School weren't generally the children of farmers. They came from some of the area's wealthier families and went on to do high-powered jobs, like my friend Bob Thomson, who ended up becoming the boss of the Royal Society of Medicine. He'd told me to pop in to see him if I was ever in London, so I turned up at this very grand office at 1 Wimpole Street, still very much the country boy, and asked to see Bob Thomson. The receptionist looked at me quite sternly and said, 'Do you mean Mr Robert Thomson?'

I've always been into boats, and as a child I had a little toy motorboat that I loved. One day it went underneath a bridge and I never found it again – I was distraught. Maybe that boat was part of why I always wanted to go to sea. My mother pushed me a bit too, saying, 'You don't want this farming life, do you?' We used to sing Methodist hymns around the piano twice a week, and there was a picture perched on top of the piano of my mum's first cousin, who was a commander in the Royal Australian Navy. He was really good-looking, in this amazing uniform. I remember thinking that I wanted to be like that chap and, years later, when I was fourteen, I applied to join the navy. My mother encouraged me, and her cousin helped get me into Thames Nautical Training College, situated on HMS *Worcester* on the River Thames in London.

First in show: Michael as a child in the Vale of Avalon (above); and ready for sea with the Merchant Navy, aged 15 (opposite).

I was fifteen when I went there in 1950, which was quite young to leave home, and I was a bit frightened. I remember going to Bath to collect my uniform, with its shiny brass buttons – I was so proud of it. On the day of my departure, I dressed in my uniform and went to say goodbye to my father, who was milking the cows. 'I'm off now, Daddy,' I said, and he just broke down in tears. I was never as close to my father as I was to my mother, and I'd never seen him cry before. I think he was touched by the contrast between me in the uniform and him doing what he was doing, sitting on a stool milking the cows. He was overwhelmed by it all. I was a young, smart, good-looking fifteen-year-old and I was making a break for it. I think that was the moment when he realised I was gone, and that I wasn't going to follow his lifestyle.

Nautical training college was an instrumental experience for me: there was a lot of discipline and a lot of pressure to get decent grades in order to go off to sea. I learnt all about navigation, using sextants, and even how to find my way by looking at the stars and the moon.

In the end I managed to scrape a first-class pass, and I joined the Merchant Navy. I was assigned to the Union-Castle shipping company and we travelled all over the world in amazing, beautiful ships. They were mail ships, so we'd bring post to and from Cape Town, while also transporting passengers and freight. We'd carry anything from bananas to animals, and because they knew about my farming background, they'd have me looking after any livestock. I once came back with two elephants for London Zoo. I had to make sure we had one on either side of the ship, so that it didn't topple.

My affection for the farm grew the further away I was – it became a very romantic thing. But the Merchant Navy was a life I enjoyed, so my plan was to do it until I was about forty and then retire and return to Somerset to run the farm.

But then, when I was nineteen, my father was diagnosed with terminal cancer and I had to come home. I phoned Union-Castle and told them that I couldn't go on the next ship because my father was ill, but my uncle also worked there, and he put a lot of pressure on me to stay. He said that he'd had reports from Union-Castle that I'd been doing really well and they had high hopes for me. But I knew I had to return to the farm. It was my duty to get stuck in, and I felt it was my rightful place to be.

I was seriously upset when my mother told me she had some bad news and that my father wasn't going to live. That was the point when I really cried. But then I had about six months to prepare for his death, although we tried not to talk about it. My mother was

quite tough. I never saw her cry. But I was at my father's bedside with my mother when he died, and I was glad that I'd come back.

After he died, the responsibility was on my shoulders. My mother said, 'You need to see the bank manager; he wants to talk to you about the future of the farm.' I'd never seen a bank manager in my life at that point. So off I went to an appointment with Mr Giddings, who told me that my mother would rather sell the farm so she could move away and start teaching again. She was only forty-seven, and she had a whole life in front of her. Mr Giddings had a customer willing to buy the farm for £12,000, but I couldn't countenance selling. The farm had been in my family for more than a hundred years and I had a deep connection to it.

In the end, the bank manager loaned me the £12,000 to give to my mother to retire. He said that he thought I wasn't a farmer and I wouldn't be able to do it, but that he'd give me a couple of years to see how I got on, and then I could always sell the farm and go back to sea. He told me he'd have the deeds in his drawer, waiting.

It was a big responsibility for a nineteen-year-old to take on, but I really got stuck in. I had to find a job in the village for the chap who was working for my father, because there was no way I could afford to pay his wages. And then I did it all myself.

It was very hard work. I spent my twenties struggling like mad to keep it going and not let Mr Giddings down. I married Ruth, a local girl I'd known since childhood, but I'm afraid I was a pretty dreadful husband. I was trying to make the farm work, seven days a week, with no help at all. We had three children, one after another, but I just wasn't in a position to have children – I didn't have any money or anything. It wasn't a happy time. Ruth did her best, but I was in a terrible place and it didn't work out for us.

I first saw Jean in Knight's chip shop in Glastonbury town, which is still there, in 1964, and fell in love. She was very beautiful and we shared similar roots, her having taught at the Methodist Sunday School in Glastonbury when she was younger. When we started seeing each other, everything fell into place. She loved the farm, enjoyed working on it and, like me, she had a passion for music.

Music had always been a big part of my life. I discovered Radio Luxembourg when I was at boarding school, and I'd listen to it every Sunday night, when Pete Murray and David Jacobs were on. Bill Haley and Bob Dylan captured my imagination, and although I never really went to concerts, I fell in love with pop music.

Before I met Jean, I'd rigged up a very primitive sound system to play music to myself and the cows in the parlour. It was a nine-foot-long pipe connected to a speaker and it made a hell of a sound. I used to play 'Lola' by the Kinks a lot – that was our big milking song.

One day in 1970, our baker lady who used to deliver bread to the farm arrived late. She told me it was because she'd been held up in all the traffic going to the blues festival. I had no idea what she was talking about. She told me it was this big event happening at the Bath & West Showground, a few miles from the farmhouse, and there were millions of people coming for it. 'That sounds amazing!' I said, to which she replied, 'No, it's horrible!'

Jean and I agreed that we should go there on the Sunday, after chapel, and it was absolutely incredible. They had Led Zeppelin and Pink Floyd and all these West Coast American bands. It was the whole flower-power era, and all the girls and blokes looked amazing. It was a very lovey-dovey affair, and emotional, too. I'd never seen anything like it in my life before – it just hit me for six.

We were standing there in this huge crowd and I turned to Jean and said, 'I'm going to do one of these on the farm!' If I remember rightly, her reply was, 'Don't be silly, you've no idea how.'

She was right, of course. I had absolutely no idea how to organise a concert. But the next morning, I called up Colston Hall in Bristol – which was the biggest venue in our area – and asked the girl for a number for the Kinks, our favourite band from the parlour. She told me you could buy a thing called the White Book from WHSmith, which was £6 and had all the numbers for talent agents in. But £6 was quite a lot for me at the time, so I said, 'Yeah, but please can you give me the Kinks' number now?' And luckily she did.

I called up their manager and said I'd never done anything like this before, but I wanted the Kinks to play a festival on my farm. He said, 'Okay, we'll do it for £500.' Looking back, I can't believe how easy it was. I decided to only charge a pound for a ticket, which was much less than the blues festival had been, but I thought, Well, we only need 500 people to pay for the band.

That was in June, and I booked them for September, so I'd only given myself three months to organise my first ever event. I was just so excited, though. I was really carried away – I couldn't think of anything else for the entire time.

I didn't think to get in touch with the organiser of the blues festival – a guy called Freddy Bannister – to ask for help. He never did another event at the showground as he moved on to Knebworth, but he did call me years and years later and say, 'So, I hear I inspired Glastonbury Festival. Am I going to get any commission?'

Of course, I had to announce to the people in Pilton village that I was putting on a festival, which was a bit of a sticky situation. My standing in the village was low because

Michael and Jean Eavis together at Worthy Farm, 1970 (below); and (opposite) the 'world exclusive' news story in the Pilton parish magazine where Michael set out his early vision for the Festival.

PILTON GOES POP. A digest of the proposed pop festival, by Mr. Michael Evis.

Thank you for giving me the opportunity to explain to the village the details of my pop music venture, at Worthy Farm.

The first, and probably the most important fact is that it will in no way resemble the "Blues Festival" at the Fair Ground of the Bath and West. One reason for this is that I have only spent a hundredth part of their costs, which accounts for my estimate of 2000 as the probable number of audience. The type of music which I envisage is basically POP with a more local appeal. It is not expected that people will come from a great distance especially in view of the fact that the Isle of Wight Festival will have taken place only 3 weeks previously.

I wish to give the image of a Festival to celebrate the incoming of the Harvest, and if the sale of tickets is sufficient to justify it, to include the roasting of an ox over an open fire.

I have booked ten groups which will provide 12 hours of "live" music from 2 p.m. to 2 a.m. on Saturday and Sunday night 19-20th September. The bands vary in type from the KINKS to the MARSUPALAMI (in which Jessica Stanley Clarke plays).

I think anyone would agree that the site of Worthy Farm is a suitable venue for such an occasion and is sufficiently distant from the village as not to cause a nuisance. I also intend to use the road from Springfields pass Stricklands shop, up Copse Hill and directly to the farm, and in this way passing only four houses and so leaving the other roads free.

I certainly do not anticipate any trouble, but if there is, I will be personally responsible. I hope to be still around when it is all over and prepared to meet any complaints. I neither expect to make a fortune nor to disappear to the Bahamas. In fact I will be fortunate if I cover my costs.

-5-

I'd left Ruth, who everyone saw as the perfect, angelic wife, and our three lovely daughters. The vicar thought I was headed for the lap of the devil, but he still let me print an announcement in the parish magazine about the festival. I think it would be fair to say that people weren't too impressed with the idea of hundreds of music fans turning up in their village, but I ploughed on regardless.

I phoned up the local paper, and the *NME* and *Melody Maker*, and asked them to write about it. Then disaster struck. The Kinks pulled out. They saw the piece in *Melody Maker* and I think it made them feel like this mini-festival run by a farmer was a bit beneath them.

And, to be fair, it was. I had nothing apart from the idea, which they had twigged. They were spot on, really.

I thought, Oh my God, I'm going to have to cancel this. But my eldest daughter, Juliet, who was nine or ten at the time, said, 'Daddy, you can't! You'll look such a fool if you cancel.' So I decided that I had to keep it going one way or another. I phoned the Kinks' agent and he said, 'Well, as luck would have it, I've got Marc Bolan from T. Rex going through to play at Butlin's in Minehead on the same weekend, and he'll do it for the same £500.' I counted my lucky stars.

I was thirty-four when I organised that first Festival in 1970.

I discovered that I could take the strain without cracking up. In fact, it turned into a bit of a buzz. The stress of it all became almost like a drug. Life before that had just been carrying on much the same, and I'd been getting migraines in the mornings. The Festival stopped them, just like that. I think the stress was good for my head.

The day of the Festival came on 19 September 1970, and a lot of nice people, hippies really, turned up saying, 'This is a really cool place! It's magic!' 'Really?' I'd reply. 'I've always found it a bit of a drag!'

It was the first time I'd met people like that, as Jean and I hadn't really interacted with anyone at the blues festival. We'd just observed. But we spoke to our guests about the big anti-Vietnam movement, which really appealed to me. And, of course, there was all that incredible music.

It was the day after Jimi Hendrix died, and that was such a big thing. It really affected people, and it felt like the Festival was a tribute to him in a way – like we were celebrating his life.

I'd never met a rock star before, and Marc Bolan turned up in this incredible car – a huge American model, about eight-foot wide – which he'd covered in velvet, because he was glam rock. The problem was, he had to drive it down Muddy Lane to get onto the site, and because it was September there were thorns everywhere.

'I'm not going down there, there are too many brambles,' he said. I was telling him it'd be all right, while trying to brush off all the thorns that were sticking in the velvet. 'Get off my car, man!' was his response. He was very cross, and clearly wishing he hadn't turned up, but I replied, 'Look, you're going to have to go down there – please. There are people waiting to listen to you.'

He made it eventually, and his show was absolutely fantastic – he was just out of this world. It was so inspiring to see the sun going down behind the little makeshift stage. And I think that set was what inspired me to carry on. I actually couldn't pay him afterwards, though, because I didn't have any money. I had to tell his agent that I'd pay him £100 a month for five months from the milk profits. And that's what I did.

That first Festival was an incredible experience, and I think people enjoyed it, but a month or two after it I was feeling pretty depressed. There's actually a picture of me on the wall in Emily's office today, in which I'm staring at the ground like I'm thinking, My God, what have I done? I can remember exactly how I felt when that picture was taken. I'd lost a lot of money and things had got out of control – in truth, I didn't know what I was doing. The event had been great, but I was absolutely penniless. It had all been hot air and magic.

I think Jean was still a bit embarrassed about the whole thing at that point. Her family did quality control at the sheepskin factory in Street, and they were real disciplinarians. They all thought the Festival was just a whole lot of hippies wandering about being lazy and not working. Jean's family did eventually come round to thinking that I was a good bloke, but it took a long time to get there.

'And it will be free . . .': Andrew Kerr, once Randolph Churchill's private secretary, moved from London to the West Country with dreams of establishing an alternative gathering.

Despite everything, I wanted to carry it on. There was already something really important about it to me.

By then, word had started to spread, and a man called Andrew Kerr, who'd been planning to do a free Glastonbury fair somewhere near the town, heard about it. He came down to see me with Arabella Churchill, Winston Churchill's granddaughter, and John Michell, a famous writer who'd developed the 'Earth mysteries' movement and believed that the Glastonbury area had a sacred power. I got to know John quite well, and he did some dowsing, playing about with hazel twigs, to work out where the first Pyramid Stage should be. A mate of Andrew's called Bill Harkin came up with the idea of the Pyramid. He was an architect and he wanted to recreate the Great Pyramid of Giza. It did look good at night when it was lit up, but it wasn't weatherproof. When it rained, the bands had to stop playing.

Andrew's gang were all slightly off their heads with LSD and they were smoking all day long, which I was a bit annoyed about. I wasn't into drugs at all – I never have been. By then, I had four children – I'd had a son with Jean – and a huge responsibility to Mr Giddings the bank manager to succeed with the farm. I couldn't muck around with stuff like that.

I allowed the 1971 Festival to happen, but it wasn't my event. It became quite a trendy thing. It really caught the attention of the media, I think because of Arabella – who was quite well-known – and all the highfalutin stuff they were saying about doing away with capitalism, the summer solstice, the anti-war movement and having a more sharing society.

A lot of their ideals seemed to fit with my Methodism, particularly being against war and having a more egalitarian society. So I was mentally on board with it all and I was excited by the concept, plus they were going to give me some rent which would help pay off my debts. But the reality was different. There were all these crazy people on acid everywhere and it was quite frightening. I had nothing in common with those people.

Then, at the end, they all ran away and left me in even more debt. It was a right mess. The farm was a state, people hadn't been paid, it wasn't a nice thing at all. Andrew didn't have the means to pay for all his ideas and I had to foot all the bills. It turned out that for all their well-meaning ideas and theories they didn't really care. They had a good time and they weren't worried about the consequences of it. I wouldn't say I enjoyed that Festival.

Arabella did come back, though. I think she realised I'd been a bit of a rock in 1971 and so she attached herself to me. And although we didn't put on another Festival until the end of the decade, we continued through the seventies with lots of unofficial, free events where people just turned up at the farm and partied for a few days. There was one of these every year, and I enjoyed hanging out with the people who came. There was a rapport developing.

In 1979, Arabella came and said, 'Look, why don't we do a proper Festival again?' She had a bit more money to put into it, and she was working with Bill Harkin again. They told me that they knew what they were doing and that I should stay out of it, which I was happy enough to do.

But then, a few weeks before the event, they came to me and said, 'Michael, we're going to have to cancel the Festival because we've run out of money.' My heart sank. We had Peter Gabriel playing, and most of Genesis – to cancel would have been a nightmare. They were like that, though; if they ran into trouble, they'd just walk away. They didn't really stand their ground.

Eventually, they told me that if I could find £15,000 we could keep the Festival going. I went to see my bank manager in Wells, by then a man called John Williams, and he said, 'You must be off your head.' I told him I really did want to borrow the money, and he told me that he'd have to escalate it to his boss in Bristol. In the end they approved the loan, but I had to give them the deeds to the farm.

It was absolute madness, really. I could have lost the farm. I'd lost considerable amounts of money on the two occasions the Festival had happened previously. And, even though the milk price was quite good at that time, I was still only just breaking even on the farm side of things. But I knew we had some wonderful people playing, and I just thought it would be a goer. And because the bank in Bristol said, 'Make sure Mr Eavis signs every cheque himself or we won't honour them,' it meant I was back in charge of the show.

It was a marvellous event. The weather was nice – I dread to think what would have happened if it hadn't been – and the bands were great. John Martyn's set that year was one of my best Glastonbury moments. Twelve thousand people showed up. It was a huge success.

SHEPTON MA...
JOURNAL

MID-SOMERSET SERIES OF NEWSPAPERS

Thursday, June 7, 1979

Vol. CXXV—No. 23

£20,000 bill for Show mudbath

THE mudbath caused by heavy rain and thousands of cars and weary feet at the Bath and West showground and its car parks has left show organisers with a £20,000 task to put things right.

But the show society had one piece of good news this week when local grain merchants Sheldon Jones stepped in to provide free grass seed, and a North Humberside fertiliser company, Wills, offered to provide fertiliser.

Together, the gifts have knocked about £1,500 off the agricultural repair bill. Show publicity officer Wendy Tucker said the most pressing job was to remove quickly the tons of straw laid down in show-ground roadways.

"We've got to get every bit up as it could stop new grass growing through," she said.

Many of the car parks will have to be ploughed, harrowed and re-seeded.

Green light for festival but with many conditions

THE CONTROVERSIAL pop festival which is splitting Pilton in half is to go ahead on June 21, 22 and 23 with planning permission.

Villagers who crowded into Mendip Council's planning committee meeting on Tuesday lined three of the walls of the council chamber, many of them having to stand because seating accommodation was insufficient.

At the end of the debate, 13 members voted in favour of giving Mr. Michael Eavis planning permission for the festival at his Worthy Farm, Pilton—but with conditions attached. One lone member voted against permission.

VOTED AGAINST

Coun. Ken Flawn, who lives at Draycott, declared: "Even if we can't stop it, but if we can stop it, we sh...

They heard Mr. Raymond Bush, chief planning officer, say that the council had received 258 letters about the festival, 149 in favour of it and 109 against. Of the 149 supporters, 61 were Pilton people. Nearly all the 109 protesters lived in the village.

"Although in theory the option to refuse the application is open to the committee, it must consider how effective such a course of action would be. The applicant is well advised, and could, even following a refusal, still ... legally continue with ...

Mr. ...

of visitors are highly conjectural."

In a report to the committee, Mr. Joe Compton, chief environmental health officer, told the members: "It is my opinion that the event is likely to be on a scale which is out of proportion with the village, its facilities and its normal pace and way of life.

Mary Britton (right) local organiser for the Cystic Fibrosis R... Royal Bath and West Show last week. The m...

Homes crisis at Shepton for first-time buyers

FIRST-TIME home ... epton Mallet ...

NORTH & EAST SOMERSET EDITION

The Western C...

FOUNDED 1736: No. 12,617

FRIDAY, 8 JUNE, 1979

Licensees lose application

COUNCIL GIVE GO-AHEAD FOR FAYRE...

THE proposed three-day "Glastonbury Fayre" on Pilton's Worthy Farm pop f... site, has been given the official seal of approval.

With only one member voting against, Mendip District Council's Planning Committee o... day granted farmer Mr. Michael Eavis planning consent for the Midsummer extravaganza, on 21st June—but subject to a list of conditions.

The Shepton Mallet Council Chamber was crammed with members of the public. The majority were objectors from Pilton.

Whilst there were 109 letters of objection, Chief Planning Officer Mr. Raymond Bush up-dated his printed report by revealing the receipt of 149 letters in support of the Fayre (61 of them from Pilton itself).

He told the meeting: "While ... is a great deal of feeling in the village against the proposal, we have equally received very sincere letters from all shades of ... public who give ... feel the fayre should take place and indeed welcome it."

In his opinion, the event was going to be on a scale out of all proportion with the village, its facilities and its pace and way of life.

"Although in theory the option is open to the committee, it must consider what effective such a course of action would be. The applicant is well advised, and could, even following ...

Candidate row claim... 'vendetta'

BY MICHAEL CHAMBER...

...pendent candidate for the Wel... ... General Election, Mr. Gra... ... a special mee...

Problem of farmer turned pop promoter

14 SEP 1970

Mr. Michael Eavis (34) the farmer turned pop promoter, has a big problem down at 17th centu... Worthy Farm, Pilton.

When his dairy herd ... ready to be milked, he ... himself on one end ... telephone taking ... orders for his pop f... next week-end.

"It's fantastic. Eve... minutes the phone ... ing and I just c... away to see to th... said farmer Eavis.

Up till the mid-... week, he said, o... tickets had been ... But now it was...

Earlier in ... learned from ... London that a ... concert over ... an announce... over the pub... tem about ... farmer who ... promoter a... ly to be ... fans on S...

Said ... have r...

18 AUG 1970 W

My fears of failure, by pop festival farmer

Western Daily Press Report...

PILTON farmer, M... Michael Eavis, was l... night questioned for mo... than an hour by his paris...

Happ... pop show

2,500 gather at Pilton for weekend

Pilton's first Blues Festival, staged at the weekend ... Worthy Farm, Pilton, was described afterwards as a "fan-tastic success" by the organiser, Mr. Michael Eavis.

And although he did not quite manage to break even financially—2,500 fans came instead of the 3,000 needed to pay expenses—Mr. Eavis is far from despondent with the result of the festival.

"The incredible response I have had from the people who did come has wiped out the gloom of not managing to make a profit," he said.

"There is no question of my having to sell the farm or any part of it," he added. "Although I don't know exactly what my loss will be as yet, I can say that it will not be too great."

Ever since the weekend Mr. Eavis' telephone has been busy with callers, congratulating him on the show, and saying how sorry they were that he did not receive better support.

GROUPS ENTHUSIASTIC

"It was great to see ev... enjoying themselves se... tinued M...

tmosphere at

The 1971 Glastonbury Fair Pyramid Stage designer Bill Harkin (pictured right in 1971) and the sketch from his dream that led to its creation.

almost to the two thousand
everal local groups came
ng the evening there was a
ence as a mark of respect
itarist Jimi Hendrix who
e previous day. The
s death, felt by

The sparsely populated 'scene' at
the Pilton Pop Festival on
Saturday afternoon.

Mr. John Bak
Store

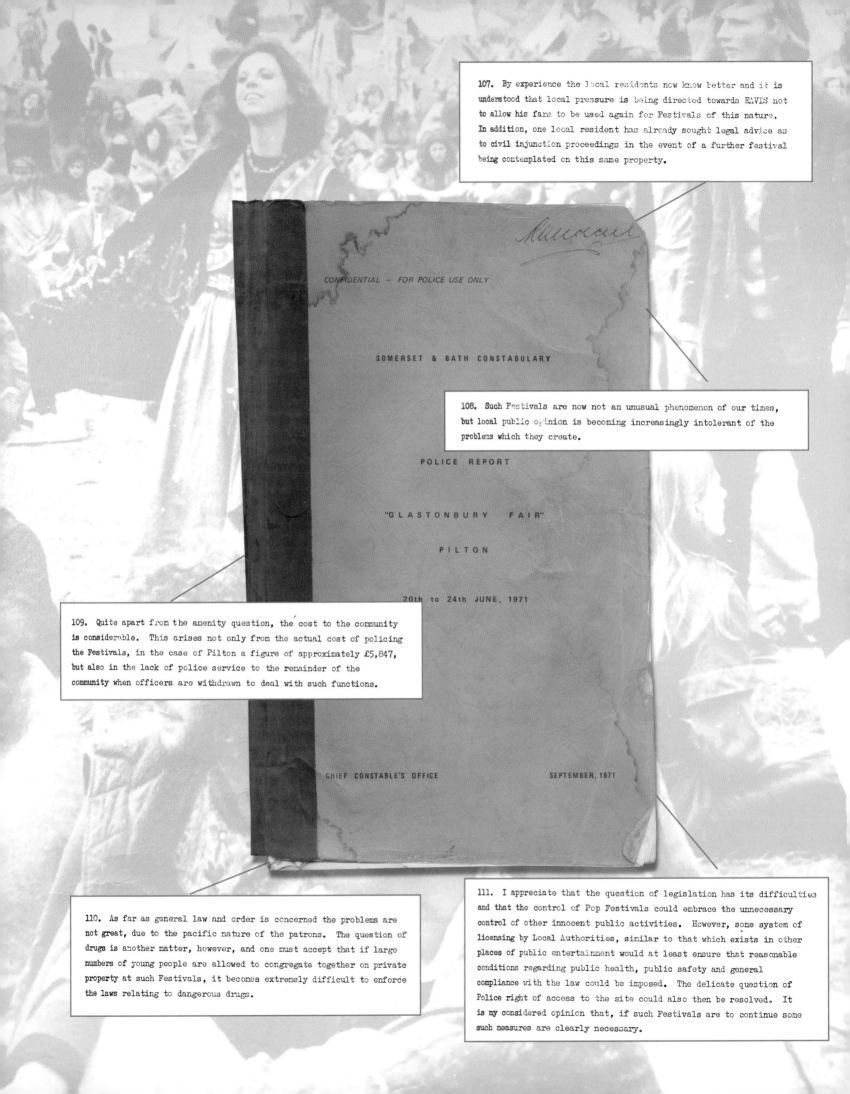

107. By experience the local residents now know better and it is understood that local pressure is being directed towards EAVIS not to allow his farm to be used again for Festivals of this nature. In addition, one local resident has already sought legal advice as to civil injunction proceedings in the event of a further festival being contemplated on this same property.

CONFIDENTIAL – FOR POLICE USE ONLY

SOMERSET & BATH CONSTABULARY

108. Such Festivals are now not an unusual phenomenon of our times, but local public opinion is becoming increasingly intolerant of the problems which they create.

POLICE REPORT

"GLASTONBURY FAIR"

PILTON

20th to 24th JUNE, 1971

109. Quite apart from the amenity question, the cost to the community is considerable. This arises not only from the actual cost of policing the Festivals, in the case of Pilton a figure of approximately £5,847, but also in the lack of police service to the remainder of the community when officers are withdrawn to deal with such functions.

CHIEF CONSTABLE'S OFFICE   SEPTEMBER, 1971

110. As far as general law and order is concerned the problems are not great, due to the pacific nature of the patrons. The question of drugs is another matter, however, and one must accept that if large numbers of young people are allowed to congregate together on private property at such Festivals, it becomes extremely difficult to enforce the laws relating to dangerous drugs.

111. I appreciate that the question of legislation has its difficulties and that the control of Pop Festivals could embrace the unnecessary control of other innocent public activities. However, some system of licensing by Local Authorities, similar to that which exists in other places of public entertainment would at least ensure that reasonable conditions regarding public health, public safety and general compliance with the law could be imposed. The delicate question of Police right of access to the site could also then be resolved. It is my considered opinion that, if such Festivals are to continue some such measures are clearly necessary.

A peaceful afternoon scene from the relatively small-scale 1971 Festival, and (opposite) the comprehensive Bath and Somerset Constabulary official report after the event; highlighted are some of the more far-sighted observations by Chief Constable K. W. L. Steele.

Overleaf: One of local newspaper photographer Brian Walker's classic shots from the first Festival.

Of course, I still had to pay the £15,000 back. Arabella introduced me to a shabby-looking character called Straight Mick who she said was in charge of all the money.

'What, him?' I replied. But she insisted. So I turned to Straight Mick: 'I'm going to need the first £15,000 off the gate to take to the bank in Wells.'

'No, no, no,' he replied. 'That is not happening.'

I told him it absolutely was happening or he could walk away from the job right now.

I got a driver, and Straight Mick eventually appeared with the £15,000 in a bag, which he was hanging onto pretty tightly. He wasn't a very pleasant character. We got to Wells, and he got out of the car clutching the bag and a baseball bat. I asked him to put the bat away as I knew lots of people in Wells and it was embarrassing to be walking around with this dodgy-looking character with a bat. 'I don't care,' he replied. 'I'm not losing this money.'

John Williams was waiting for us at the door of the bank. He looked pretty shocked to see Straight Mick arriving with his baseball bat, holding a bag of cash. It was like we were bank robbers in reverse. I've seen John in the last few years and he still laughs about it now. But he got the £15,000 back, and I got my farm back.

So I suppose we ended the seventies on a bit of a high. But I was forty-four by then and knew what I was doing – I was able to stand on my own feet. That third Festival was definitely the best we'd had, with the biggest attendance, and it won a lot of respect from the general public. By the time we got round to the next one – in 1981 – it was my show and I was fully in charge of everything again.

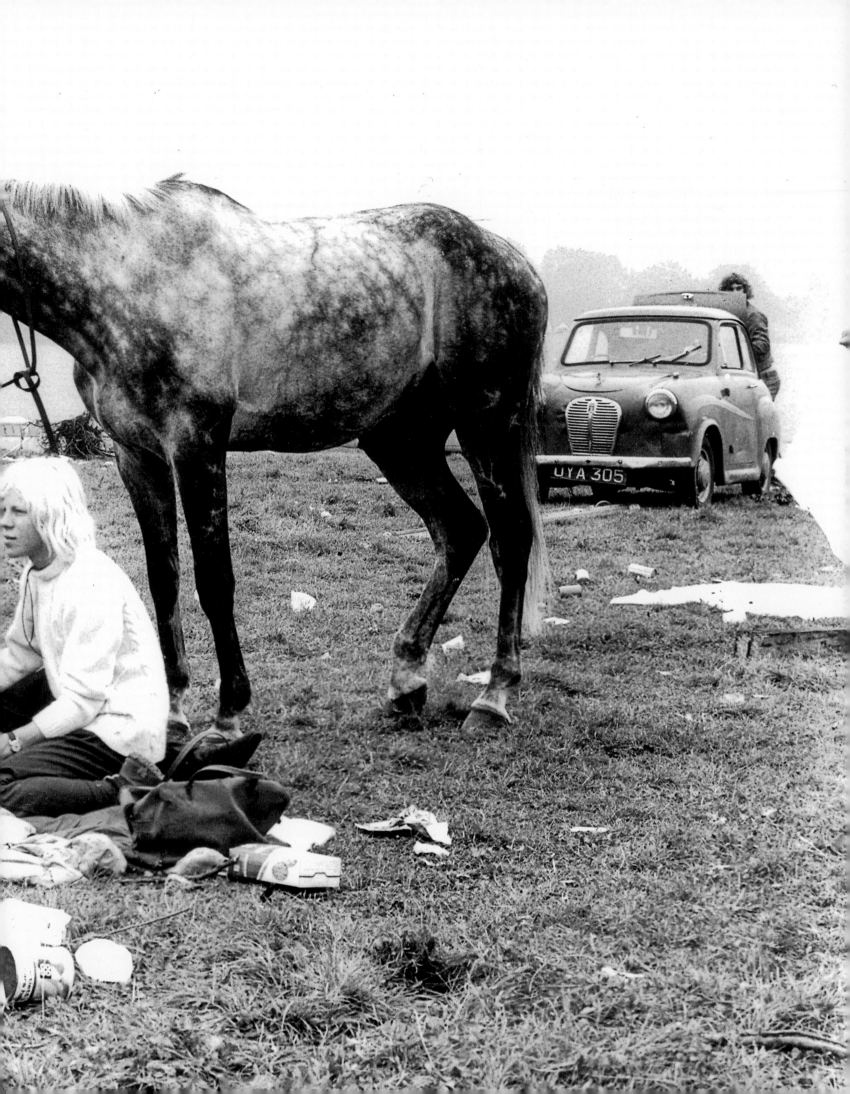

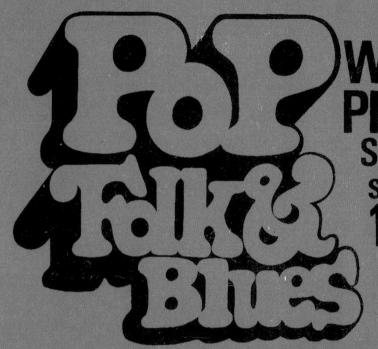

POP Folk & Blues

WORTHY FARM PILTON Shepton Mallet Somerset starts on **Saturday, 19th. September** and goes on over

Sheltered fields for camping! All food at fair prices! All farms milk FREE, and Ox roast!

THE KINKS
STEAMHAMMER
DUSTER BENNETT
ALAN BOWN
WAYNE FONTANA
STACK RIDGE
AMAZING BLONDEL

IAN ANDERSON and IAN HUNT
MALSULAMI
ORIGINN

with MAD MICK and DEREK JAMES

Lightshow · Lightship/ Diorama and Films, Freaks and Funny Things

TICKETS £1 each

(by post from M. EAVIS, ESQ, WORTHY FARM, PILTON. SHEPTON MALLET, SOMERSET

Worthy Farm: Pilton: Somerset: 17th Century:

1970

CAPACITY: 2,500
TICKET PRICE: £1

Inspired equally by the Bath Festival of Blues and Progressive Music at the nearby Bath & West Showground (featuring Led Zeppelin, Frank Zappa, Jefferson Airplane and Pink Floyd) and his own deeply ingrained spirit of Methodist non-conformism, Michael Eavis decided to launch his own event in the peaceful Vale of Avalon at the end of the summer of 1970. The site was the 110-acre dairy farm passed down to him through the family; the original theme was 'Harvest Festival', complete with ox roast and free milk. Potential attendees were promised the Kinks, sheltered camping, light shows, DJ Mad Mick, Alan Bown, Duster Bennett and Stackridge for just £1. Unfortunately, the headliners pulled out soon after the tickets were printed. They were eventually replaced by Marc Bolan's T. Rex, who took the gig on the way to another show at Butlin's in Minehead. News of Jimi Hendrix's tragically early death also came just one day before the gates opened. Despite the setbacks, over 2,000 people eventually gathered at Worthy Farm, with the *Central Somerset Gazette* praising both audience and organiser with the headline 'Happy Atmosphere at Pop Show'.

Marc Bolan, pictured here on stage at Glastonbury in 1970, was the last-minute replacement for The Kinks.

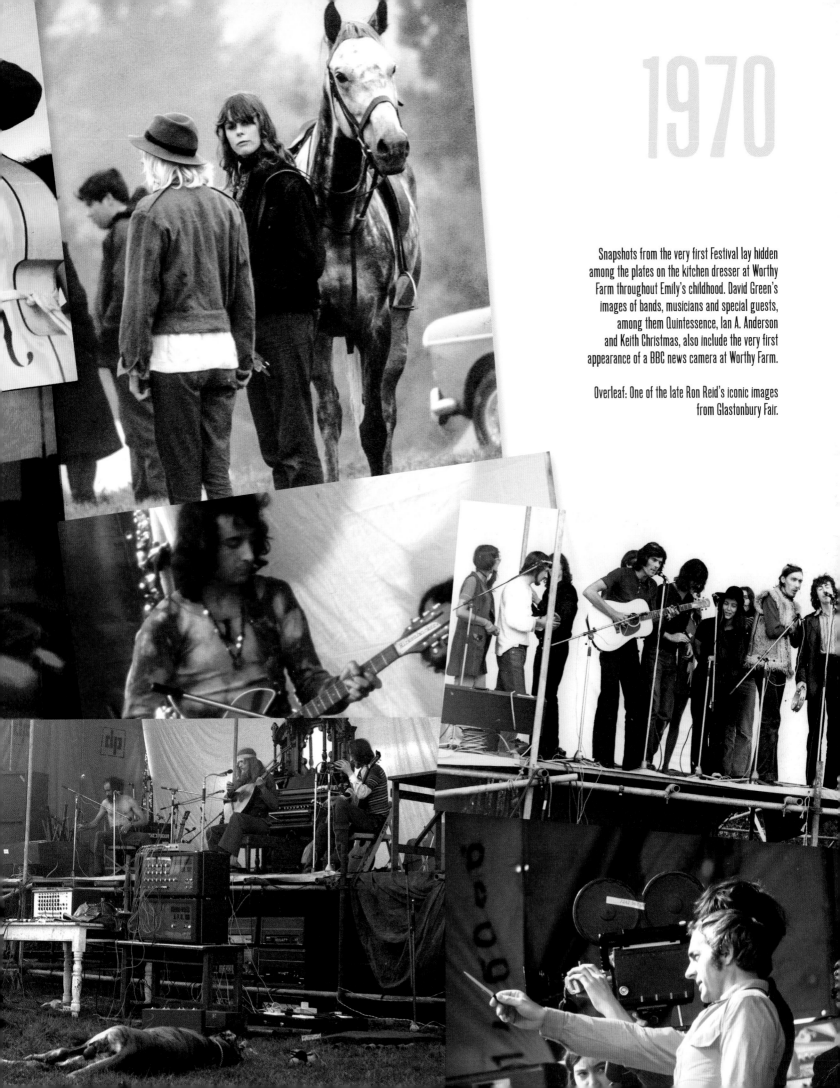

1970

Snapshots from the very first Festival lay hidden among the plates on the kitchen dresser at Worthy Farm throughout Emily's childhood. David Green's images of bands, musicians and special guests, among them Quintessence, Ian A. Anderson and Keith Christmas, also include the very first appearance of a BBC news camera at Worthy Farm.

Overleaf: One of the late Ron Reid's iconic images from Glastonbury Fair.

Thomas H. Green
Writer

I've been to Glastonbury Festival eighteen times. I've written tens of thousands of words about it. I've dived into it bodily, wholeheartedly, revelling in the idyllic and the depraved, the mind-fried and the utopian. It's woven its way into my heart. I've wept in its fields when my life seemed broken (while the Wombles played – it was that line about how Uncle Bulgaria 'can remember the days when he wasn't behind the times'), and I've been so high my insides glowed with a confetti of joy as 808 State loosed their fireworks to the sky. I've even been on Worthy Farm during a fallow year, sat at night beside a gnarled, centuries-old oak tree contemplating, as owls hooted, Anne Goode's white-lit, two-storey crucifix emblazoned on darkness across the valley.

But here's a funny thing. I wasn't initially keen. In the 1980s I resisted going to Glastonbury. I had this idea in my head of a brown swampland inhabited by multiple damp, blanket-draped replicas of comedy hippy Neil out of the The Young Ones. For those too young to recall this TV sitcom, Neil, played by Nigel Planer, was a lank, energy-sapping, flares-wearing mope who'd drone phrases such as 'vegetable rights and peace, man'. He was pejorative perceptions of hippiedom incarnate. I thought then that Glastonbury would be full of such pasty long-hairs eating mung beans and listening to interminable prog 'jams'. I sure as hell didn't need that in my life.

But, persuaded by my arty, hippy-friendly younger sister, I finally made it there. What did I find? What do you think? Pasty long-hairs, of course, eating mung beans and listening to interminable prog 'jams'. It's true! But there was also so much more. Aside from the music, theatre, circus, the acid, the sheer scale of the lunacy, something was alive at Glastonbury that Britain was moving away from: the true and brilliant face of all that sixties and seventies stuff, the counterculture. Here at the Festival, it still hummed with energy, woven with something bawdy, ancient and rustic. What was going on? Where did these tribes appear from? How did this happen? If they – we – all got together, we could surely change things for the better. I left feeling that way. And I have done every time since. Well, that and, to paraphrase Pulp, as if I've 'left an important part of my brain somewhere in a field in Somerset'.

It's now thirty years since I first attended Glastonbury. The 1960s are even further back in history. They've become worn, the very idea of them fatigued by endless reportage. The whole decade's been kernelled down to grainy video clips of round-faced girls with ironed hair dancing in parks, all flowery kaftans and body paint; propeller-buffeted snippets of American conscripts scurrying from Huey helicopters into tall-grassed jungle clearings; everything evocatively soundtracked by Buffalo Springfield's mighty 'For What It's Worth'. They've craftily rendered the sixties a naïve aberration, a stylistic footnote lit by kaleidoscopic oil-wheel bubbles, a Sgt. Pepper's fancy dress party.

Don't believe it. The sixties' impact is everywhere and ongoing, alive in multitudes of idealistic movements buoyed, consciously or otherwise, by pop-art politics and Marshall McLuhan, alive in so many organisations seeking social justice, individual freedom and planetary welfare. This sixties is certainly still thriving at Glastonbury Festival. From a therapy tipi, high in The Green Fields, which advertises the use of tantric sex to 'heal co-dependency issues', you can wander all the way down to the giant screens beside the Pyramid Stage that powerfully push the global charity WaterAid. Activism and ideas thrive amid the pursuit of pleasure – why should they be separated? – and, as ever, American anarchist mystic Hakim Bey's notion of the 'temporary autonomous zone' springs to mind.

Like all explosions, the outer regions are hit after the epicentre. So it was with the 1960s. For those not in the urban hubs of San Francisco, Swinging London or similar, it took a while for the shock waves to reach them. In the case of a 34-year-old Pilton dairy farmer and his wife, who attended the Bath Festival of Blues and Progressive Music in 1970, it took until the end of the decade. Glastonbury carried the torch on, blossoming ever-after, often as if the sixties had never stopped. But there was always more to it than a fire lit by Led Zeppelin on a late Sunday evening in June.

Methodism came into being in the mid-eighteenth century, reconnecting Christianity with the working man through big outdoor events (see where I'm going here). John Wesley, Methodism's founding figure, emphasised that the way to heaven was through service to the community, through actively helping your fellow man. It was not an inward-looking philosophy, but a religion of positive action.

Michael Eavis has never been minded to worry much about what God is or may be. He's about getting on with things. There must have been a glimpse of something, some sort of vision, when he put on that first Festival in 1970. A lover of music, he was ripe and ready for an adventure, and the counterculture's appeal was as much down to its sense of mischief and fun as its politics. From the start, the Festival was bedded deep in the sometimes whimsical utopian dreaming of the sixties. Eavis was to eventually join the dots between this and his own heritage.

It's been said that after the financial losses of the 1970 Festival, Michael Eavis wasn't really into the idea of the Festival throughout the seventies. The suggestion is that the hippies basically ran things at the 1971 Festival, with Eavis on the sidelines. Then, after a number of fallow years, the ramshackle 1979 event only happened at the insistence of Arabella Churchill. All of the above is true, but it misses the point. Eavis was there in the middle of the Festival every time, helping out, getting stuck in, on point with logistics, guiding and chivvying towards greater efficiency, learning the mindset of this rising generation of scattershot idealists. He absorbed the convictions and aesthetics of the high sixties, but did so during the seventies, and at the decade's end he was ready to take the bull by the horns, even putting up the deeds to his farm for a loan with Barclays Bank. This was a punt that could have destroyed his livelihood.

Still the profits were donated to the UN Year of the Child charity. The true seeding of the contemporary festival, its values and overall feel, happened right there and then.

I was on the big wheel once at Glastonbury in the early 1990s, revolving gently around on a warm, breezy Friday afternoon with an old pal, and we saw a UFO. It was stock still in the sky, a bright pinpoint of glinting light even on this sunny day, and it skittered suddenly, superfast, to another point and stopped again, dead, for around thirty seconds, then shot off at hyperspeed, presumably towards whatever galaxy it had come from. Maybe they didn't have their own Glastonbury there. Who knows. No one would believe us, they scoffed and laughed, perhaps because our giant black pupils spoke of a red microdot and half a purple om each. But Worthy Farm has long been conducive to such things. The original esoteric acid-heads of the early 1970s, consciousness permanently expanded to the eternal unlike we fin-de-siècle dabblers, went to the area poring over John Michell's book *The View Over Atlantis*. This tome suggested that here was a key mystic location connected by ancient science-magic to a global and fantastical psycho-spiritual network (yup, them ley lines).

Michael Eavis wasn't convinced. If we must choose a book to represent him, maybe it might be E.P. Thompson's *The Making of the English Working Class*, a radical 1963 history that posits the worth of every artisan and craftsperson and charts the forgotten underground rebel cultures of everyday working people. In the mid-eighties, Thompson, of Methodist stock himself, came to Glastonbury, invited by Eavis, and held forth from the main stage on various occasions, once giving a speech that concluded with his iconic affirmation that Britain 'has not only been a nation of money-makers and imperialists, it's been a nation of inventors, of writers, a nation of theatre and musicians, an alternative nation, and it is this alternative nation which I can see in front of me now'.

Eavis is clearly no longer short of a few quid, but it hasn't changed him much. He seldom veers from the Festival's original vision, whether that be standing up for the travelling community in small or large ways, or his patronage of everything from Somerset hospices and arts centres to the Bhopal Medical Appeal. The sweet spot between his own pragmatic religious non-conformism and the sixties and seventies outsider values provides the parameters for what his Festival is and can be. It's a perspective inherited by his children, most especially Emily, Michael and Jean's youngest born in 1979, who seems to have absorbed that essential Glastonbury ethos through her childhood at Worthy Farm, sharing her summers with Festival Folk, her winters planning the Festivals to come alongside her parents in the farmhouse. In my outsider's view from the hill, it surely must have been that upbringing that allowed Emily to become Michael's most trusted reference point throughout her teenage years, and a force to be reckoned with as the millennium approached. In the Brave New World of the noughties, and the rebuilding that followed the epic over-attendance in the Bowie year of 2000, it was Emily who upheld her mother's legacy. And since getting more fully involved as Co-Organiser over the last decade or so, she has managed to put her stamp on the Festival and take it into a new era while still retaining the original vision. In 2016 it was Emily, alongside Michael, who hammered out Glastonbury Festival's famous 'Company Rules'.

I have been to many festivals. I watch them grow. I watch commerce slush slowly in, an incoming tide littered with possible profit but also plasticity and ugliness. There's a nibble at first, just to boost the festival's ability to pay its way, then it proves irresistible, addictive, free money to allow an incremental invasion by consumer tat. One family festival I attend regularly now has a Waitrose marquee and a Range Rover stall.

Glastonbury has changed drastically too, of course. There are those who argue that it's lost touch with working people, that it's wandered off course and bears no relation to the Festivals of the 1970s. This is a recurring theme of its many critics, and I can relate to it, for I have a confession: I had my own years of doubt. I once reckoned the Glastonbury Festival was no longer its true self and therefore not worth attending.

After the 2000 Festival I clambered up on my high horse. It had been messy that year. Quite apart from the crammed *Mad Max 3* Bartertown aspect, due to a mass influx of the ticketless I was frazzled before I even got there. A close friend was nicked at Castle Cary train station on arrival for carrying way too many things he shouldn't have been. And my personal life was in pieces, choking on powder and infidelity. I was, in retrospect, 'fragile'. Then the Festival announced it was going into partnership with the dreaded Mean Fiddler organisation (later rebranded as Festival Republic). To some of us, this lot were the pantomime baddies of festival culture, ruthlessly commercial money-suckers, and now they were to raise an impenetrable wall around our festival. How dare they? This was surely the end.

I'd been to every 1990s Festival, clambered in on a few occasions assisted by affable Scousers, but in spring 2002 it was over for me and Glastonbury. We were done. I'd had the best years. Now it was just a place for students and middle-class fluffies. Those 1970s countercultural connections were done. I could move on and join the masses watching it on telly from my sofa, telling anyone who'd listen that 'I used to go when it was good'.

I started a family. Time passed. Then, in 2007, *Q* magazine unexpectedly called and said they were a body short for their Glastonbury review team. Could I help? Well, why not. They were all very organised. I didn't much care for their cucumber-salad cool. Bloody music journalists, a bunch of Londoners standing in a field trying to recreate their office politics, all attempting to outwit each other with sub-Wildean bon mots. Also, I was assigned a bunch of landfill indie bands on The Other Stage at the same time Shirley Bassey was playing. I missed 'Goldfinger' to watch the Rakes.

So it was crap, then? No, it was a revelation. How had I been so wrong? Here it was, the mecca, still intact within its Cold War walls. Eavis and his daughter had simply changed the model. My snippy travails paled compared to the crunch point they'd reached as the new millennium approached and then arrived. Jean Eavis died in 1999 from cancer, the bereavement scorching the family. They'd originally planned to retire the Festival in 2000 but, instead, were now emotionally wrenched another way. Two generations of Eavis came together to reinvent it, to move it forward while holding fast to the unique community-arts bacchanal his wife and her mother had co-piloted for three decades.

By 2007 I'd missed four Glastonburys. I'd missed Paul fucking McCartney because my deluded kangaroo-court judgement had sent me clambering up my own rectum. The new Glastonbury sold 125,000 tickets, but what about the other tens of thousands in attendance? The freaks were still here, the creatives and their mates, the party people, the south-east corner, the weirdos, the healers and spirit-guide oddballs, the tipi hippies, not to mention the many locals given work, some of whom, ten years hence, would benefit from the Eavises' financial backing of the Maggie's Farm affordable-homes scheme in Pilton.

It was all going on. The 1970s were alive and well, nurtured: the mushroom people, the UFO nuts, the Mick Farrens and the Steve Hillages, E.P. Thompson's alternative nation of dreamers and creatives harboured. Newbies mixed with multi-generational heads and politicos, and thus the good word spreads ever-outwards. Even Billy Bragg agrees, so that seals the deal, right? The 12-foot steel wall changed the Festival's character but the game wasn't over. And it still isn't. Glastonbury pushes on, riding the ley lines like a water-park flume into the splash pool of its own benign madness.

It's almost impossible now to see the late sixties and early seventies as they were, all that L.P. Hartley stuff about the past being a foreign country. So maybe Glastonbury embroiders it, embellishes, even sentimentalises on occasion, sure. I'll take that. Why not? It's a party, a celebration! I'll take that organic on a bed of mixed-herb bulgur wheat with wild garlic pesto, local cheddar and fresh coriander. I'll take that in the Left Field Tent as they argue about 'gender equality on the cuts frontline'. I'll take that quiver-fizzin' my barnacles off to New York death metal in a disembodied tube train. I'll take that ravin' in 3 a.m. darkness in far-flung fields, and I'll take that baked in circus sunshine with psychedelic cricket commentators from Mars. I'll take that once a year, that old counterculture flickering into wild life, its romance intact, unsullied. And, until I die or it stops, I'll see you next year for more.

Melanie
Musician

It was 1971 . . . the year of the Pyramid, the year all of us believed we were heralding in a future that would include our true purpose in being here. After Woodstock, after the Isle of Wight — Glastonbury, England.

'Peace will come':
Melanie on the Pyramid Stage in 1971.

We envisioned a world without war and insanity. That Pyramid seemed to be the culmination of all of this. Internally I was hoping I was worthy, as I was not one in the crowd of revellers and true believers who came to experience what was about to happen; rather, I was what was about to happen, or part of what was about to happen.

Fires. Fires everywhere. And stoves burning. I literally couldn't breathe. I was handed a mug of homemade brew from some guys who could have been right out of *Blade Runner* and I think I even drank some. I trusted. And I knew right then that when we can trust each other, we can have peace. The Pyramid will lift and I will be there and we will ascend . . .

The moment passed. Festivals started going a bit south just a few years later. The agenda seemed to turn more towards hard rock and male; the vibe became just a bit less wonderful. But I'm a free-thinker, still. Free-thinking was the calling card of the 1960s and I still believe in that. You can do this, that's okay. And you can do a bit of that too, that's okay. Now you have to be labelled. You have to be this, you have to be that, 100 per cent. It's all slogans. If I ruled the world, things would just gradually get better. But then again, I don't rule the world. I just do music.

Again, you know my recollections may be short in the outer observance of details. My recollections come through webs, veils, shadows of how I felt. I seem to remember being helped, being hoisted onto the stage by these motorcycle types. Then I remember seeing another snippet and it didn't look like anybody was helping me at all.

The story of my life is much too long and complicated and most of it untrue . . .

ALL FREE

Glastonbury Fair will be held at Worthy Farm, Pilton,
near Shepton Mallet, Somerset, from Sunday June 20
to Thursday June 24, encompassing Midsummers Day.
It will be a fair in the mediaeval tradition, embodying the
legends of the area, with music, dance, poetry, theatre,
lights and the opportunity for spontaneous entertainments.
There will be no monetary profit - it will be free.

Pictures and images

1971

CAPACITY: 12,000
TICKET PRICE: FREE

After losing money on the first Festival, Michael was approached by Andrew Kerr and Arabella Churchill (both then based in west London) about the idea of staging the Glastonbury Fair, a meeting of like-minded souls who could provide an alternative to the existing festivals that they felt had become too commercial. Initial site visits left Kerr unsure of the farm's suitability due to the string of pylons that ran through it, but he soon decided that Worthy Farm was the right setting for what he saw as being a free festival featuring music, dance, poetry, theatre and spontaneity. He moved into the farmhouse, which soon became a drop-in centre for organisers and crew as well as performers and their friends. The anarchic qualities of the Festival's set-up were captured by legendary movie director Nicolas Roeg in the documentary film *Glastonbury Fayre* (eventually released, along with a triple vinyl album, in 1972), while Michael and Andrew's connections managed to persuade a host of key acts to perform, including David Bowie, Melanie, Traffic and Quintessence. An estimated 12,000 people attended, and the centrepiece of both the film and the Festival was the very first Pyramid Stage, designed by engineer Bill Harkin and constructed on a ley line between Glastonbury and Stonehenge.

Opposite: The 1971 programme, published after the event and only available with the triple album released in 1972, celebrated the Festival's move to midsummer and the desire to avoid monetary profit.
Left: David Bowie pictured on the steps of Worthy Farm, three days before he eventually took to the stage in 1971.

Julie Christie

Actor

Glastonbury, 1971. No one knew what lay ahead. Except that my friend's band were playing and that the spiritual leader Guru Maharaj Ji was coming. A whole load of magical snapshots. A naked guy on his motorbike, penis laid out tidily in front of him, manoeuvring through the seated crowds.

A huge carthorse with an entire family astride, ranging from the smallest child to a Viking-like dad. Jean Shrimpton taking photos with a snazzy camera and looking elegant and collected among the moving mass of shawls and beads and Saharan carpets. Beautiful strangers. Music without stop throughout all the hours of the days. No self-consciousness. Pure magic, not of this world.

This page: Glastonbury's original supermodel shoot, 1971. Oscar-winning actor Julie Christie (right) takes a break with (left to right) fashion icon Jean Shrimpton, model Dee Palmer and *Withnail & I* costume designer Andrea Gayler. Photograph by Paul Misso, who captured all the production stills for the film *Glastonbury Fayre*, directed by Nicolas Roeg. And (opposite) Chris Difford (left) and Glenn Tilbrook on stage in the 1970s; they later teamed up with Jools Holland to form Squeeze.

Chris Difford
Squeeze

I first went to Glastonbury in 1971, having gone with a friend in his sixties London taxi that we also slept in. I remember seeing Hawkwind, sitting cross-legged on the grass, stoned as could be, lights trickling across the sky and the PA only just coping with the volume of space-age jamming. They were the Take That of our day and seemed to play everywhere I went.

It was a warm atmosphere, and not once did I feel out of place or without a friend. I had come from a skinhead council estate; suddenly I felt like I could fall back into the arms of music and love. There was always someone playing an acoustic guitar onstage. There seemed to be no limit on how long people played for in those days, which was lovely – unless it was shit. Mostly it was like floating on a magical carpet of chords, words and harmony.

Sleeping under the stars and smoking too much weed was the order of the day. I strummed my battered guitar around the fireside and seldom made it to see who was on stage, but I had a good time and floated from one song to another with all the joy that youth can bring. Glastonbury has always been the Eden of music venues, a poetic valley of dreams and cherished hangovers. Eventually, in 2017, we played on the Pyramid Stage. Our time had come after so many years strumming in the distant fields. To walk onto that stage and get that kind of response from the crowd forty years after our first big hit was a really important point in our journey. It felt very spiritual. And it was so emotional too. I'd never seen the whole band come offstage and burst into tears like we all did that day.

If I stand for long enough I can still hear 'Silver Machine' wafting across the valley, reaching me through the smoke of a small fire to keep me warm on a Somerset Festival morning.

GLASTONBURY FAYRE 1979

Summer Solstice
JUNE
21 22 23
WORTHY FARM
PILTON
Nr SHEPTON MALLET
SOMERSET

Steve Hillage   Sky   Tim Blake   Barry Ford Band
John Cooper Clarke   Leyton Buzzards
The Good Missionaries   X-Dreamysts   Sex Beatles
Nik Turner's Sphinx   Carol Grimes   Matumbi
John Martyn   U.K. Subs   Clayson and the Argonauts
The Pop Group   The Only Ones   Raja Ram
Patrick Fitzgerald   Etc. Etc.

Theatre, dance & mime from: Footsbarn Abracadabra   Continuum
Incubus Cunning Stunts Many Ways of Moving Matchbox Purveyors
Natural Theatre Company   Beril & The Peril Headless Wonder
All Women Cabaret, and many more!

Plus: Camping and van space   Wholefoods   Welfare
Crafts Clowns Market Yoga Medical & legal services
Giant childrens play area   Lecture area

Tickets £5 from all Virgin shops or by post from
Glastonbury Fayre,   57 Elgin Cres., London W 11
Please enclose an S A E
All profits to Unicef International Year of the Child

1979

CAPACITY: 12,000
TICKET PRICE: £5

After an eight-year gap, the Glastonbury Fayre returned to the Worthy Farm fields, with Michael, Arabella Churchill and Bill Harkin crafting a three-day event around the concept of the Year of the Child. The Children's Field was created for the event and led to Arabella's Glastonbury Children's Festival in the town itself, as well as the creation of the Children's World charity (which still exists and works with special schools in Somerset and Avon). In the intervening years various impromptu gatherings had occurred as bands and passers-by turned up around the solstice. In fact, a whole fleet of them arrived in 1978 and staged their own private party.

In 1979, over 12,000 revellers enjoyed Peter Gabriel, Steve Hillage, the Sensational Alex Harvey Band and the Footsbarn Theatre company. The roots of the modern-day Festival were delivered in miniature, from fairground rides to cinema tents, from Festival Welfare Services to newsletters printed on site. Craft and food stalls rubbed shoulders with an area boasting alternative medicine, with all the attractions taking place in a space not dissimilar to today's Pyramid field. However, the £5 ticket price didn't bring enough returns, and the financial loss was subsidised by Michael and Jean Eavis. After the Festival weekend, sporadic events began to happen in the wagon shed next to the farmhouse, with Ginger Baker's Air Force and Jimmy Page, among others, playing. The success of these smaller gigs whetted Michael's appetite for more, and the Festival would return under his guidance in 1981.

Arabella Churchill's Children's World organisation (top) played a major role in setting up the 1979 event, the first to feature alternative stages (bottom).

1979

Clockwise from top left: John Martyn on the main stage; Peter Gabriel and friends; the Markets Area in 1979; headliner Steve Hillage; the Leyton Buzzards.

Haggis McLeod
on Arabella Churchill

After we were married, I once asked Arabella if she was middle class or upper class, and she said, 'Darling, I'm aristocracy.' She was Winston Churchill's granddaughter, and she grew up in this rarefied world of nannies and holidays in the south of France where playmates on the beach included Jackie Onassis. It was a very establishment upbringing and I think she felt there was a lot of pressure on her to do establishment things. After she'd been to finishing school in Switzerland there was apparently society talk of her marrying Prince Charles.

In 1968, when Arabella was still only eighteen, she was made the Azalea Queen, which was essentially Miss United Nations. Her father's secretary was a free-thinking guy called Andrew Kerr, and he was a big formative influence on her. Arabella was due to go to America to be crowned live on TV, and Andrew tried to convince her to refuse the crown and deliver a speech against the Vietnam War.

At the last moment Arabella pulled out of going, but she did write a letter saying that she was horrified by Vietnam and she believed in the global peace movement. That caused quite a stir in her circles, and I think it was one of the reasons she ended up running off down to Somerset with Andrew's crowd. It was all a big two fingers to the establishment.

Oposite: Arabella Churchill at Worthy Farm in 1971.

Andrew had got into Arthurian geometry – which has Glastonbury Tor as a sacred location – and he was looking to do a festival in the Somerset area. That's how he ended up working with Michael on the 1971 Festival, and Arabella moved to the farmhouse to be a big part of that.

Arabella had great connections and she was able to help financially support the Festival, so I can see why Michael was keen to have her involved. And even though she was from a privileged background, she was happy to get her hands dirty and throw herself into it. She always had a really strong work ethic.

I think she liked the rural life and so she stuck around. Michael took over the running of the Festival finances from Arabella and Andrew after 1979, but she asked if she could set up a children's area and then a theatre field, and Michael trusted her enough to let her do both.

She'd always had an interest in children, having worked with a charity in Biafra (part of Nigeria) when she was a teenager. She christened the first kids' area Children's World in 1979, and that went on to become a registered charity which to this day provides educational, social and emotional benefits to disadvantaged children.

I think the reason she asked to do a theatre area was that she thought it was something the Festival needed to have. In truth, she was winging it: she once confided to me that when she started the theatre area back in 1981, she had no clue who to book or how to book them.

But she always had that Churchillian can-do spirit, and it took off. That little theatre tent has grown and grown into what has now become the Theatre and Circus area: three fields filled with some of the best theatre, circus and comedy on the planet, with over 400 acts doing more than 1,500 shows. Arabella created the absolute focal point in England for all those artists to come together. The Festival isn't now just on the bucket list of every gap-year student, but also the world's comedians, dancers, circus artists, poets and street-theatre companies.

My involvement began in 1985 when, as a young, up-and-coming juggler, I was invited along to perform by Arabella. But I didn't actually meet her until 1987, when she'd booked me to play at her kids' festival in Glastonbury town. We became an item, and she almost immediately became pregnant with our daughter, Jessica. She said, 'Right, we're going to have to get married now. My family won't like it if we don't.'

Not long after, Arabella invited Michael and Jean round for dinner. I think they were keen to meet this young juggler who'd won Arabella's heart. I'd seen Michael at the Festival – I have vague memories of watching him digging trenches – but that was the first time we'd met.

Michael, as is his way, came straight to the point: 'So, when are you going to make an honest woman of Arabella?' Ten minutes before this he'd told me in absolute confidence that although he and Jean had been living together for twenty-eight years, they weren't actually married. So I replied, 'I'll marry Bella if you marry Jean.'

A few weeks later, we had a secret double wedding at Shepton Mallet registry office; we were the witnesses for each other. It was quite a mad, surreal moment. There was literally nobody there apart from the four of us. When we came out, Michael was looking through the hedge at the council buildings, making sure nobody could see him.

Arabella died much too young, in 2007. But since her death I have, along with a core team of around 300 crew and volunteers, striven to keep the ethos that she instilled in us as the Theatre and Circus area has continued to grow and evolve: Work hard, never give up and always treat people as you would like to be treated yourself.

Glastonbury remained a huge part of Arabella's life right until the end. She loved being involved with something that was doing real good. It was certainly a long way from the astonishing youth that she'd had – she would mention in passing things like meeting Martin Luther King at the US Senate, being romantically linked with the Prince of Sweden and buying the Clash their first PA – but I think she'd be very proud of what we're doing and what the Theatre and Circus area has become. And that's all her legacy.

1980s

GLASTONBURY PROGRAMME FESTIVAL

£2

GLASTONBURY FESTIVAL 1985

GLASTONBURY CND FESTIVAL 1981
WORTHY FARM PILTON SOMERSET
Glastonbury
19 20 21 JUNE
FRI SAT SUN
THREE DAY TICKET £8

PPY END
T PARTY
DENTOPS

Rag Tag
en

NBURY
1986
TON MALLET, SOMERSET.

GLASTONBURY
CND FESTIVAL 1986
20 21 22 JUNE, WORTHY FARM, PILTON, SHEPTON MALLET, SOMERSET.
TRADERS LICENCE

1984

Glastonbury 1987

GLASTONBURY
CND FESTIVAL 1986

GLASTONBURY
CND FESTIVAL 1987
19-20-21 JUNE · WORTHY FARM,
PILTON, SHEPTON MALLET, SOMERSET.

Michael

After the dramas of 1979, I wanted some time to catch my breath, so we didn't have a Festival in 1980. We'd been through so much in the seventies, and definitely finished the decade on a high, but I really needed some space to think about where we were going next.

We went back to farming seriously again, and I milked all the cows seven days a week. The farm was doing okay; there were no wages to pay, because Jean and I did everything ourselves. But I soon realised that I was very keen to come back with a Festival in 1981, and to do it on my own. I think organising it had got into my veins. I couldn't shake it.

1981 was the year I decided to join up with the CND (Campaign for Nuclear Disarmament). I'd already been involved with them locally after somebody had found a secret bunker in the Mendip Hills which was guarded by soldiers with guns. Everyone was very worried about that; it was all top secret, but we wanted to know what was going on in our area, so we formed a local CND group in Shepton.

Emily being born in 1979 also had a lot to do with me getting involved with the CND. I felt a great need to protect her, because she was so tiny. She really made me think, 'I'm not going to let her get blown up by a cruise missile!'

We spent a lot of time having meetings and going on marches, and I even helped out with the Greenham Common protest. Fay Weldon, who lived in Pilton, was the leader of that gang who set up camp at RAF Greenham Common to protest against the cruise missiles being stored there. The Peace Camp was all women, but Fay asked if I'd do the loos, so we went out there with a lorry load of them and got a local digger to dig the long drop trench. A council chap tried to stop me, but I pointed out that there were thousands of people there, with no loos, and I was putting them in for free. He eventually let me continue.

So when it came to the 1981 Festival, I called up Bruce Kent, the CND's general secretary who was always in the papers, and asked if they'd like to be involved. At the time our image was slightly shabby and I wasn't totally sure the Festival was going to work. We were still losing money and the whole event hadn't really caught on with paying customers, but I thought the CND could help.

Bruce said he liked the sound of me and invited me up to their offices in Seven Sisters Road, London to meet him. The idea was that they'd help promote us and we'd give them the proceeds and rename it the Glastonbury CND Festival. I was a bit nervous, but he said, 'No, I love it, Michael! We're pleased to be a part of it. I'm with you, whatever you want to do.' I walked away thinking, 'Oh, thank God for that!'

They had this enormous mailing list with 350,000 people on it – a fantastic target audience of the kind of people who'd be interested in the Festival – and they let us put our flyers in the envelopes for free, as long as it didn't go over the weight of the stamp. Previously, we'd just put the posters in the goods van on the London train at Castle Cary and leave the rest to them. So now, with the CND's help, we were getting incredible nationwide publicity for nothing, at a time when we still weren't really very well known. It was of huge value for us. The whole success of the Festival was actually down to that, I think.

I'd managed to book Taj Mahal to headline that year through Wilf Walker, a guy I'd met who worked at the Portobello Hotel and at the time was running the Notting Hill Carnival. In those days we always seemed to book our acts through random connections like that. Taj Mahal ended up playing Glastonbury quite a lot in the eighties. Back then we'd feed the acts in the farmhouse, and Taj Mahal used to sing to the children before they went to bed. The kids would line up on the stairs to listen; it was like something out of *The Sound of Music*!

Below: 'Always in the papers': Monsignor Bruce Kent of CND speaks from the Pyramid Stage in 1982.
Opposite: 'A little bit of magic': The Pyramid after the crowds had gone in 1981 (top), and the wooden CND sign stored in the barn (bottom).

1981 was also significant because it was the year of the first permanent Pyramid Stage. I really liked the idea of the Pyramid after the first temporary one we'd built in 1971. The pyramid shape has a little bit of magic. I decided to construct it out of telegraph poles and building it was such good fun. Those poles were just about everywhere back then. You'd see heaps of them at the side of the road, so we started collecting them for the Pyramid and eventually had enough to build the pyramid of my dreams.

According to legend, that Pyramid doubled as a cowshed in the winter, but it never really happened like that. The truth is that when the planning people from the council came to check on it, I told them it was an agricultural building because I knew the rules were more relaxed for those than for a stage. But then they came back with some blokes and some ladders. Turns out 29 feet was too high for an agricultural building. I offered to cut off the top, but it went to the planning committee. In the end, the chairman of the planning committee okayed it. He was a Quaker, and I think he had the same sort of non-conformist streak that I do as a Methodist. 'It's a good show, we'll pass it,' was all he said.

That year's Festival did really well. Thanks to the publicity we got through the CND, we suddenly had people coming down from Manchester, London, Liverpool, Cardiff,

Glasgow and all over the place. I think, in a way, Maggie Thatcher coming to power contributed to the success of the Festival in the eighties. Little did she know it, but Maggie gave us a real political drive, something to fight against. We went on lots of demonstrations against her, and we had political speakers attend the Festival every year.

We did, however, get some opposition to the CND's involvement. Some people on the crew were jealous of the CND taking over what they thought they'd begun. They thought the politics of the CND were really wicked compared to their hippy ideal of love, peace and lots of dope. They thought the CND was a left-wing conspiracy in league with communist Russia.

For the 1982 Festival we got a schoolmaster in nearby Evercreech to make a huge CND sign for the top of the Pyramid Stage. But one morning I went down to get the cows in at about half past five and it had gone! I thought I'd gone mad. I went out on a motorbike to look for it and eventually found it after some of the crew had ripped it off and rolled it away.

Then in 1983, while Bruce Kent was giving a speech from the main stage, an aeroplane appeared in the sky trailing a banner that said, 'The Kremlin loves you'! I was outraged. I phoned up our fireworks chap and asked if he had a rocket that could reach the plane. He told me he only had one, and it would cost £100. I asked

him to fire it off right away and within minutes the rocket was hurtling towards the plane and exploded all around it. Of course it didn't actually hit the plane, but it was fantastic, it really was.

After the Festival I had a summons from the police saying I'd been causing danger in the sky. As luck would have it, I ended up in court at the same time as the pilot, who himself had infringed the no-fly restriction. The courts fined him £600, which was quite a lot of money in those days. He pointed at me and, angrily said, 'Well what about him? He nearly shot me out of the sky!' Everyone, even the magistrates, started laughing. They were all on my side because I was a bit of a local hero by then, and I wasn't fined anything!

There's always been conflict like that, but I did thrive on the aggravation because I knew I was on the right side of the argument. I remember at school, I never wanted to do boxing, but once I'd got punched and had a bloody nose, that was it – I was a killer! I'd always rather be the first to be punched. Lead from the back foot. Maybe that's the Eavis way.

I turned out to be quite good at dealing with interpersonal conflict too. I first realised that in 1979 when taking on Straight Mick. I didn't get scared, you see; I had the self-confidence to challenge people and stay calm. My mother established that in me – she thought I could do no wrong. I needed those skills in the eighties as at that time we seemed to be constantly arguing with the council, the locals and the police. The new licensing law came in in 1982, which resulted in even more rows with the council. They actually told me that if I fundraised for someone other than the CND, they'd give me a licence but I reminded them that they weren't allowed to make a political decision, it had to be based on health and safety. In the end I had to challenge the council over the licence in court that year. Luckily, the chairman of the magistrates' bench was well on side.

It felt like turning a massive oil tanker, but as the decade went on the Festival was becoming increasingly popular. The bands were getting really good too. Landing The Smiths in 1984 felt like a very big moment. They were the top band in the world at the time. I'd actually booked them in the previous October when they played at Bristol University. I spoke to Morrissey and said, 'Do you fancy doing Glastonbury?' He didn't really know what it was, but we managed to persuade them.

With The Smiths' help, 50,000 people came through the gates that year. The Festival was growing like mad – it was crazy. I'd begun to become quite prominent and well-known, and although I'd been a shy child growing up, I found that I quite enjoyed the newfound attention. In fact, I loved the publicity. And even though there was a lot of stress – there were days when I couldn't eat my breakfast – it always felt that there were more people with me than against me.

It was a very exciting time, but I don't think the success ever went to my head. Even now people are surprised that I still drive the same battered old Land Rover. They tell me I haven't changed, and I do think that's true. My self-esteem comes from doing the right thing at all times, if I possibly can. That's down to the Methodism. I don't think we've lost money since 1979, but I've got a fundamental belief in giving away the profits we make. I never started going to the Bahamas for the winter or anything. In a funny sort of way, it's quite a selfish thing really. For me to feel good about myself, I need people to feel good about me. So we've got to give the money away.

That said, back then I was extremely busy between the farm and the Festival, and that meant I probably wasn't as good a father as I could have been. I just didn't have much time between milking cows and organising a festival. I did the best I possibly could, but I don't think I did parenting quite like I should have done. It's certainly been wonderful to be able to spend so much time with Emily's children – my grandchildren – since they were born.

After starting the decade so well, 1985 was a tumultuous year, and that was all due to Michael Heseltine, one of Thatcher's colleagues who everyone called Tarzan. He closed down the Stonehenge Free Festival, which led to the Battle of the Beanfield, during which the police smashed up all the travellers' vehicles. Because we're only about 40 miles from there, the travellers all decided to come to our Festival instead. Eventually even the police started to divert them down here themselves.

It seemed like hell on earth at the time – the travellers could be quite intimidating and were uncontrollable, really – but I think it turned out to be another real turning point for us. It was a totally different mob of people than we'd been getting: poor, working class, fed up of being booted around by employers and the government. Theirs was a battle cry against everything. They certainly thought I was a bastard too, initially, until they realised I wasn't really too bad.

I paid one of the neighbouring farmers to let me use a 30-acre field down in the valley for the travellers to park up. He was a real Tory, who ran the hunt, but he was happy to accept £5,000 for that old field! And that was what became the Travellers' Field, which then became the south-east corner. The legacy of that is still alive today. A lot of those incredible, creative, fired-up people who would've been going to the Stonehenge Free Festival still run the south-east corner venues now. Thank you, Tarzan, for that.

The arrival of the travellers does also go some way to explaining why drug-taking started to take off at the Festival in the eighties. Suddenly there were dealers all over the place. People always thought I'd be into drugs, but I've always been very anti them. Taking drugs and getting off your head didn't fit into my Wesleyan grounding in social responsibility. My drug was organising the Festival.

In the beginning, I did turn a blind eye to the drugs. Back in the early days, Andrew Kerr had even made badges for everyone saying 'Don't tell Michael'! The Festival was producing a hell of a lot of money for the CND, for Greenpeace and for the local area, all the things I really care about. And most people seemed to be having a good time, even with the drugs. So I suppose I had to compromise with the devil a little bit.

But by the mid-1980s it did start to get out of hand. Suddenly the drug dealers were fighting each other over who got the best spot, and there were even shootings between them. It was really horrible, and not what the Festival was about, so I had to bring the police on board to stop it.

That was another thing I learnt in the eighties: that I couldn't always do everything myself. I had to learn to delegate, because the Festival was getting massive and I realised I would have a nervous breakdown if I didn't get people in to help. So I brought Malcolm Haynes on board to do the dance area and Tony Cordy to run the Kidzfield and Liz Eliot to organise The Green Fields. Those three are all still here. I seemed to be able to choose the best people. Either that or I got lucky.

Jean also eventually came round to the idea of the Festival. She put up with a hell of a lot with me, because I must have been a nightmare. I was quite excited and geed up by it all, but she was so loyal to me. Without that loyalty, I would never have succeeded. She supported me to the hilt and I will always remain grateful for that.

By the end of the 1980s, the Festival was attracting crowds of 80,000 people and the media was starting to like us: even the deputy editor of *The Times* was telling people Glastonbury was the best place on earth. I'd struggled all the way through my life, but it didn't feel like we were struggling any more. I absolutely loved it.

Official praise for organisation of CND pop festival

GLASTONBURY CND Festival. has been mir... year's

The observatic... Mendip I... chief envi... officer Mr...

"Consider attending, t... produced problems either...

"The atmo... relaxed and complaints," s... in a ...

... each town council and...

... were in a situation where... we had to relax extra rese... nue to make the banks... balance. We had to find...

... district," she... "The reso... suspend the f... lost by eigh...

... Mr E Jackson-Stavem... Wright said... district and discussed with... had consistantly opposed... said the matter should have...

TOUTS PUSHED U... FESTIVAL FIGURE

FARMER Michael Eavis has received complimentary comments from Mendip District Council's chief environmental health officer, Mr Joe Compton following this year's CND music festival on his Worthy Farm, Pilton.

"Considering the numbers attending, this year's festival produced remarkably few problems, either p.o.p. of

---

A Farmer who cultivates peace

Farmer Michael Eavis and daughter

... to have been buried. Whether e... ...GGITT and DOUGAL TEMPLETON spen...

...ys of glo... ...ne ...ne is ...ire ...for ...part ...acre

...0,000 came ...he had final ...appoint ...grin). It ...tion the ...received. ...port for ...t marks ...th such a ...d:

...nt to the ...with the ...alf year old ...older, you ...tective and ...ure of your ...y child being ...a fox . . . or ...poisoning." ...thing about it. ...I know how. ...he future of his ...plains why this ...has been playing ...r over a decade ...Worthy Farm's ...son were first ...when Mike paid a ...two miles up the ...n Mallet: "I was ...the spirit of the ...finity for the people ...a great escape from ...ertainment' in these ...like clay pigeon ...ing and skittles really ...o me. This was a new

ystical

...ie Glastonbury legend ...unched appropriately ...the hey-day of free ...Z and the tail end of ...love era. Middle-and ...ss drop outs turned up in ...London, attracted to the ...ystical associations of the ...like a great idea," ...all these

...to make sure eve... applied a frugal farmers' approac... to the organizing. What 1 felt w... needed was a compromise between... commercial and free festival, wi... any profits going towards a caus... CND was the obvious choice, t... most pressing campaign with... with which many musicians had... affinity."

It's clear then that the CND... raisers are as much a produ... financial reality as pacifist ide... Glastonbury '81 was the only... festival last year to make a... Fun-loving, philanthropic... he may be, but Michael Ea... now shown himself to be on... shrewdest and most... respected promoters in th... business.

problems

Persistent and not a litt... well. His involvement wi... has caused him and his fa... of problems. Local opp... often been vociferous b... points out, it mostly... those people who b... moved to Pilton and... preserve the picture p... of the village:

"There's a lot of... Generals who've... here. They hate the... and they like CND... real local commu... whom I've known t... be sympathetic an... that I've stuck it ou... despite the opposi... was a problem at f... stick and my fa... suffered wit... phonecalls and... but things have...

tra

THREE weeks... Worthy Farm...

..."It was a crazy night,"

In ...1971 G... be forg... favou... Conve... her?!)... young... put i... perfor... Rathe... affair... was th

Mil... a mea... to fin... their

WATER THE WORLD

WATER is something we all take too much for granted. We don't give any thought to turning on a tap, we simply expect that clear water will rush out. It might taste strange but usually it's safe for whatever purpose we need to use it – cooking, drinking, washing.

It comes to us from a variety of sources. Some is withdrawn from rivers which routinely contain treated sewerage and industrial wastes from higher upstream. Another source is catchment – reservoirs, often miles from the place of use, collect rain and spring water draining into them. The third main source is groundwater trapped in porous rock layers and which is pumped to the surface for use. It's generally reckoned that groundwater is one of the best sources, having good flavour and needing less treatment than river water.

This treatment which water receives depends on the initial quality. Cloudy river water is quickly transformed by settlement, filtration and disinfection into something suitable for pumping into the pipes. Chemicals are added sometimes to control the hardness of the water and to prevent it dissolving the pipes in which it flows. Groundwater often only needs the minimum of disinfection to ensure its safety. However, pollution of rivers and streams by industrial and agricultural effluent is a growing problem in some parts of Britain. Chemical lution is difficult to remove from water; elaborate detection ems guard river intakes, and on a warning of a serious ard the only action possible is to close the intake until the ted water has passed downstream.

But pollution of groundwater is a worse problem to solve. tes can be turned into cancer-causing nitrosamines in human stomach, and nitrates are the main ingredients of tificial fertilizers which farmers have been applying to land for 40+ years. Unlike natural forms of nitrogen are held well by the soil, the artificial ones are easily dis- by rainfall, leach into the watercourses and percolate the soil and underlying rocks until they reach the earing layers, a journey taking decades. As a result, a high-nitrate water is beginning to filter into some water, taking the nitrate content towards dangerous and little can be done about it other than finding altern-

water distribution system has grown ...

MAN & MISSION

Interview: Tom Archer
Pic: John Evans

"One option would be to put up the ticket price, but I can't see how we could do that by much more. Another is to cut the costs, but that would mean weakening the event. We should make money this year, but I'm worried about next year."

In fact Michael is seriously talking about 1988 being the first year with no Glastonbury Festival. His family would welcome a break from the stress of having a big money music event run from their home. He would miss it of course

---

GLASTONBURY '8 CAMPING FOR NUCLEAR DISARMAMEN

28th June, 1986 New Musical Expre...

...ney – who come on strong with 'Horse Overboard' and 'Birthday Girl' but soon get bogged down with a lumpy sound that makes O'Hagan's harmonies ugly and Coughlan's aggression over-powering.

And if you want blues there's **Robert Cray**, hitting the highway, wondering where he's going. But fine axeman that he is, the uninspiring rhythms behind the quickfire solos left me cold – he's norra patch on Carlos Santana. Less serious, and in a different vein, it's **Robyn Hitchcock**, looking like a bad trip to Top Shop and demanding 'Tell Me About Your Drugs'. Here goes . . .

Amid the vendors flogging white lightning and yellow microdots, we're offered **Simply Red**, who begin with the mediocre 'Red Box' and the depressive 'Picture Box' dub. Hucknall's vocals al... ... take you to a higher plane 10 ft too tall.

lack flares and... laces.

"Provided or... time drugged or... a fine place" s... prior commitment... with us today, ... **Thompson**. A... Prof reminds u... (CND funds), to... save the plane... mingly points... future of man... sponsibility. ... urinating on... bog rolls or... listening to t... Can this be

Peace, love and pyramids

The ultimate in self-build, high-tech, pyramid-shaped cowsheds was causing the planners at Mendip District Council a few problems last week. Built and designed by a local farmer and his friends, the 'cowshed' has only seen service to date as a colossal stage structure for the recent Glastonbury Rock Festival. But the farmer, Michael Eavis, insists that the steel-clad pyramid is really an agricultural building, and it

A sympathetic chief planning office... Ray Bush, told a colleague: 'We hav... never seen a cowshed built on three... floors before and we found it a little... difficult to swallow that it was pure... agricultural building. Having said... however, it is not in a very prominent... position and it certainly looks no w... than a lot of other farm buildings.

Farmer Eavis accepts that he shoul... have got planning permission in t... place. 'We messed up the forms... we put in for it', he said. Work o... shed took about three months... complete and cost about £6000.

The good father

The Rev Richard Hayes, who se... last Sunday on a sponsored bicy... to Jarrow from St Paul's, Ruislip... West London, is, I am sorry

Home life meets headline news: Michael and Emily in the press (left); Michael and Jean at Bridgwater Market (right) and selecting poles for the Pyramid Stage in 1981 (below).

Pilton festival promoter wins in court case

[MI]CHAEL EAVIS, promoter of the celebrated Glastonbury [fe]stivals on his Worthy Farm at Pilton, has successfully [def]ended five prosecutions brought by Mendip District [Cou]ncil alleging contraventions of five of the 24 [cond]itions under which he was licensed to stage last [year]s Festival.

[In] an all day hearing [at Sh]epton Mallet [Magistrat]es Court, all five [were] dismissed.

[He] had been told by the [so]licitor, Mr David [...] is was the first time [prose]cution had been [brought] under the [air pr]ovisions of the [Environ]ment Act.

[Wit]nesses in the all-[day... Mr.] Donald Aitken, [... of] the Festival [Welfare] Trust, said [that the] Glastonbury [festival ob]tained an [...] among [... of] the country [... of] its national local government expert on the organisation of large open air festivals.

Chief Inspector Tony Pink gave evidence of discussions with the organisers of the event about points of access, emergency telephones and other questions. Later he paid visits to the festival when it was in progress, and found obstructions on emergency routes, a route made up so that it was not suitable even for four-wheel drive vehicles, (although this was remedied later in the day). When he asked for a loud speaker message to warn people about the difficulties of returning if they left the site, the system was not immediately available.

A man with a sick child wanting to leave urgently could find no way out, and the chief inspector had to ask for a key to an emergency exit which was chained and padlocked.

Replying to Mr. David Wood he agreed that Mr. Eavis did his best to comply with all the regulations. He agreed that Mr. Eavis appealed for no more people to visit the site and also stopped special buses which were on their way.

He did not know that one of the telephones at the farm had had the number changed so that there would be no incoming calls and the telephone would be available.

APPRECIATIVE

Fire Officer Keith Furlonger agreed that generally Mr. Eavis and his staff were appreciative of the fire service's needs, but at the same time were concerned about [... even]ts.

[Mr.] David Burton, Mendip [Envi]ronmental Health Officer, [said] he had been liaising with Mr. [...] ever since...

difficult to deal with people who were prepared to leap through hedges to gain unauthorised admittance. He had employed 850 people on the site, including a security patrol.

He did not agree with Mr. Burton's estimate of 37,000 on the Sunday afternoon. "People were coming and going all the time," he said. In retrospect, bearing in mind that people had come for specific performances and had then left, and after studying aerial photos, he now considered it unlikely that there were more than 30,000 people on the site at any one time.

LOCKED

He said it was obvious that gates would have to be locked to prevent unauthorised access, but he was sure the fire officer had said that in the event of an emergency the firemen would have no difficulty in cutting through a padlock and chain.

He had done all that he could to comply with conditions about roads and the telephone. British Telecom could not install a special line in time, and so the number of an existing telephone was changed.

Replying to Mr. Wood, he said most of the money from the festival went to CND. There was no profit motive involved in his alleged technical breaches of the conditions. He employed 25 people permanently, and he intended to apply for a licence for another festival this year.

Dr. Christopher Howse, of Shepton Mallet, who said he is a member of the local branch of CND, was the co-ordinator for medical services.

He told the court...

Emily

Emily and Michael backstage in 1985 (opposite), and the violin lessons that led to Emily's first appearance onstage (left). The Snoopy Club card became Emily's first official stage pass for the whole of the 1980s (above).

I was born in 1979, so my memories of the early eighties are a little hazy. But I can't remember life without the Festival – it's always been a part of my existence.

If you'd met me as a five- or six-year-old and asked what I thought of the Festival, I think I would have said I was a bit apprehensive about the whole thing. There was a different energy to the event in those days; it had a very unpredictable nature. It felt as though we were doing something unruly and wild, and the characters who came with that were in equal parts exciting and, at times, terrifying. And it was all so close to home – the Festival medical centre was literally in our house, and was teeming.

Back then, there was a whole culture around getting in without paying full price. It was quite loose and fun. There'd be touts outside offering deals to get you inside the fence, which was much easier to breach than the one we have now. People were quite elaborate with their ways of getting in. Lots of them would try tunnelling or climbing over, and I remember some people even using branches to try to catapult themselves in. I saw others trying pole-vaulting and trampolines! We actually used to drive around the fence and put people in the back of the Land Rover to bring them in. This all worked as a bit of a Robin Hood policy – as long as enough people bought tickets, we were happy to help people who couldn't afford it get in.

Because pretty much anyone could get in. It was a real melting pot, and that did mean there were more drug dealers on site. I remember seeing people in lots of different states. In the end, it was a good life lesson, and it definitely put me off drugs. My parents never touched them either. I don't have a problem with people enjoying themselves any way they want, but I think the natural high you get from this event is more powerful than any substance. The moment you see the site emerge over the horizon as you get close, it just gives you a massive rush.

I'd spend the Festival being carried around on my dad's shoulders or on my mum's hip. I remember that Van Morrison played a lot in the eighties, and we would always go and pick him up from Castle Cary train station and then there'd be a long discussion in the car about what he'd play.

During the 1985 Festival, when I was still only five, I was up at the farmhouse, practising my violin with my friend Joe. Someone said, 'Wouldn't it be funny if you guys were on the Pyramid?' I don't know how it happened, but within about five or ten minutes we were up there. The Style Council were just about to play the headline slot, so there were something like 40,000 in the audience, and we were just pushed onto the stage. I can remember someone going, 'Dim the lights! Dim the lights! She's going to freak out if she sees how many people are in this field!' So we walked on and I played 'Twinkle, Twinkle, Little Star', with Joe turning the pages on the music. I'll never forget that moment, the feeling of seeing all those faces looking back at me, many of them grinning. But the most overriding memory is the fear that I felt. I walked offstage and said to my mum, 'Mummy, my legs feel like jelly.' The crowd were going mental and the stage manager said I was going to have to go back on for an encore. I ended up doing it five times with the same response, but after the sixth, when I tried to play another song I didn't know as well, they didn't cheer me back on again. It was an amazing experience, but it put me off joining a band for life.

creativity. That's how Glastonbury became the ever-evolving city that it is now.

Thatcher actually became an unwitting catalyst for it. Her extreme views triggered a real passion in people like my parents to be positive and bring people together. It brought a real political edge to the Festival that has lasted to this day. That's how the CND became involved with Glastonbury, and it's why we were always at Labour Party meetings or on marches. We'd call the marches 'Maggie Outs'. In fact, apparently one of the first things I ever said was, 'We're going on a Maggie Out today!'

Despite the tension, my parents were incredibly close through that time. They really were very much in love. And although my dad was the figurehead of the Festival – the one with the drive and tenacity – my mum was always there to offer amazing support to him. He's quite impulsive, and she was the anchor of it all. The heart of the Festival. The one who was always concerned about how people were feeling, and about looking after them and protecting us all.

The Festival ended the eighties in a much better place than it had begun. My parents had formed a really steely partnership that could withstand anything. They were so close – they needed each other. And the Festival needed them both too.

There were loads of great, ridiculous moments like that, but I think my dad relished it! It was hard to walk through the village and have some people shout at your parents – we were total outsiders. As it got nearer to Festival time, there would sometimes be vicious graffiti about my parents sprayed on signs and roads around the area.

Ultimately, we were choosing not to fit in, and to do our own thing. My parents did have lots of fun, but there was definitely stress too, and there were often meetings in the kitchen with serious-looking bank managers, or court cases as my dad was facing prosecution. He'd be very tense; after all, there were a lot of things to worry about.

There was definitely a part of me that would see the strain we were under and think, 'Are you sure you want to do it?' I was worried about them, and started to relish the Festival's fallow years that began in the eighties. I still do. It's always nice to drop off the radar for a bit.

But despite all the stress, the Festival grew really quickly in the eighties, and got better every year. I remember when we started to get TV coverage and positive reviews in the national press, and it felt like such a novelty for the Festival to be praised. I started to hear all these accents on site that I'd never heard before – big groups of people came on pilgrimages from places like Glasgow and Manchester. And, towards the end of the eighties, even the kids at school began to understand what it was.

A lot of that growth was down to my parents letting so many varied people in to work on the event, and trusting them. They were extraordinary at that. This was a time when there was a lot of fear being spread by Thatcher's government, who were pushing a more self-centred culture, with the whole idea of there being 'no such thing as society'. But my parents gave these very alternative people a lot of freedom and space and, eventually, budget to come in and just create amazing stuff. And as the trust between them grew, so did the

Opposite: Michael, Jean and Emily on a 'Maggie Out' march in London (top);
Michael and Emily visit a photobooth (bottom).
Above: Best friends Emily and Joe Fletcher, aged six.
Overleaf: Hawkwind play on the Pyramid Stage below the disputed CND symbol.

Glastonbury

C N D F E S T I V A L 1 9 8 1
19 20 21 JUNE WORTHY FARM PILTON SOMERSET

Bands

INTRODUCED BY PETE DRUMMOND

**Aswad   Decline and Fall   Ginger Baker   Gong
Gordon Gilltrap   Hawkwind   John Cooper Clarke
Judy Tzuke   Matumbi   New Order   Nick Pickett
Robert Hunter   Roy Harper   Supercharge   Taj Mahal
Talisman   Tim Blake**

(Other bands have indicated their desire to play but do not wish to be publicised)
There will also be a number of speakers including
Bruce Kent, Edward P. Thompson and Sir George Trevelyan

Theatre and films

European Theatre of War, Eye to Eye, Matchbox Purveyors, Tony Crerar, Greatest Show on Legs, Ekome,
Attic, Crystal Theatre, Forkbeard Fantasy, Dance Tales, White Horse, Skullduggery, Emerging Dragon
Blowsabella, Fire-eaters.
Films showing every night from 9pm – 3.30am

Children's Area

Inflatables by Airspace and Groundwell, Palfi the Clown, Zippo, Ekome (African tribal dancers),
Jacolly Puppets, Bath Puppets, Donkey Team, Bristol Playbus, Steam Railway, Playskool, Plus, Adventure
Playground, Stage and Marquees.

In addition to the above events there will also be a large market area, food stalls, medical and legal
services and free camping. Three day advance tickets are £8 each, children up to 14 years old get in free.
The fee for a stall is £40 this entitles two people to trade at the Festival for three days.

Applications for TICKETS to:– C.N.D. (Festival) 11 Goodwin Street, London N4 3HQ. Applications for STALLS to:–
Festival Office, Worthy Farm, Pilton, Shepton Mallet, Somerset BA4 4BY. All Cheques and Postal Orders to be made payable
to GLASTONBURY C.N.D. FESTIVAL. Please enclose an S.A.E. with your applications.

As membership of the Campaign for Nuclear Disarmament grew, the first Festival of the 1980s took on a new name: Glastonbury CND Festival. Michael was back in full charge of the event, convincing an initially reluctant National CND that with proper management the Festival could be turned into a profitable venture, with proceeds going to the Mid-Somerset CND campaign. In return, National CND promoted the event and handled ticket sales. Around £20,000 was eventually donated to CND by Michael Eavis.

This was also the year that the second Pyramid Stage was built, on the same spot as the 1971 structure. Constructed from telegraph poles and ex-MOD iron sheeting (spotted by Michael at Taunton cattle market), it took three months to build and was to be used as a cowshed and animal food store in the winter months.

1981
CAPACITY: 18,000
TICKET PRICE: £8

The 1981 Festival attracted curious locals as well as young Festival-goers. Opposite: scenes from 1981, including an early version of the Kidz castle (top left). The departing crowds left behind their memories and, in some cases, their clothes (bottom right).

Peter Hook
New Order

I am listening to our performance at Glastonbury on 20 June 1981 as I write this. There are many comparisons between our performance and the festival: we were both young, chaotic, sloppy and relaxed, indulging in a sense of enjoyment without worrying about the future.

It is strange that both of us should have to grow up, almost together. Both becoming more mature, more important, more experienced, more responsible, more professional. Less fun? NEVER!

I still use my four appearances at Glastonbury as a yardstick of my career. Whenever I need to impress someone or gain a little leeway, it's always that fact that I pull out.

From the first time, being welcomed into the family home and having Michael show how to make Aga toast while Emily played with her dolls on the floor – I had never heard of an Aga then, but I proudly own one now, and whenever I make toast it is with that recipe and those thoughts in mind – to the most recent, when opening with the Haçienda Classiçal and making the opening tribute to the victims of the Manchester and Grenfell tragedies, I am very proud of my association with the Festival. I fondly remember finding Joe Strummer's memorial stone, and all my lost weekends with Bez and Keith Allen, when I was performing in a different way.

Now, the Festival and I are both older gentlemen, and take things at a slower, more deliberate pace. But, believe me, the smile on my face whenever our paths cross takes a long time to fade, and in some ways never does ...

Peter Hook (in background, right) as a younger gentleman; on the Pyramid Stage with New Order in 1981.

MUSIC
**VAN MORRISON
JACKSON BROWNE
RICHIE HAVENS ASWAD
JUDY TZUKE   STEEL PULSE
JOHN COOPER CLARKE
CLIMAX BLUES BAND
THOMPSON TWINS U2
THE BLUES BAND TALISMAN
A CERTAIN RATIO**

THEATRE
**ALEXEI SAYLE DAVID RAPPAPORT INCUBUS
GREATEST SHOW ON LEGS ATTIC THEATRE EKOME
FREEFORM THEATRE TRUST FORKBEARD FANTASY**

FILMS
**Dr STRANGELOVE BEING THERE AIRPLANE
DERECK JARMONE & TOYAH in THE TEMPEST
SECRET POLICEMANS BALL CHINA SYNDROME
MY BRILLIANT CAREER**

**SPEAKERS LASERS FOOD
CHILDRENS WORLD CAMPING**

GLASTONBURY
CND FESTIVAL 1982

**FRIDAY 18th SATURDAY 19th & SUNDAY 20th of JUNE. Worthy Farm, Pilton, Somerset.
Advance Tickets £8 from C N D (Festival) 227 SEVEN SISTERS ROAD, LONDON, N4.**
All Cheques and P.O.s to be made payable to **Glastonbury C N D Festival**. Children under 14 admitted FREE.

Design - John Andrews

1982

CAPACITY: 25,000
TICKET PRICE: £8

CND increased its role within the Festival, Western Region CND taking control of the entrance gates and Mid-Somerset CND taking charge of the Festival's press, advertising and information services. This was also the first year the CND logo appeared on top of the Pyramid Stage, where it remained throughout the decade.

Parts of the event were filmed for a Thames TV music documentary, broadcast later that year. It was also an extremely wet and muddy year: Somerset's highest rainfall for a single day in forty-five years was recorded on the Friday. Although conditions were challenging, the post-Festival welfare report concluded that 'the facilities and services coped much better than last year in far more difficult circumstances'.

Babylon by bus: reggae legends Robbie Shakespeare and Sly Dunbar arrive at Worthy Farm in 1982 in a line-up that also included the late, great Dennis Brown, Black Uhuru (above), Aswad and Talisman.

Clockwise: The Pyramid Stage in 1982; headliner Van Morrison; an unlicensed market trader spots a potential customer; Aswad's Brinsley Forde kicks back.

Billy Bragg
Musician & Left Field Organiser

Thursday night had become Friday morning when we arrived straight from a Music for Miners benefit in Bristol. The only light came from campfires, hand torches and a waning moon. Every space seemed to be taken by tents, through which lines of people snaked across the site. The only way to make progress was to verbally negotiate with whomever's private space we were walking through.

The atmosphere was reminiscent of a kind of West Country Kumbh Mela: as far as the eye could see there were pilgrims waiting for the dawn, while in the distance the dark shape of the Great Pyramid, focus of this ceremonial gathering, rose out of the Somerset Levels.

But for now, the only noise to be heard above the murmuring throng was the sound of hawkers offering their dodgy wares. 'Hot knives!' was the call from the hedges, repeated every hundred or so yards, calling the faithful to partake in the most primitive of sacraments. Thirty thousand people camped out under the stars; it was a stark contrast to the world unfolding beyond Worthy Farm.

It was June 1984. Just three days before, five thousand miners picketing Orgreave coking plant were attacked by lines of mounted police. Hundreds were hospitalised, including their leader, Arthur Scargill, in what was later described as a police riot. It was one of the most violent clashes in British industrial history, and the working class took a severe beating.

Since Margaret Thatcher came to power in 1979, the whole country had taken sides. The miners' strike had heightened that division, forcing people to ask, 'Which side are you on?' Glastonbury Festival nailed its colours to the mast in 1981, donating profits to the Campaign for Nuclear Disarmament. The CND symbol that sat like a magic eye at the pinnacle of the Pyramid Stage was a beacon to the tribes who stood in opposition to Thatcher and all she represented: lefties, crusties, feminists, peaceniks, Rastafarians, vegetarians and all sorts of esoteric madmen and women left over from the sixties. The Pyramid acted like a giant orgone generator, and we gathered together in its shadow to recharge our activism in solidarity and song.

It was behind this stage that I awoke that first morning at the Festival, having spent the night sleeping in the beaten-up Volvo estate that Andy Kershaw and I had been using to tour the UK that summer. Ablutions backstage would be seen as pretty basic now, but given the state of those available to the punters, they were luxurious – a portable toilet block with urinals, a couple of cubicles, plenty of toilet paper and a sink to wash your hands.

These were the days when rock festivals were nothing more than a gig in a field. Facilities were basic, the organisation ad hoc, but people came nonetheless. For a few days, you felt part of an alternative society where the vibes were more important than the material experience. And the vibes at Glastonbury were stronger than anywhere else, mostly because of the remote location of the site.

All the festivals that I'd been to before were in cities. If it started to rain at Reading Festival, you could walk into town, buy a bag of chips and get the train home. Likewise Knebworth. Glastonbury was a whole different experience. In the days when fewer young people had cars, it was a trek to get on site, and once you were there, well, there wasn't anywhere within walking distance to seek respite, apart from that little shop on the bend in Pilton that was always overwhelmed with festival-goers buying loads of Wagon Wheels to see them through the weekend munchies.

For five days in June, Glastonbury Festival was a kingdom unto itself, the green and pleasant land of Blake's 'Jerusalem', rising from the Levels in the misty dawn like Arthur's Avalon. For, whatever the elements threw at

us, we were all in it together, castaways from straight society enjoying a few days of spiritual anarchy until the whole thing upped and vanished on Monday morning like a crusty Brigadoon.

Plus, Glastonbury had something that you couldn't find at Reading or Knebworth: the summer solstice. The two events didn't always line up, but when they did, magic happened. One year beneath canvas, I was awoken by a distant rhythmic banging. Nowadays, of course, that would be a sign that The Glade was still going strong, but back in the eighties, nights were quieter at Glasto, and this noise had crept into my dreamy consciousness. A constant three beats of a bar – 1-2-3, 1-2-3, 1-2-3 – it was hypnotic, irresistible. The first light of dawn was illuminating the tent as I slipped out into the misty morning, drawn to the sound. I climbed up through the site until I came to Carhenge, the base camp of the Mutoid Waste Company.

There, I found perhaps a thousand people, gathered around the Skull Bus that led the Mutoid convoy. Standing on top of the vehicle were a crew of skinny white dreads, orchestrating the rhythm with wooden staffs that were part weapon, part wand. Everybody in the crowd was beating out the 1-2-3 on anything they could lay their hands on: tins, rocks, sticks. I grabbed a nearby Coke can and began hitting it with a stone – 1-2-3, 1-2-3. Soon, my individuality had been submerged in the music of the mob.

I gleaned that we were summoning the solstice sunrise, and as it appeared the rhythm picked up pace until a metallic cacophony greeted the moment that the orb of the sun left the ground. As it did, the Skull Bus lurched into life and, belching smoke, set off downhill at high speed towards the Pyramid Stage. Suddenly the spell was broken, and we awoke from our trancelike state to look at one another in amazement and smile at the dawn.

Could that still happen at the Festival today? I doubt it. People would be too busy filming it on their phones to let go and become one with the solstice. But for me it was the quintessential Glastonbury experience, something chanced upon that captures your imagination and, for a moment, takes you out of yourself. Totally free, totally unscheduled and totally bonkers.

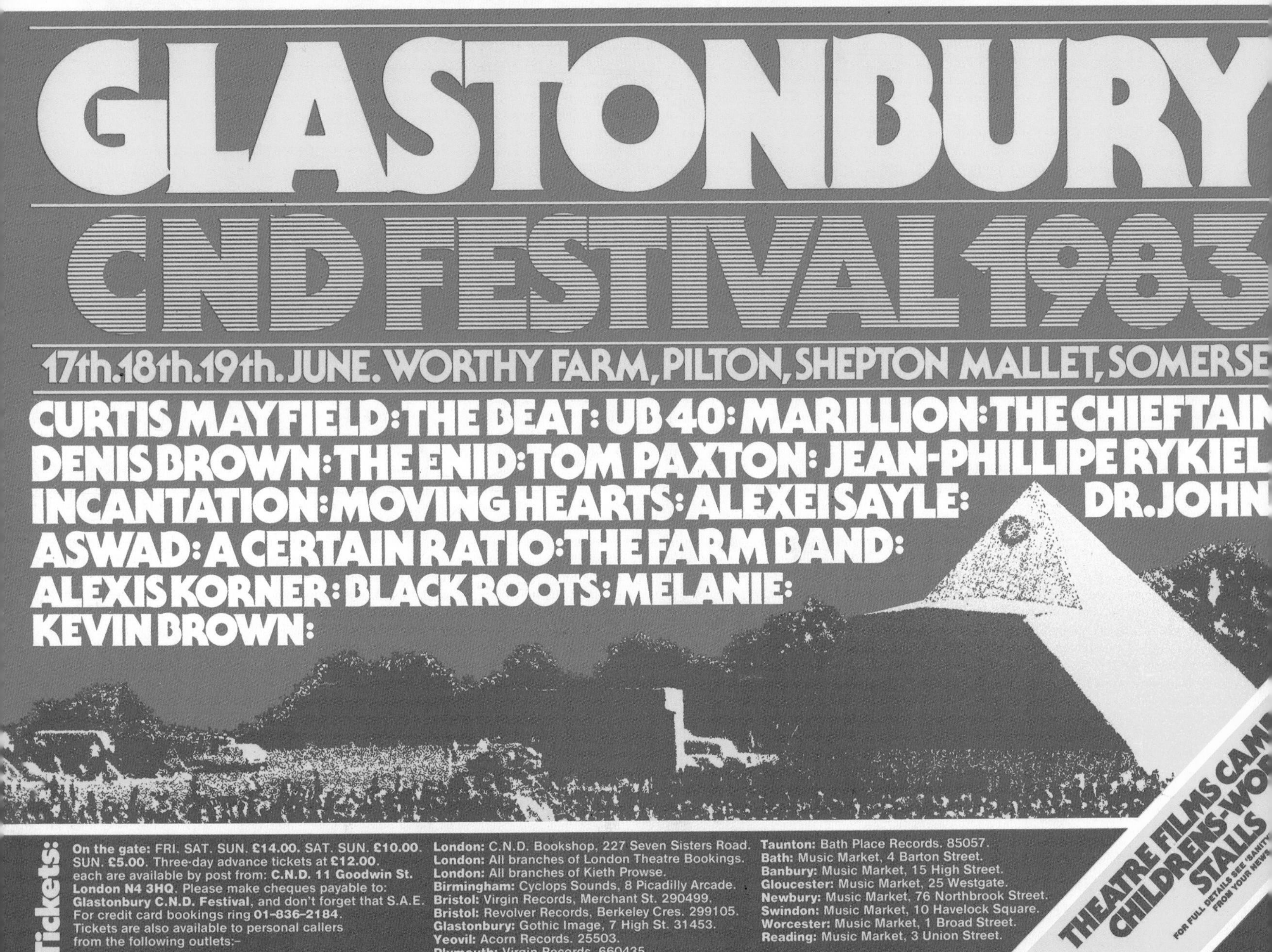

GLASTONBURY
CND FESTIVAL 1983

17th.18th.19th. JUNE. WORTHY FARM, PILTON, SHEPTON MALLET, SOMERSE

**CURTIS MAYFIELD : THE BEAT : UB 40 : MARILLION : THE CHIEFTAIN
DENIS BROWN : THE ENID : TOM PAXTON : JEAN-PHILLIPE RYKIEL
INCANTATION : MOVING HEARTS : ALEXEI SAYLE :   DR. JOHN
ASWAD : A CERTAIN RATIO : THE FARM BAND :
ALEXIS KORNER : BLACK ROOTS : MELANIE :
KEVIN BROWN :**

Tickets: On the gate: FRI. SAT. SUN. £14.00. SAT. SUN. £10.00.
SUN. £5.00. Three-day advance tickets at £12.00.
each are available by post from: **C.N.D. 11 Goodwin St.
London N4 3HQ.** Please make cheques payable to:
Glastonbury C.N.D. Festival, and don't forget that S.A.E.
For credit card bookings ring **01–836–2184.**
Tickets are also available to personal callers
from the following outlets:–

London: C.N.D. Bookshop, 227 Seven Sisters Road.
London: All branches of London Theatre Bookings.
London: All branches of Kieth Prowse.
Birmingham: Cyclops Sounds, 8 Picadilly Arcade.
Bristol: Virgin Records, Merchant St. 290499.
Bristol: Revolver Records, Berkeley Cres. 299105.
Glastonbury: Gothic Image, 7 High St. 31453.
Yeovil: Acorn Records. 25503.
Plymouth: Virgin Records. 660435.

Taunton: Bath Place Records. 85057.
Bath: Music Market, 4 Barton Street.
Banbury: Music Market, 15 High Street.
Gloucester: Music Market, 25 Westgate.
Newbury: Music Market, 76 Northbrook Street.
Swindon: Music Market, 10 Havelock Square.
Worcester: Music Market, 1 Broad Street.
Reading: Music Market, 3 Union Street.

**THEATRE FILMS CAM
CHILDRENS-WO
STALLS**
FOR FULL DETAILS SEE 'GAMI
FROM YOUR NEV

Curtis Mayfield (opposite, centre) delivers one of Glastonbury's
first legend slots in 1983.
Overleaf: From donkey rides to 'dread at the controls',
Glastonbury offered a diversity unmatched anywhere else.

1983

CAPACITY: 30,000
TICKET PRICE: £12

The Local Government Act became law, giving local authorities the power to regulate outdoor events. For the Festival to go ahead, a Public Entertainment Licence had to be obtained from Mendip District Council, which set the crowd limit and regulated conditions for all on-site services.

At Worthy Farm, the ever-growing Children's Area was very well received, with the local paper describing its donkey rides, play equipment, model-railway circuit, face-painting and entertainment as 'heaven on earth for the young'. Glastonbury Festival's own on-site radio station, Radio Avalon, also made its debut this year, and has continued to broadcast from the farm during the event (latterly as Worthy FM) ever since.

CHECKPOINT KIWI

TICKET CHECKPOINT

PLEASE SHOW PASSES

LOST CHILDREN
LOST CHILDREN KEPT
HERE TILL 6PM THEN MOVED TO

WEST END
PLAYGROUND

4 for £1

83

FESTIVAL
BADGE
30P

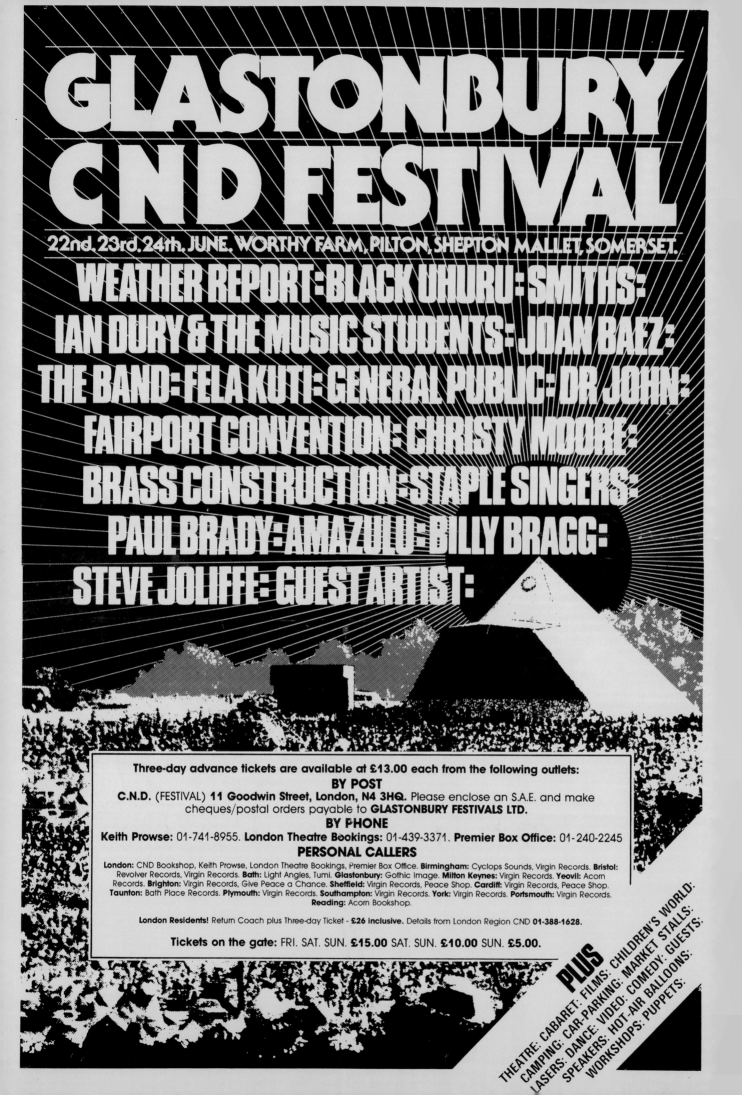

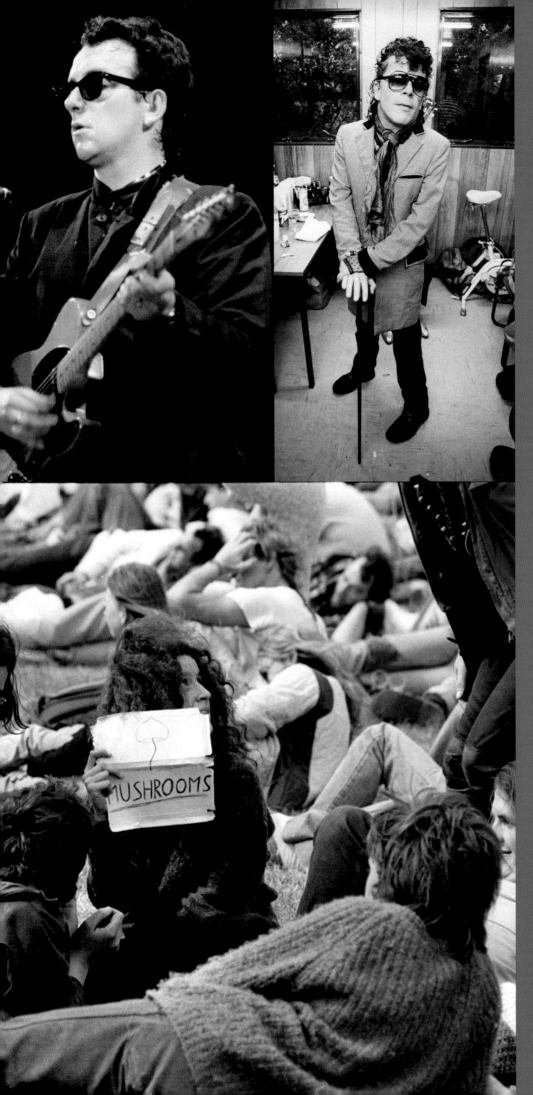

1984

CAPACITY: 50,000
TICKET PRICE: £13

On 17 January 1984, at Shepton Mallet Magistrates' Court, Michael Eavis successfully defended five prosecutions brought by Mendip District Council for breaching the 1983 licence, and immediately applied for a new licence with a 15 per cent increase in numbers. After a series of packed public meetings and debate in the local press, the licence was duly granted.

The site expanded to include the Green Collective for the first time (current Green Fields Area Organiser Liz Eliot is a willing volunteer), while the PTA at Emily's primary school in West Pennard raised funds by stewarding on-site parking.

Up at the farmhouse, Dan Stewart arrived to head up a signwriting team based in an abandoned railway goods wagon, and helped with the creation of the distinctive Glastonbury font. One of the first newly painted sings read 'SITE FULL'.

On the Pyramid, The Smiths delivered a Saturday-night headline set now remembered as one of Glastonbury's defining musical moments. But at the time Morrissey wasn't convinced. 'It wasn't the best of our performances,' he said, 'and there was some animosity from certain sectors of the crowd. It is quite strange when you're singing to people who obviously do not like you . . . It sounded a very attractive prospect, but I don't think The Smiths worked at Glastonbury.' The following morning, renowned historian E.P. Thompson (author of *The Making of the English Working Class*), personally recruited by Michael, delivered his famous 'Alternative Nation' speech.

Elvis Costello (top left), Ian Dury (top right) and one of the many unofficial Festival signs in the crowd (left). Overleaf: Captured from the side of the Pyramid, rock photographer Paul Slattery's classic image of The Smiths in 1984.

The Festival's size and reputation grew exponentially in the early eighties, allowing Michael and his trusted agents (particularly Paul Charles at Asgard) to attract some of the biggest names in music to the line-up. Malcolm Haynes also arrived from Bristol in a Transit van packed with speakers and amplifiers to inject some dance music into proceedings (and he remains Area Organiser of Silver Hayes to this day).

Meanwhile, the purchase of Cockmill Farm and the land at the end of the disused railway line increased the site by over a hundred acres. This extra space turned out to be extremely useful, as 1985 saw an influx of travellers following the Battle of the Beanfield, in which the police violently prevented the Peace Convoy from entering nearby Stonehenge for the traditional free summer solstice festival. Many travellers diverted to the Glastonbury site instead.

Then, on the Thursday of the Festival, it began to rain very hard. By the time the bulk of the

crowd arrived, the newly enlarged site was a mudbath, and Welfare were handing out free bin liners with holes cut out as makeshift ponchos. Artists' coaches and trucks were ferried in via a new Stage Road, completed only hours before the gates opened. Despite the weather, the crowd's Glastonbury spirit remained strong, and the mud-soaked masses seemed determined to enjoy themselves. That said, most artists would probably have preferred it if throwing mud at the stage hadn't become this particular Festival's defining trend.

Celebrated as Glastonbury's first real 'muddy one', 1985 saw appearances from Joe Cocker (bottom, far left), the Boomtown Rats (left), Echo and the Bunnymen (above) and the Bishop of Bath and Wells (above left).

Jean, (in foreground), Emily and Michael visit the CND hot-air balloon after a trial flight before the Festival in 1985. Opposite: An early traffic jam in the Markets quarter (top); message boards kept people in touch before the arrival of mobile phones (bottom).

GLASTONBURY

CND FESTIVAL 1986

stage 1

Friday:
PSYCHEDELIC FURS
RUBY TURNER
THE POGUES
WATERBOYS
AMAZULU
THAT PETROL EMOTION
HOWARD HUGHES
& THE WESTERN APPROACHES
RODNEY ALLEN
(Local Guest)

Saturday:
THE CURE
LLOYD COLE &
THE COMMOTIONS
BLACK UHURU &
THE WAILERS
JOHN MARTYN
LATIN QUARTER
LOUDON WAINWRIGHT III

Sunday:
LEVEL 42
MADNESS
ROBERT CRAY BAND
SIMPLY RED
CHRISTY MOORE
GIL SCOTT-HERON
THE HOUSEMARTINS
BUDDY CURTESS
& THE GRASSHOPPERS

stage 2

ARIWA POSSE · BRILLIANT CORNERS · TED CHIPPINGTON · DREAM SYNDICATE
FOREST HILLBILLIES · FRANK CHICKENS · FUZZ BOX · GO-BETWEENS · HALF MAN
HALF BISCUIT · JAZZ BUTCHER · PELLY & JERRY · MICRODISNEY · NIGHTINGALES
PHRANC · THE POTATO 5 · RENT PARTY · ROBYN HITCHCOCK & THE EGYPTIANS
DAINTEES · ZAP D · THREE MUSTAPHAS THREE · WOODENTOPS · JUNE BRIDES
MIGHTY LEMONDROPS · FISSION BROTHERS · LEN BRIGHT COMBO · SHENNONS
PAULINE BLACK & THE SUPERNATURALS · MUMBO JUMBO · BLOOD FIRE POSSE
EDWARDO & ANTONIO · CRAIG CHARLES · ALAHA · ZINICA

Accoustic Stage

BILLY BRAGG · LOUDON WAINWRIGHT III · MINT JULEPS · CEILIDH with ARRAN PILOT · RAG TAG
JOHNY COPPIN & PHIL BEER · NICK PICKETT · RORY McCLOUD · RUMILLAJTA · MELANIE HARALD
CAJUN MUSIC · FLAMENCO GUITAR · FOUR FRENCH MEN · MARIA MULDOUR · KEVIN BROWN
ANDY WHITE · JAMES CANN · SCREAMING ABDABS · STRING QUARTET · WILD ETHNIC DANCING

Classical

JOHN WILLIAMS, GERALD GARCIA (guitar) ALAN SCHILLER (piano), MICK TAYLOR (sitar)
FRANCIS MONKMAN (synthesiser), Buckingham Piano Quartet, Ariel Ensemble, Etesian Winds,
Christine Bunning & David Mason Darryl Way with Electric Chamber Ensemble, Anthony Pleeth,
Myriad Piano Trio, Triple Echo Cello Quartet, Richard Stagg, Miranda Fulleyglove Trio Shakuhachi.

FRINGE THEATRE

La Bouche · Denise Black & The Kray Sisters · Sensible Footwear · Fallout Marching Band
Northern Black Light Theatre · Akimbo · Joolz · Centre Ocean Stream · Malcolm Hardee · Zippo & Co
Spare Tyre · Laughing Stock · Two Fingers · Attila the Stockbroker · Skint Video · Flying Patrol Group

Speakers: Edward Thompson · Paul Johns · Ann Clwyd M.P. · William Peden · Petra Kelly & Bishop of Dudley

THEATRE • FILMS • CHILDREN'S WORLD • CEILIDH • VIDEO • FOOD
CLASSICAL MUSIC • STALLS • CABARET • CAMPING • CLOWNS
GREENFIELD • LASERS • WORKSHOPS • FOLK MUSIC • COMEDY

This Event is the most effective Anti-Nuclear Fund Raiser in Europe

1986

CAPACITY: 36,000
TICKET PRICE: £17

As the Festival continued to grow, difficulties arose in recording the exact number of people on site. Actual tickets sold gave some indication, but it became clear that plenty of people had arrived without them. This year, however, Mendip District Council took a different tack on the licence conditions, setting no limit on numbers but compelling the Festival to provide 'sufficient facilities' for all those attending.

For the first time a spotter plane circled Worthy Farm capturing aerial photographs in an attempt to quantify the size of the crowd. Inside the event, the expanding Theatre area shifted to a new location with two marquees and an open-air stage, and also hosted the HQ for the Glastonbury Global, the first (Xeroxed) newspaper to be produced on site. The Children's Area also found itself in a new home, a quieter and soon to become permanent location near the Acoustic Stage. Its other near neighbour this year was the short-lived Classical Stage, programmed by John Williams.

The Cure headlined for the first time, and most of those in attendance, and particularly the music press, heralded a vintage year. But for Michael and Jean, it proved a stressful experience, and it was far from certain that Glastonbury 1987 would go ahead.

Previous page: Mike Scott of the Waterboys (centre),
That Petrol Emotion (bottom left) and Ruby Turner
(bottom right) at Glastonbury in 1986.
Opposite: From the garden gate — 1986 snapshots in
Jean Eavis' family album.
This page: An early Glastonbury bootleg — The Cure's
gig on cassette, complete with setlist, exhumed from
the loft at Worthy Farm. Unlicensed C90 cassette
recordings of Glastonbury gigs, sold under the counter
at market stalls, were the must-have collectors' items
of the 1980s.

THE CURE. GLASTONBURY.1986

Intro:
SHAKE DOG SHAKE.
PLAY FOR TODAY.
THE KYOTO SONG.
PRIMARY.
CHARLOTTE SOMETIMES.
A STRANGE DAY.
IN BETWEEN DAYS.
THE WALK.
A NIGHT LIKE THIS.
ONE HUNDRED YEARS.
PUSH.
A FOREST.
SINKING.
CLOSE TO ME/LET'S GO TO BED
GIVE ME IT./BOYS DON'T CRY/
FAITH.
PORNOGRAPHY.

SPITFIRE TAPES 1986

Glastonbury

1987

CND FESTIVAL 19-20-21 June 19-20-21 June

— Worthy Farm, Pilton, Somerset —

MAIN STAGE

ELVIS COSTELLO ▲ VAN MORRISON ▲ THE COMMUNARDS
NEW ORDER ▲ THE ROBERT CRAY BAND ▲ LOS LOBOS
BEN E. KING ▲ TAJ MAHAL ▲ TROUBLE FUNK
THE RICHARD THOMPSON BAND ▲ COURTNEY PINE
HÜSKER DÜ ▲ PAUL BRADY ▲ MEN THEY COULDN'T HANG
THE WOODENTOPS ▲ THE MIGHTY LEMONDROPS
MICHELLE SHOCKED ▲ MISTY IN ROOTS
WORLD PARTY ▲ RODNEY ALLEN

STAGE TWO

EL SONIDA DE LONDRES   MEKONS   THE OYSTER BAND
GAYE BYKERS ON ACID   THE BLUE AEROPLANES
BRILLIANT CORNERS   CHORCAZADE   THE CHILLS
STUMP   ROBYN HITCHCOCK & THE EGYPTIANS
ANDY SHEPHERD QUARTET   EDUARDO NIEBLA &
ANTONIO FORCIONE   BEN BADDOO & THE ALAHA BAND

ACCOUSTIC STAGE

RICHARD THOMPSON   ARNOLD BOLT   JACKIE EVANS   NICK PICKET
PRIOR STRING QUARTET   THE THREE CABALLEROS   SCREAMING ABDABS
CHARLIE HERNSHAW QUINTET   THE GLEE CLUB   ANDY WHITE   Music from
South America and Eastern Europe There will also be late comedy and guests on this stage.

THEATRE:

SKINT VIDEO   ATTIC THEATRE   THEATRE ROTTO   RICHARD CUMING
CENTRE OCEAN STREAM   JIVING LINDY HOPPERS   UNITED MATRONS
DAVID MICHELSEN & MANNA   DOCTOR FOSTER'S TRAVELLING THEATRE
PANIC PUPPETS   MALCOLM HARDEE & THE GREATEST SHOW ON LEGS
BEAVERS   SHIKISHA   The best of straight-and alternative theatre, cabaret, stand up comedy, mime,
dance, drumming, harmonica-virtuosi, clowns, stilt walkers, jugglers, special effects and many participation workshops.

WOMAD FIELD

CIEGO DE NAGUA (DOMINICAN REPUBLIC)   FRANCO & T.P. OK JAZZ (ZAIRE)
GWERZ (FRANCE)   TANGO AL SUR (ARGENTINA)   FARAFINA (BURKINA FASO)
ALAAP (INDIA/UK)   KRISHNA MURTI SRIDHAR (INDIA)   MUZSIKAS (HUNGARY)
AIT MENGUELLET (ALGERIA)   GASPER LAWAL (NIGERIA/UK)   SELDA (TURKEY)
FLORA HOLTON (USA)

THEATRE ▲ FILMS ▲ CHILDREN'S WORLD ▲ GREENFIELD
CABARET ▲ CAMPING ▲ CLOWNS ▲ CEILIDH
COMEDY ▲ WORKSHOPS ▲ FOLK MUSIC
LASERS ▲ FOOD ▲ STALLS ▲ VIDEO

1987

CAPACITY: 60,000
TICKET PRICE: £21

With Mendip District Council initially refusing to grant a licence, it wasn't until May that the decision was overturned on appeal and the Festival was given the go-ahead. Yet less than a month later, a stunning line-up was revealed that featured a host of international acts across the growing number of stages. This year saw the launch of the WOMAD field, with music from Zaire, the Dominican Republic, India, Argentina, Burkina Faso and Turkey.

Around the site, Glastonbury's penchant for the unexpected continued with the solar-powered Croissant Neuf Stage. And former TV sports presenter turned professional conspiracy theorist David Icke took to the Pyramid to preach his gospel – he would later announce that he was the son of the Godhead and predict the imminent end of the world.

Joe Rush, founder of the Mutoid Waste Company – who'd first arrived with the travellers diverted from Stonehenge in 1985 – built Carhenge, a stone circle made from scrap cars, in the Travellers' Fields in the south-east corner of the site. He then led a legendary night-long drumming session around it, sowing the seeds for what would become the Festival's late-night areas.

The 1987 Festival ends with a record £130,000 contribution to CND funds – and a decision to take a 'fallow year'.

Top: Courtney Pine.
Centre left: Jimmy Somerville of the Communards.
Centre right: The Mutoid Waste Company's Carhenge.
Left: Michelle Shocked.

Suzanne Vega

Musician

Being offered the headline spot at Glastonbury in 1989 was incredibly special. In the summer of 1979 I was the wardrobe mistress for the miracle plays at Glastonbury Abbey. While my friends jumped the fence and went to the Festival, I spent my nights at the local library reading and writing poetry, hoping to make some headway as a songwriter, little dreaming that in ten years I would be back — to headline!

However, it wasn't all plain sailing. A female fan had developed an unhealthy obsession with my bass player, Mike Visceglia. He'd refused her advances, and she became angry, making violent threats, and Scotland Yard was called in. Right before we were due to go onstage, I was told that I was also the target of these threats, and we were advised not to perform that night. I told them that of course I was going to play, so they gave me a bulletproof vest. The vest's owner was three times my size, so we gaffer-taped it closed, and I wore my assistant's denim jacket over it. Mike had to play offstage, surrounded by two bodyguards.

The whole set felt surreal, like it was happening underwater. Every song felt like it was twenty minutes long. In the end, there was a curfew, and we had to cut the set short, but looking back it was a thrilling moment. I was the first female headliner, and when Beyoncé headlined in 2011, I can remember thinking, 'Oh yes, I've done that!'

John Cooper Clarke

Poet

THE FUCKING VIEW IS FUCKING VILE FOR FUCKING MILES AND FUCKING MILES THE FUCKING BABIES FUCKING CRY THE FUCKING FLOWERS FUCKING DIE ...

That is one of the less-celebrated stanzas of my poem 'Evidently Chickentown', and I'd like to think it had some resonance for the motley crowd who turned up to see me perform on the Pyramid Stage at Glastonbury Festival in 1982, even if it was a bit much for the telly people who were there trying to film everything. A brave call that, and I wouldn't mind seeing that footage again sometime. Show what you like, use what you like, just don't make me look like a cunt.

I'd toured some venues in America the year before, and at the first gig I was still reading the poem with 'bloody' in it. The way it was first written. On the second night, at the Ritzy in New York, I was told bloody ain't a cuss word there. So from then on I did it right – got the engine of the poem going, put a tiger in its tank. Thank you, the Land of the Free, for that.

I was on at Glastonbury between the Polecats, riding high in the charts with 'Rockabilly Guy', and Black Uhuru, joined by Sly and Robbie. Reggae, rockabilly and poetry, there's an eclectic booking policy right there, the 1980s in a sandwich. Far from being the pop-up megacity it was to become, Glastonbury back then really was a shared experience, with all us performers gathering below the stage, hobnobbing between bits of wood, metal and plastic with the stage above our heads.

Opposite: Suzanne Vega on the Pyramid in 1989. Above: John Cooper Clarke delivers the uncensored 'Evidently Chickentown' in 1982. Overleaf: No ordinary backyard — Jean Eavis captures the essence of 1980s Glastonbury in this family snapshot.

THE FUCKING FOOD IS FUCKING MUCK THE FUCKING DRAINS ARE FUCKING FUCKED THE COLOUR SCHEME IS FUCKING BROWN EVERYWHERE IN CHICKENTOWN.

I'm just not the countrified type but despair is the same wherever you are. I was wearing Anello & Davide shoes, top dollar, and the first thing I did with Judy, my PR, was check the exits. Told her to keep a car handy, because I wasn't going to damage my footwear.

I did hear, some time later, that people in the nearby village of Pilton had made complaints about the foul language broadcast over the valley. I can confirm that was me. Thanks a lot for not calling the police on me. I wouldn't have had a leg to stand on.

GLASTONBURY FESTIVAL

16–17–18 June 1989

This event, at Worthy Farm in the Vale of Avalon, has over 1,000 acts on 10 stages covering the complete range of contemporary performing arts, and offers a major stimulus to the morale and finances of the Campaign for Nuclear Disarmament. At £28 for the whole weekend this must be by far the best value in the country.

PYRAMID STAGE: ★ ELVIS COSTELLO ★
★ VAN MORRISON ★ SUZANNE VEGA ★ special guests ★
ALL ABOUT EVE ★ AMABUTHU ★ THE BHUNDU BOYS
FAIRGROUND ATTRACTION ★ HOT HOUSE FLOWERS ★ FELA ANIKULAPO KUTI
MAHLATINI & THE MAHOTELLA QUEENS ★ YOUSSOU N'DOUR ★ PIXIES
THE PROCLAIMERS ★ DAVID RUDDER ★ THROWING MUSES ★ ALEXEI SAYLE
MARTIN STEPHENSON & THE DAINTEES ★ THE WATERBOYS ★ HEATHCOTE WILLIAMS
WOMACK & WOMACK ★ THE WONDER STUFF
introduced by ANDY KERSHAW and JOHNNY WALKER ❦

THEATRE & CIRCUS: ★ MR. ADAMS & MR. DANDRIDGE ★ DERRICO ALZANAS ★
BRIAN ANDRO ★ ANIMATE THEATRE ★ TONY ALLEN ★ ARIADNE PRODUCTIONS ★ ATILLA THE STOCKBROKER
AVANTI DISPLAY ★ AVON TOURING COMPANY ★ BALLETICO FANTASTICO ★ BALLS-UP JUGGLERS
BASIC STRATEGIES ★ THE BEAVERS ★ BERNIE BENNETT ★ BLACK MIME THEATRE
THE BMX FREESTYLE DISPLAY TEAM ★ PADDY BRAMWELL ★ REX BOYD ★ LES BUBB ★ ZAK CARLINO
CENTRE OCEAN STREAM ★ CIRCO BESERCO ★ CIRCUS BURLESQUE ★ CIRQUE DU TROTTOIR ★ CLOAK 'N' DAGGER
COMIC CAPERS ★ DESPERATE MEN ★ THE ENGLISH SHAKESPEARE COMPANY ★ FAULTY OPTIC ★ FLUKE
THE FLYING ALLIGATORS ★ FOUR MINUTE WARNING ★ FRANTIC ANTICS ★ FREEFALL MACHINE
THE GAMBIAN ACROBATS ★ THE GAMBOLLING GUIZERS ★ SEAN GANDINI ★ BRENDA GILHOULIE
THE GRAND THEATRE OF LEMMINGS ★ GROUNDWELL ARTS ★ HAGGIS & CHARLIE ★ HAIRY FAIRY ★ ANNIE HALL
MALCOLM HARDEE ★ HARP START'S RANDOM SOUND ★ JOHN HEGLEY ★ NEIL HERD ★ HI-FIVE
ROY HUTCHINS reads "WHALE NATION" ★ THE INFLATABLE THEATRE COMPANY ★ JACKIE JONES
THE JONGLEURS ★ JOOLZ ★ THE KATHKALI DANCERS ★ DES KAY ★ JONATHON KAY ★ KEIR HARDEE ★ LA BOUCHE
JOHN LEE ★ LOS PRIMOS ★ LUMIERE & SON ★ CHRIS LYNHAM ★ JOHN MOLONEY ★ MARK MIWURDZ
MOON SHADOW PUPPETS ★ MOP & DROP ★ JOHN MOWAT ★ MUMMERANDADA ★ NATHANIEL OF WESSEX
NATURAL THEATRE COMPANY ★ NICK NICHOLAS ★ NICKELODEON ★ NO FIT STATE CIRCUS ★ NO MEAN FEAT
THE NORFOLK MOUNTAIN RESCUE A-TEAM ★ NO STRINGS PUPPET THEATRE ★ NOT THE NATIONAL THEATRE
OMELETTE BROADCASTING ★ THE ODDBALLS ★ THE PALLACY TRAPEZE RIG & SCHOOL ★ PARACHUTE THEATRE CO.
THE PEOPLE SHOW ★ THE PIONEERS KENYAN ACROBATIC SHOW ★ PUBLIC PARTS ★ THE QUEENS OF ARTS
RACHEL ★ JERRY SADOWITZ ★ MARK SAUNDERS ★ SCRATCH ★ THE SEA MONSTER ★ SENSIBLE FOOTWEAR
FRANCOISE SERGY ★ SEB SHAW ★ SKINNING THE CAT ★ SKINT VIDEO ★ SPLATMAN ★ THE SQUEAKERS ★ STOMPY
DAVE SUICH ★ SWAMPS CIRCUS ★ TAK 'N TAT ★ THIN AIR ★ MARK THOMAS ★ TEATRO DE EXISTENTIALE
ANDY WATSON ★ WAX 'N' WANE ★ THE WHALLEY RANGE ALL-STARS ★ LUCY WISDOM ★ YSKALNARI ❦

ACOUSTIC STAGE: ★ AND ALL BECAUSE THE LADY LOVES ★ BALHAM ALIGATORS ★ RUBY BLUE ★ THE BLUES BAND
MARTIN CARTHY ★ SONJA CHRISTINA ★ CLEA & MCLEOD ★ BRENDAN CROKER & THE 5 O'CLOCK SHADOWS
THE DUBIOUS BROTHERS ★ FIGGY DUFF ★ JOHNNY G. & THE WALCOT STRINGS ★ HULLABALOO
INNER SENSE PERCUSSION ORCHESTRA ★ FLACO JIMINEZ ★ FLYING PATROL GROUP ★ THE LATE ROAD LUNATICS
DAVID LIPMAN ★ LOS PRIMOS ★ RORY MCLEOD ★ MIRO ★ EARL OKIN ★ OVER THE MOON ★ THE OYSTER BAND
RANDOM SOUND ★ THE STAR RHAPSODY STEEL BAND ★ LUCINDA WILLIAMS ★ MALCOLM WOOD ❦

ONE EARTH ARTS VILLAGE & GREEN FIELD: ★ ADZIDO ★ AK47 ★ AFTER HOURS ★
SAM ALEXANDA SCHOOL OF SAMBA ★ ALIEN CULTURE ★ LENNY ALSOP ★ SU ANDI ★ APU
THE ARMAGH RHYMERS ★ BEN BADOO DRAMA GROUP ★ BALATON ★ MURRAY BOOKCHIN
EDDIE CHAMBERS ★ JENNY CHAPMAN ★ THE COMMON GROUND EXHIBITION ★ CROISSANT NEUF
DARTINGTON GAMELAN ORCHESTRA ★ THE DODGY JAMMERS ★ ENCHANTED BOX ★
HASSAN ERAJI & ARABESQUE ★ THE ERITREAN CULTURAL TROUPE ★ THE ESSENTIAL DANCE BAND ★ FIGGY DUFF
THE FREEDONIAN STATE ORCHESTRA ★ CY GRANT ★ INNER SENSE PERCUSSION ★ INVISIBLE OPERA COMPANY
JIGGERY POKERY ★ JULIVIA ★ JUNCTION JUGGLERS ★ PETER KEMPIDOO ★ BRUCE KENT ★ KUMINA DANCE GROUP
BRUCE LACEY ★ LANZEL AFRICAN ARTS ★ JOHN LITTLE EAGLE & THE SIOUX DANCERS ★ MABSANT ★ MASKARRAY
MEET YOUR FEET ★ MORCIRE ★ MYSTERY THEATRE CO. ★ NIOMINKA BI N'DIAXAS BAND ★ HENRY NORMAL
ONDINNOK AMERINDIAN INITIATION CEREMONY ★ OUTBACK ★ PASSING MOTIONS ★ PRANA ★ JOHN PERKINS
JONATHON PORRITT ★ RAG MORRIS ★ DEN RAY & DREAMWAVE ★ RHYTHMSHOP ★ RICHARD & DREW
GRAHAM RUSSELL ★ NAHID SIDDIQUI ★ SOUL IN MOTION ★ SPINNING TALES ★ BETHLEHEM TAYLOR
PETER TEMPIDOO ★ NICK TOCZEK ★ TRIBAL LAUGHTER ★ NIK TURNER'S FANTASTIC ALL-STARS
THE UTTERLY AMAZING ONE-WOMAN MULTI-DIMENSIONAL PYROTECHNIC FIRE SHOW ★ VIAL MILA
JAKI WHITREN & JOHN CARTWRIGHT ★ LULI WISSAM ★ WRECKLESS ERIC ★ MANDY DE WINTER
MOHAMMED YUSUF ★ ZOOTS & SPANGLES ★ ZUMZEAUX ★ ...Green Futures Arena: Debates and Speakers

CHILDREN'S AREA: ★ BALLETICO FANTASTICO ★ BOING CREATIVE SOLUTIONS ★ MARTIN BRIDLE ★ CRACKPOTS
DANDELION PUPPETS ★ DR. FOSTERS TRAVELLING THEATRE ★ FACEPACK ★ ROSY GIBB ★ GROUNDWELL ARTS
HARP START ★ INSTANT MUSIC ★ TERRY LEE ★ MOUSE CHILDRENS THEATRE ★ NICADA PUPPETS
NO FIT STATE CIRCUS ★ LIVING DAYLIGHTS ★ PARACHUTE THEATRE CO. ★ RUBBERFACE ★ RYVEETA
SCAT THEATRE CO. ★ RANI & JUGNU SINGH CHILDREN'S THEATRE CO. ★ SOUND SCULPTURE
THE STAR RHAPSODY STEEL BAND ★ ZURIYA ★ ...chairoplanes, donkey rides,
inflatables, swingboats, trampolines, space tumblers ❦

Still more to come — but a few of these names need confirmation

Sponsored by **NME**

This year the Police have been invited by the Organisers to patrol the whole site with a view to preventing crime & drug dealing

1989

CAPACITY: 65,000
TICKET PRICE: £28

Despite the tactical year off, Michael and Jean's battles with the local council (and, with a few notable exceptions, the local population) continued. The 1989 Festival only went ahead after Michael invited the police into the organisation and planning of the event. Underneath the line-up, the poster reports that: 'This year the police are invited by the Organisers to patrol the whole site with a view to preventing crime and drug dealing.'

The late running of preparations also necessitated an advance poster declaring that the huge list of performers – over a thousand acts over ten stages – had 'still more to come, but a few of these names need confirmation'. Elvis Costello and Van Morrison again headlined and were joined by Suzanne Vega, who played even though her bass player received death threats leading up to the weekend.

The international flavour continued with Fela Kuti, the Bhundu Boys, Mahlathini and the Mahotella Queens, and Youssou N'Dour all gracing the Pyramid, and the likes of Lanzel African Arts and the Eritrean Cultural Group becoming part of the One Earth Arts Village and The Green Fields, which also offered a school of samba, an Ondinnok Amerindian initiation ceremony, Bruce Kent, a one-woman pyrotechnic show, debates, speakers and a Green Futures arena, which looked to focus on new eco-friendly opportunities.

This year also marked the arrival of Glastonbury's now famous 'dancing figures' logo, designed by Hilary McManus.

The Proclaimers hail the sunshine at Worthy Farm (centre). Breached fencing (top) and the arrival of the travellers' convoy (left) led to record numbers on site.

Infrastructure and security remained an issue all the way through the 1980s, but Michael was always on hand to greet new arrivals.

Overleaf: The dawn of a new decade: photographer Stuart Roy Clarke's 'Sleeping Bag Girl' celebrates the Monday morning of the 1989 Festival.

GREEN KIDZ
C.N.D.-
PART OF A
GROWING
PEACE
MOVEMENT
IN BRITAIN...
Womens peace alliance
Roland
GREENPEACE
GREENPEACE
Dont Miss WHEN You Piss!
STOP

Michael

The Festival had got a bit out of control towards the end of the 1980s. It was good fun, but the fence didn't work and it was getting busier and busier. The travellers had brought a lot of issues with them and everything just felt a bit haphazard. So it wasn't an enormous surprise when the council refused to give me a licence for a music festival in 1990. But I didn't for a moment consider giving up. I just decided that we'd call it a theatre festival instead.

I rang Arabella Churchill, the Theatre and Circus Area Organiser, and said that I needed her headliner, Archaos – a huge French circus troupe – to switch to the Pyramid Stage. She wasn't overjoyed about me taking her prize act, but I told her I had to save the event.

Luckily for me, the little old bloke who did licensing for us at Mendip wasn't really on the ball. He'd worked for the council all his life, but he'd semi-retired and wanted a quiet life. So when he was landed with us, he said, 'Michael, I don't want all this grief.'

'Well, look, this is a theatre festival now. It's not a music event,' I replied.

He just said, 'All right, then,' and that was it. We got the licence. We've called ourselves the Glastonbury Festival of Contemporary Performing Arts ever since.

We did obviously sneak a bit of music onto the Pyramid Stage – we had The Cure, Happy Mondays, Sinéad O'Connor and various others – but officially Archaos were the headliners. They did an incredible show, too. There were jugglers with chainsaws, they had cars driving up and down the metal outside of the Pyramid, and there were tightropes running from the top of the stage out to the oak trees in the field. It was extraordinarily dangerous, but absolutely fantastic. The *Daily Telegraph* said it was the best theatre show they'd ever seen in this country.

Unfortunately, 1990 is mainly remembered for the riots after the Festival. I had a new security firm that year from Wolverhampton, and they were basically these tough guys who'd done judo at the Olympics. I got them in because we'd been losing control of the travellers and the drugs, and it was all going a bit Wild West. When some of the travellers began building a full-scale bar in the middle of the Pyramid field without any sort of licence or permission, I told them they couldn't do that, and they just replied, 'How are you going to stop us, man?' So I went back twenty minutes later with the guys from Wolverhampton and they just took the whole thing down.

The new security firm really gained control that year, confiscating drugs and clamping down on illegal activity. We had to get on top of things if we wanted to keep the licence, and it did work. But the travellers had had free rein for a few years, and they didn't like the new regime at all. On the Monday night after the Festival hundreds of them marched on the farmhouse, chanting away, throwing Molotov cocktails. They burned fifty Land Rovers. It was incredibly scary. I managed to get Emily and Jean out of the house and up to the village for their safety.

Even the security guys were scared. They got in their coach and did a runner back up to Wolverhampton. They'd done a good job, but they thought they were going to get killed. The lead guy told me, 'We'll never come back here again!' And they never did.

So that just left me and a dozen police with riot shields. I thought I was going to lose the farm, but the police were so brave and held the line, eventually bringing things under control. Unfortunately, the TV cameras caught the whole thing, and it did look like seriously bad news. I thought we'd never be able to do the Festival again after that. I decided we had to take 1991 off – we needed a rest.

Surprisingly, though, I got the licence in 1992 without any problems. The council weren't

Opposite: 'It could have been a lot worse': the second Worthy Farm Pyramid burns to the ground ten days before the Festival in 1994. A replacement stage was rapidly sourced, but the Pyramid did not return until 2000.

weren't as bothered about the riot as I thought they'd be, and the village didn't really complain either. There were always a few people in Pilton who were fiercely against the Festival, but lots of the villagers were beginning to see some revenue from it by then, with parking and accommodation and everything, so that was winning them round.

The Festivals from 1992 to 1994 were when things really started to take off and the Festival started to become what it is today. The explosion of dance music and Britpop into the mainstream in the early to mid-1990s definitely helped us. I didn't really like the whole dance thing myself – I thought it was a bit mindless and lacking in soul – but it was clear that I couldn't hold back the tide on that one, and it's gone on to become such a big part of the Festival.

I did really like a lot of the bands that came through around that time, though, Primal Scream being one of my favourites. I had an old radio up in the roof of the milking parlour, and I was milking the cows one morning when their new song, 'Movin' on Up', came on. The Italian guy I was milking the cows with didn't like it at all, but I thought it was fantastic. I had to climb up to the radio to turn up the volume – and then I was on the phone at 9.15 a.m., booking them to play in 1992.

By 1994 we had so many amazing bands making their debuts at Glastonbury: Oasis, Blur, Radiohead and Pulp. Plus we had Orbital proving me wrong about dance music by doing an incredible headline set on the second stage. It was the perfect year for the Festival to be screened on national television for the first time, with Channel 4 airing the whole thing live.

I don't think you can underestimate how important TV coverage has been for us. The CND had helped bring us to a bigger audience in the early 1980s, and suddenly we were now broadcasting live into the homes of people across the UK. It is a huge part of what's brought us to where we are now.

In all honesty, I didn't love Channel 4's coverage. It just didn't feel like the right style for us, and the advert breaks felt like they were threatening our integrity. That was why I phoned Mark Cooper from the BBC and asked if they'd like to come on board from 1997. They've been there ever since. They're much more sympathetic to what we do, and it's unbelievable the number of people who see their coverage now – something like 20 million people every year.

Of course, 1994 was also the year the Pyramid Stage burned down just before the Festival. I vividly remember looking out of our bedroom window and saying to Jean, 'My God, the Pyramid's on fire!' Emily was understandably really upset about us losing that stage.

I was annoyed too, because I thought it might have been my fault. We always put a light at the top of the Pyramid just before the Festival, and I'd asked my man Bill Egan to put a more powerful lightbulb there because it didn't look bright enough. And although Bill didn't think an overly powerful bulb was the cause of the fire, it's usually what's blamed.

I do wonder if it was sabotage. There was a huge campaign against wind turbines at the time – people were really upset about them spoiling the countryside. But I thought they were a good idea and I'd put one on the site as a gesture to support Greenpeace. Our phone number was still in the telephone book then, and one day I got a phone call from a very annoyed chap who said, 'I'll burn your fucking Pyramid down if you don't remove that turbine.' I didn't remove it and, of course, the stage did burn.

Whether or not it was him, I don't know; there was never an official investigation. But I didn't worry too much about it. I'm not the sort of person to sit down and cry. I've got a great ability to deal with a tragedy and turn it into something else. It fires me up in a way. My main concern was getting a replacement stage, and I was on the phone the next morning, saying we needed one within ten days.

The other big drama was our first shooting, in 1995. There were no police on site back then and there were still quite a lot of drug dealers around, so it could be a bit wild. I think some of the dealers had an argument about being on each other's patch, and five people got shot. I couldn't believe it when I was told. Luckily, they were all okay, the public weren't involved and the council didn't really dwell on it afterwards. It could certainly have been a lot worse.

We had a fallow year in 1996, but that turned out to be unexpectedly dramatic too, as I was diagnosed with bowel cancer. I was ill enough to think I could have died. It was a horrible six months, but I was very lucky, and in the end I had a good prognosis, which was a huge relief.

When I was asked if I would stand for Labour in the 1997 general election, I said, 'Do you know what? I'm so happy to be alive that I'll do it!' I knew I couldn't possibly win – this is not a Labour area – but, to be honest, I didn't want to. I couldn't have juggled being an MP alongside being so busy with the farm and the Festival, but it gave me the chance to stand up for the things I believed in. And I actually did pretty well. The Labour vote went from 2,000 to 10,600, and *Hansard* reported that I had the biggest percentage increase in the whole of the south of England.

When we came back with the Festival in 1997 I was feeling quite buoyant about everything. Both this year and the following, 1998, were wet years, but I have great memories of both – particularly Radiohead in '97 and Bob Dylan in '98. The Festival was still undergoing unbelievable growth. Suddenly we had all these big companies wanting to sponsor us, and we even had a proper bank on site – things we couldn't have dreamed of in the 1970s. We were still doing something that we really believed in, and it was working.

Jean still thought I was a bit crazy and that I didn't really know what I was doing, which was probably fair enough. When she left school she made sheepskin coats at the Morlands factory in Glastonbury, where things had to be done thoroughly and properly. Jean always did everything right. She didn't like the elements of danger, unpredictability and law-breaking that the Festival brought with it.

She was incredibly loyal, but I don't think she ever had her heart and soul in it, really. And the Festival takes over everything. Getting phone calls in the middle of the night was normal for us. So when Jean said, 'We're having no real life together any more,' I promised her that we'd end the Festival in 2000 – the year I turned sixty-five – and then have a nice, normal farming life together. I do have my doubts that it would have actually happened, as I was getting a huge sense of satisfaction from the Festival by then. But it sounded good at the time and it placated Jean.

And then Jean died from cancer shortly before the 1999 Festival. I was devastated. But through my grief I realised I wanted to keep going with that year's Festival. I thought, Well, what else have I got? In a way, the Festival had always been my mistress, and I threw myself into it.

That was when Emily came back from London to help out. I'm not sure she'd been totally into the Festival before that either, but it was growing on her. We've always got on really well together, so we

made a good team. We still do.

The whole site went silent in honour of Jean at the 1999 Festival. I was down at the Pyramid Stage for it, standing among the crowd. Everybody was completely silent – you could have heard a pin drop. It was extraordinary. It was an emotional moment for me – I had a lump in my throat – and I felt very proud to see how much all these people respected Jean.

Jean might not have totally gone along with the whole event, but I couldn't have done it without her support. She's a very big part of why Glastonbury became what it is now. It meant a lot to me that she had that tribute.

If you care about this area, vote for someone who *does* something for it.

Michael **EAVIS**

Labour

Above: Michael and Jean Eavis in the
crowd at the Jazz World Stage
(now West Holts) in 1998.
Opposite: A page from the Wells Labour Party
general election campaign leaflet in 1997.

Emily

Left: Emily and Robert Smith in The Cure's makeshift dressing room in 1990; the windows were taped over so the band could watch the World Cup.
Opposite: 'I started to get more freedom in the nineties . . .'; Emily rises to a Britpop occasion in 1995.

I was ten at the beginning of the nineties, and in many ways the Festival and I went through our teenage years together. By the time I was twenty so much had happened in my life; I'd discovered politics, music and culture – and was doing what teenagers do. By the end of the decade I'd completed my A-levels and started training to be a teacher at Goldsmiths, University of London. Everything I experienced was surrounded by the Festival, which was also changing dramatically. For a start, it was happening more frequently, but it was also growing and attracting a different crowd to the eighties. Suddenly there were ravers and indie kids who perhaps wouldn't have been there before. It was more diverse, and everything felt like it was shifting on its axis – morphing into something new.

I started to get more freedom to explore the Festival. Before then I was pretty inseparable from my parents; I'd always be on my dad's shoulders or my mum's hip. The nineties was when I began to go off on my own or with my friends. My parents actually thought I'd got lost one year. I heard an announcement from one of the two main stages: 'Michael and Jean have lost their daughter, she's ten years old and blonde. If anyone sees her …' I was like, 'Oh, hang on, that's me!'

I really started to get into the music in 1990. I became a proper music geek and immersed myself in all the fantastic artists that were coming through. There were a lot of bookings being decided around the kitchen table, and my dad would say, 'Who do we want to see?'

So I'd chip in. Even now, we rely on young people to give us their thoughts – we're constantly asking kids who they'd like to play here.

I was really into Happy Mondays, and they were booked to play the 1990 Festival. Their singer, Shaun Ryder, was the first musician that I was really excited about meeting. But it didn't go quite as I'd imagined. He was coming to say hello when he just collapsed on me. He didn't even bend his knees, he just went over like a domino, right on top of me.

I'm not a big fan of hanging around in artists' dressing rooms at the best of times, so I tend to avoid that area. When people ask me, 'Can I get a backstage pass?' I always tell them not to bother. Shows aren't designed for people backstage; they're designed for the public. We spend all our energy making Glastonbury the best we can for the people out front. We do try to look after the bands as best we can, but backstage is definitely still the least exciting area of the Glastonbury site.

The Festival was becoming more popular in the early nineties, but I still didn't have friends who wanted to go. The 1994 Festival – my first as a teenager – was the first year my mates from school came along. Their parents were definitely a bit sceptical because the Festival still had a dodgy reputation, but my mum said they could all sleep in the farmhouse and we'd just wander down to the main stage.

I brought about ten friends, and my mum laid out mattresses upstairs for everyone. We had such a great time – it was an amazing Festival that year. Dance music and Britpop were coming to the fore, and we had all these genre-defining acts like Orbital, Radiohead, Oasis and Elastica playing for the first time.

But the 1994 Festival nearly went up in smoke before it even began – literally. I vividly remember one of my sisters waking me up at about four in the morning saying, 'Emily! Emily! You won't believe it – the Pyramid's burning down!' It felt like I was having a nightmare, but I looked out of the window and all I could see was the smoke. We got out of bed, walked down the hill and sat there in the field watching in disbelief as the Pyramid burned to the ground. The fire brigade couldn't do anything because it was already caving in by the time they arrived. We just had to watch it collapse in front of us. It was a terribly sad moment.

No one ever really got to the bottom of what caused the fire, but there was a lot of speculation about it. My life up till then had been spent on that Pyramid. It was a permanent thing in our lives. We'd all helped choose the telegraph poles it was built from in 1981, and it was where I'd played since I was tiny. I treated it like a doll's house. Once I was a teenager, it was where I hung out with my friends and had my first cigarette. Losing it was my first experience of grief.

The 1995 Festival was probably the pinnacle of the nineties, for me. That was the year Britpop really exploded. Suddenly the sort of

bands that we'd always had on the bill were becoming household names. It was one of those rare moments when alternative culture and the mainstream meet, and it was a total blast. I was about to turn sixteen and Blur, Oasis and Pulp were all coming to perform at our farm. Growing up, it felt quite normal to have lots of musicians coming here. But to me, as a teenager, those Britpop bands were superstars, people whose music I loved and felt part of. It was a very exciting time.

That was also when I first camped on the site and just enjoyed the whole experience without having any responsibility. The weather was great – it was blisteringly hot – the music was amazing and everything just felt euphoric. It was a really special few days.

Looking back now, I think it was so important that I had that time. In a way, it showed me what all the fuss was about. Now, when people tell me about their first experience of the Festival, I can really connect to that buzz and excitement, because it's what I felt in 1995.

We took 1996 off, and then 1997 and '98 were really wet, muddy years, but there were some monumental musical moments. Radiohead in '97 will always go down as one of the best sets we

have had here; the music took on a deeper meaning during what was probably one of the biggest downpours we've ever had. The crowd stood still, wellies lodged in the deep mud, and I looked around thinking I would never forget that moment. It was magical.

By then I was already starting to take on some of the stress that comes with being involved in organising the event, and more responsibility was slowly creeping in. I would do anything to have another experience of the Festival like I did in 1995, but I know I'll never experience it like that again. So I'm still clinging to that memory!

The huge success of the Britpop bands and some of the dance acts that were coming through – like The Chemical Brothers, Underworld, Prodigy and so on – definitely helped the Festival become more popular and well known, particularly when it started to be shown live on TV, which first happened with Channel 4 in 1994. It's funny to think now, but we couldn't believe it when they rang up and said they wanted to put Glastonbury on TV. And then when the coverage moved to the BBC in 1997 it really went up a level, although it did take a lot of time and hard work to get to where it is now.

Back then, the BBC coverage seemed to involve them having a couple of presenters in a VW campervan backstage, with a few CND signs and a plastic cow or two, going, 'Whoa! We've landed in outer space,' in front of a fake backdrop of the Festival. It didn't feel like they were communicating the reality of what was happening here, which is actually quite hard to convey on film. We spend all year trying to get every detail of this Festival right, and if they paint the wrong picture to the millions watching at home then it can be very frustrating. But I think the quality of what the BBC does now is incredible. If you speak to bands, a lot of them will say it's one of the only events they will allow to be filmed because the production values are generally so good.

The BBC coverage has been brilliant for a long time now, and it reaches a huge audience, with over 20 million people tuning in over the weekend. And that's a very useful thing in helping us attract artists to an event that doesn't pay acts anything like as much as other big festivals do. Glastonbury is an extremely expensive event to put on and we spread the budget across the whole site evenly. We want Theatre and Circus, or Arcadia, to be as important as the Pyramid Stage because that's what we are about as a festival. That, coupled with the fact that we aim to give £2 million to charity each year, means we don't have vast artist budgets like some other events. Bands know that when they play here, it's different to a standard arena show: they're taking part in a giant cultural event that is about so much more than the music. From headliners on the main stages to circus performers and stewards, everyone is here because they want to be here.

The funny thing was that, even when the live TV coverage began and we had shows like Radiohead's 1997 headline set getting huge audiences on the BBC, the future of Glastonbury still didn't really feel secure. My dad would say every year that this would be the last Festival, and people thought it was some kind of scam to make headlines. But my parents did genuinely think that. The Festival wasn't being run like a long-term business, and it was a hugely stressful and time-consuming thing to organise. There were still no offices, all the phone calls came to the farm and there would be people knocking on the door all the time. So even though Glastonbury was making a stamp on contemporary culture, it still didn't feel like it was long term. In fact, my mum and dad always said they were going to retire in 2000, which would have meant the end of the Festival.

That's why, in 1998, I went off to Goldsmiths to become a teacher. The Festival wasn't something that could provide a solid job, or even anything semi-permanent. And I didn't think about trying to get a job in the wider music industry. If anything, my experience of music-industry people at the Festival had put me off that. My granny was a headmistress, and I spent a lot of time with her and liked working with kids, so I always thought I'd be a teacher. It wasn't something I really questioned, and I was really enjoying it at Goldsmiths. I had a placement at a primary school in East Ham, which I loved.

But then, in 1999, when I was nineteen, my mum became ill with cancer. My life stood still during that whole time, and I deferred my course to move home and look after her and my dad. Losing my mum had always been a fear of mine – we were so close and she was such an anchor to all of us, keeping the whole ship steady – and the reality of life without her seemed unbearable.

She was so worried about my dad. In hospital she would say, 'Can you look after him? Can you cook him dinner tonight?' He was quite old-fashioned in that respect, and she was very concerned about how he was going to look after himself. But I was like, 'It's okay, I can deal with this. I will completely take this on. I will look after my dad.'

Mum died peacefully in May 1999. At that extremely difficult time, the Festival became a life raft for me and my dad. We had a month before the gates opened, and that year's Festival became a huge tribute to her. We had the burning of a phoenix in the King's Meadow, where we planted an oak tree overlooking the farm, and R.E.M. did a tribute to her from the Pyramid Stage on Friday night. Losing my mum was by far the hardest thing I had experienced, but the atmosphere and the support among the crew and the Festival-goers was amazing. People really carried us through.

It all culminated in a tribute to my mum on the Pyramid Stage on the Sunday morning, which was one of the most moving moments I've ever been part of. I was late and running through the fields to get there, where everyone was just standing in silence. I've never seen that many people be silent. I was floored by it. It felt like people understood the importance of my mum and her role in it all.

The whole reaction gave us a bit of hope. The 2000 Festival was meant to be the last year of Glastonbury, but after 1999 my dad and I thought, Actually, maybe we should keep going, because what else are we going to do? I put my course on hold and stayed at the farm to look after Dad and work on the Festival together.

I look back now and think I was actually quite young, but at the time I felt like an adult. Losing Mum at that age changed me completely, and my life took a turn in a different direction. Dad and I became a unit, supporting each other during that difficult time. I am also extremely lucky to have some incredible friends who helped me through it.

Dad and I still talk about Mum often, and it feels like all of the subsequent Festivals have been a tribute to her. That's what makes the evolution of the Festival so special and meaningful. I will always see it as a testament to my mum's amazing life and my parents' bond.

The Festival ended the eighties in a much better place than it had begun. My parents had formed a really steely partnership that could withstand anything. They were so close – they needed each other. And the Festival needed them both too.

Michael and Jean share a reflective post-Festival moment in 1998, and (overleaf) the music press and the newspapers chart the unfolding Glastonbury story, including the many heartfelt tributes to Emily's mother Jean.

GLASTONBURY 199
The world's best dirty weeke

NME
NEW MUSICAL EXPRESS

Treading the duckboards w
SUEDE × STEREOS × THE
TEENAGE FANCL
LEMONHE
CRO
VELVE

US BJORK × U2 × 200EUROPA
AKA DEMUS & BITER

£1.95 · AUGUST 1995

SELECT
25th BIRTHDAY SPESH

elastica
prodigy
orbital
pj harvey
gene
cure
black crowes

oasis

supergrass
and a cast
of thousands...

Glastonbury

40-page pull-out
blitzkrieg!

'REE GLASTO POSTER!
3ft x 2ft DOUBLE-SIDED SPECIAL: spy-in-the-sky 'copter shot *plus* top live stuff!

COURTNEY STEPS OUT – PAGE 3

NME
MUSICAL EXPRESS

THERAPY?:
taking
the piss
at Donington

WOBBLE &
RES CRANBERRY
ESTED DEVELOPMENT
NE TEMPLE PILOTS
IS × GREEN DAY
IN DALE × LUSH
T STATIC × RIDE
E CHARLATANS
RANK BLACK
HE CROW

MIGHT OF THE
LIVID DREAD
RAGE AGAINST
THE MACHINE
fire up for
tonbury

75p $(US)3.75

NME
NEW MUSICAL EXPRESS

VOLUME 4

www.nme.com

GLASTS FROM
THE PAST

The history of **the world's**
greatest festiva
as told by NME & Melody Make

Thursday 16

to spen
your ho

AR
RO

PILTON festival
today counting
blaze and ticket
rocked him to the
The famous 13-yea
for his world famou
next week, was destro
Booking agent Jamie
glary at his Glastonbu
And festival workmen
in the centre of Glastonbu
investigations into the c
ing havoc are being carrie
"I and another stage fi
cast build another stage fo
be the same without the py
"It was my choice to
pyramid from telegraph
became the symbol of the fi
On Friday night sea
Nottingham, are are
involved in running fight
Jooper's Fun Pub licensee
ups started in Silver Street

Mother of Glastonbury

Favourite photograph from Michael Eavis's family album

THE FARMER'S WIFE WHO MADE TEA FOR THE STARS AND COULD CALL OASIS 'OUR BOYS'

Working behind the scenes at Glastonbury Festival: Jean and Michael Eavis and daughter Emily

A TRIBUTE by CHRIS BINDING
Deputy Editor, Western Daily Press

DAWN at Worthy Farm. A fresh and glorious May morning, the meadows lush and vibrant, buttercups basking in the glory of the rising sun.

Michael Eavis strides out to gather in his dairy cows, the way he always has, gazing out across his blessed acres. A timeless thing.

But on this dawn there is a sadness in the air that even the birdsong cannot disguise. For Michael Eavis has lost his wife, his partner, his soul-mate.

And Worthy Farm has lost a dear friend.

He was at Jean's bedside when she died at 4.30am, comforting and reassuring as he had been for the last three months, the worst three months of their 35 years together. Years of turbulence and triumph in equal measure, but through them all the joy of jointly creating the greatest festival of modern music in the world.

For, make no mistake, Jean Eavis was no silhouette in the background of the Glastonbury Festival, no timid wife basking in the glory of her husband's inspiration. Jean and Michael Eavis were a partnership in every sense.

"She was my moderator," said Michael. "She knew when I was going over the top, getting something wrong. She would rein me in, put me in my place."

They did everything together. The good things, the sad things, the ordinary things. For despite the fame the festival has heaped on this couple over the years, they remained intensely private; a working, caring partnership with Jean as the steadying force, as genuine, good-hearted and generous a woman as you could meet.

She preferred a stroll along Burnham sands to the glitz and falseness of the countless music award ceremonies she attended with Michael. She would always go of course, always be there at his side, but her heart was set firmly at the farm she loved, with her flowers and her pastures and her family.

They spent 20 years together before finally deciding to marry — at a joint ceremony with their great friend Arabella Churchill — Winston's granddaughter — and her groom, juggler Haggis McLeod.

That relationship brought two children of their own, Patrick, a doctor, and 19-year-old Emily. And there are the three each from previous marriages.

Eight children, drawn together today to grieve.

But, though Worthy Farm will surely never be the same again, nor is it a place where broken hearts are left to wither. Jean would have had none of that.

"I haven't had the time to look too far into the future. But I know Jean would not want us to stop everything because she has died. The festival was our life and she loved it, she loved to see young people enjoy themselves. She cared enormously about that and the great causes that benefit from it," said Michael.

Not that everything pleased her. She found it hard to cope sometimes, especially when bad weather turned her beloved farm into a quagmire and the litter mounted up.

Emily remembers seeing her mother, armed with a bin bag, marshalling the litter pickers last year as the crowds left and the cleaning up operation began. "She was a doer, a hands-on person. She couldn't just sit around and watch everyone else working. She had to join in and get things done herself."

A visit to Worthy Farm was always something to look forward to.

You never left without a cup of tea and a piece of home-made pie, whatever your reason for being there. And often the visits were from environmental health officers, gathering information to prosecute Michael over alleged breaches during the festival. Or angry neighbours doing their best to stop the annual invasion of music fans.

Fiercely protective of Michael, she would filter out those she felt wished him ill. "She was a good judge of character, very outspoken sometimes if she felt someone was a bit flaky, trying to take us for a ride," said Michael.

But if she took to you, the welcome you received was as warm as the glow from the kitchen Rayburn.

And many a pop star has savoured the hospitality of the Worthy Farm kitchen.

The Gallagher brothers, from Oasis, became firm friends, Jean referring to them as "our boys". The couple visited them in London and received personal invitations to their glittering events.

But, rather than the music, it was the wider attraction of the festival which appealed to her most. The spirit of an event which brings such joy to so many.

And, somehow, this year's event must not lose any of that. There will be dark days ahead for Michael and his family as the enormity of the loss sinks in. But the music must go on, and next month's event will, as much as anything, be in tribute to Jean Eavis, the Mother of Glastonbury.

Her funeral, to be held on Saturday morning at Pilton Methodist Chapel, will not be a sombre occasion. "We intend this to be a celebration of Jean's life. She was a warm, intelligent, attractive and honest woman and I want everyone to take joy in who she was," said Michael.

There will be hymns, of course, for Jean was a devout Methodist. But Michael also plans a special, personal tribute to the woman he loved — the Bob Dylan song, If Not For You will be played in her memory.

"It says everything I want to say about how I felt about her, better than anything I could say myself. I hope people will understand it," he said.

Bob Dylan, who fulfilled a long-held ambition by playing at Glastonbury last year, would surely be honoured to know that his words meant so much.

If not for you
My sky would fall,
Rain would gather too.
Without your love I'd be...

NEWS

Jean Eavis, without whom the Glastonbury Festivals died. **Simon Roiser**, a personal friend who has bee '70s, gives a personal appreciation.

Jean Eavis 1939-1999

Jean Eavis could have been 'just a farmer's wife' - and an excellent one she was. She could handle a muck-scraper and a frying pan with equal skill; breakfasts she cooked after milking (before health food was invented) had to be eaten to be believed.

In the '60s she had enough on her plate as a single mother bringing up Alison, Sandra and Juliet in a Glastonbury council house. Then she met Michael. In the early days of their romance they would enjoy rare moments together on Burnham Sands, but this brief idyll changed for ever when they gatecrashed the 1970 Blues Festival at the Shepton Mallet Showground and were enchanted by the spirit of the event. When Michael invited 1,500 hippies to join them on Worthy Farm that September, and another 14,000 in June 1971, she wondered if she'd ever have him to herself again.

The festival-free years of the '70s gave Jean the time to devote herself to bringing up Patrick (born in 1966) and the three girls, and making Worthy Farm a place of welcome. The apple store became a living room, and...

or it flooded the transport was a Mini twine trim. Most of th was let as flats, and wh painting walls she'd life stories of a stream eccentric tenants.

Bands still play the wagon shed tea for Ginger Martyn. She l Laine remark make off wi...

TV deal raises pop festival's profile to the global stage

— 4 — WESTERN DAILY PRESS, THURSDAY, MARCH 24, 1994

BRISTOL AND SOMERSET
Sunday Independent
THE WEST'S OWN SUNDAY PAPER
JUNE 28, 1992 45p

UNDER SIEGE

Pop festival nightmare of armed robberies and drugs

THE annual summer nightmare dreaded by landowners and country people arrived in the West Country this weekend.

Some 75,000 rock fans converged on Somerset for the three-day Glastonbury Festival.

WHAT'S PADDY UP TO NOW?

PADDY Ashdown had a gentle, helping hand for a lady yesterday.

But it was all in a good cause.

N ATTACK S PILTON

Report by Mike Chamberlain

---

oodbye

...the "death of the...
...g" policy of banning...
...lete success.
...ved temperatures of 80
...small-scale sound
...was little after-hours

...all," said Eavis. "The
...they don't like the raves.
...hat's fine. But it drives
...away from the event saw
...ce and a 31 vehicle
...Glastonbury, on Friday.
...s attempted to stage their

...9-year-old twins Stephen
...ton, were seriously injured
...ing over the fence, were
...r entrance. Stephen was
...st fully recovered, as NME

...stival on Friday, a festival-
...ent outside the site. The
...eved to have been pushed
...mping over the 12ft perimeter
...nel and was charging punters
...as also arrested in possession
...housand pounds in cash.
...ulated clashes with punters,
...e of people who attended the
...rests, mostly for drug offences.
...0 worth of drugs. The biggest
...d theft of, or from, tents.
...48.

For Luck' may still go ahead.

394   Tel (0935) 74551   N & E SOME

Bill Drumm...

● LEMONHEA
DANDO make

● THE world-famous Pilton pyramid went up in flames early on Monday.

The damage is put on £65,000. Arson is suspected.

Festival organiser Michael Eavis...

Norm
Harri
& Son

TRERUFFE GARAGE
Redruth 217751
MoT Testing Station
Service & Repairs
MoT while-U-Wait
including 3-wheelers

CARNARTHEN STREET

THEATRE CIRCUS

GLASTONBURY FESTIVAL

of Contemporary Performing Arts

22-23-24 June 1990

MUSIC DANCE

This year, the Festival celebrates its 20th anniversary
with 12 stages and over 1000 acts
including:

**Ry Cooder & David Lindley • The Neville Brothers
Aswad • Deacon Blue • Sinéad O'Connor
Happy Mondays • Hot House Flowers • De La Soul
Jesus Jones • James • Manu Negra
Delamitri • Green on Red • Blue Aeroplanes**

Archaos *Cirque de Caractère from France*

Theatre — 250 shows a day including:

**Nola Rae • Jonathan Kay
Omelette Broadcasting • Tony Allen
Skint Video • Mark Miwurdz • Shikisha
Jools • Malcolm Hardee • Jenny Bone
Centre Ocean Stream • Kathakali Dancers
Mummerandada • Skinning the Cat
Les Bubb • Compass Theatre Company**

Extended Green Field covering 60 acres

World Music Stage
check music press for details

Tickets £38.00

Advance only — NONE for sale at the gate

Includes camping, car parking, VAT and all on-site events
Accompanied children under 14 admitted free of charge

1990

Retitled the Glastonbury Festival of Contemporary Performing Arts to reflect the ever-growing diversity of the entertainment, the Festival celebrated its twentieth anniversary. A World Music Stage was unveiled, amid an expansion that included a line-up of over a thousand acts across twelve stages. Key to the Festival, and the eventual granting of the licence, was the booking of Archaos, a fifty-seven-strong roaming circus troupe, to headline the Pyramid Stage. The elaborate preparations involved flattening the Pyramid apex to allow Archaos to winch scrap cars all the way up the side of the structure. The event also included music from Aswad, The Cure, Sinéad O'Connor, Happy Mondays and De La Soul, and an extended sixty-acre Green Fields area.

For the first time professional car-parking teams were employed, as well as increased policing, with the cost equating to 12.6 per cent of the cash raised by the Festival. Donations to CND and local charities still topped the £100,000 mark. The police presence led to some tension over the weekend, with unrest between travellers and site security erupting into violence on the Monday evening. Michael's support of the travelling convoy, whose tenure at Stonehenge and Glastonbury had become part of the summer solstice in the UK, was well known, but change was needed to secure the Festival's future; 1991 would be a fallow year.

This page: Happy Mondays on the Pyramid Stage in 1990 (top), and (left) Sinéad O'Connor.
Previous page: Photographer Liam Bailey captures the magic of a 1990s Glastonbury dawn.

1990

Archaos literally topped the Pyramid Stage in 1990, spearheading Glastonbury's rebirth as a Festival of Contemporary and Performing Arts, for licence purposes at least (top left); on the rest of the Worthy Farm site the cider, the crowds and the music continued to flow.
Overleaf, clockwise from top: Lou Reed, Tom Jones, Joan Armatrading and Robert Plant at Glastonbury in 1992.

GLASTONBURY FESTIVAL
of Contemporary Performing Arts
26-27-28 June

*For everything that lives is holy, life delights in life,
Because the soul of sweet delight can never be defil'd*
Blake

Performers include:

MUSIC: *a special guest that we can't announce plus*
Lou Reed • Morrissey • Buddy Guy • Carter USM • Primal Scream
Shakespears Sister • The Fall • The House of Love • The Levellers
Teenage Fan Club • The Shamen • Blur • Curve • Lush
Ned's Atomic Dustbin • Youssou N'Dour • Hugh Masekela
Manu Dibango • American Music Club • Benjamin Zephaniah
Billy Bragg • The Blue Aeroplanes • Chris Whitley • Richard Thompson
Runrig • Daisy Chainsaw • PJ Harvey • Saw Doctors
The Senseless Things • Television • Airhead • Back to the Planet
Bates Motel • The Belltower • Catherine Wheel • Cud • Dodgy
Dr Phibes • The Family Cat • Fat Dinosaur • Frank and Walters
Flowered Up • Gary Clail • Jah Wobble • Joe Louis Walker
Kitchens of Distinction • K-Passa • Midway Still • The Moonflowers
Ocean Colour Scene • The Orb • Ozric Tentacles • RDF • The Real People
Sandkings • Senser • Spiritualised • The Stairs • Strangelove

ACOUSTIC: Alison Moyet • Alias Ron Kavanagh • Baba Yaga
Bare Naked Ladies • Ivo Papasov • Julian Dawson • Richard Thompson
Robin Williamson • Sharon Shannon • The Ukrainians

THEATRE: *Over 100 acts, including:* Alan Parker – Urban Warrior
Andy Smart – Vicious Boy • Attila the Stockbroker & John Otway
Ben Baddoo • Bim Mason • Blood, Earth & Medicine
Brickbat Volunteers • Charlie Chuck • Commotion • Forkbeard Fantasy
Jim Tavaré & Al Murray • John Hegley & The Popticians • Joolz
Knee High • Les Bubb • Loreena McKennitt • Malcolm Hardee
Miles and Millner • Natural Theatre Co. • Rob Newman • Roy Hutchins
Skint Video • Stewart Lee • Talking Pictures • Theatre de Complicité
They Wouldn't • 3-D • Tragic But Brave Co. • Tommy Cockles

CIRCUS: *Over 100 acts, including:* Circus Delirious • Circus Space
Club Meeting • Cycloid – the Human Gyroscope • Deb Pope • Firenoise
The Flying Dutchmen • Foolhardy Folk • Fooltime • Le La Les
Nik Turner's Fantastic All-Stars • No Fit State Circus • Ollie & Herbie
Raging Rodeo Bull • Rex Boyd • Rudi Wallenda's Exploding Car
Sean Bridges • Sheinbar Variete • Skin and Blisters • Skinning the Cat
Swamp Circus • 3-D • Trapeze Rides • William Shrew's Laser Robot

CINEMA: 20 of the best recent films, shown throughout the weekend

Huge and varied entertainments for children in the Children's Field

OR wander through and participate in the delights of 60 acres of
Green Field, including everything from alternative technology
in the Green Futures Arena to the Field of Avalon
and the Sacred Space with its Stone Circle!

National
Music Day
June 28

in aid of

GREENPEACE

Supported by
NME

Tickets £49.00 Advance: 0272 767 868
INCLUDES CAMPING, car parking, VAT and all on-site events
Accompanied children under 14 admitted free of charge

☎ **Infoline: 0839 66 88 99***
Calls charged at 36p per minute cheap rate, 48p per minute at other times

Probably the most exciting event of its kind anywhere in Europe this summer

1992

CAPACITY: 70,000
TICKET PRICE: £49

A change in the political climate and what was believed to be the end of the Cold War also changed the Eavises' perspective on donations. Following a personal letter from Michael Eavis to Peter Melchett of Greenpeace, the charity, along with Oxfam, became Glastonbury's main beneficiaries – the focus on green initiatives having taken centre stage in the Festival's thinking. Numbers remained the same for 1992, as the array of musical veterans – Lou Reed, Van Morrison, Hugh Masekela, Buddy Guy, plus unannounced special guest Tom Jones (but not the billed Morrissey, who pulled out) – became more eclectic. But the gig of the weekend was Primal Scream in full Screamadelica mode. The Theatre and Circus area continued to expand, with over 200 acts featured, and Tony Cordy, activist and traveller, was recruited to launch the Kidzfield in its now permanent location.

'Our first ever festival gig was Glastonbury in 1992. I was against us playing because I saw festivals as a leftover from the drab seventies hippy culture, all muddy fields and appallingly dressed low-energy people sitting on the ground smoking dope – nothing at all to do with rock and roll. However, Alex Nightingale, our manager at the time, convinced us it would be a good thing to do.

We performed on the Friday night and the atmosphere was incredible. We did the Screamadelica set, and it felt like a real moment. It was the biggest crowd we had played to, and the audience and the band truly came together as one. After our set I went out exploring the Festival. I think it was the first time they had acid-house raves at Glastonbury. All I remember is darknesss and an endless sea of partly glimpsed faces, as if lit by torchlight, and sparks of energy flying all around. The weekend really meant something and I'm glad we played. It was magical.'

Bobby Gillespie
Primal Scream

Photographer Grant Fleming rode shotgun on the Scream's tour bus for Glastonbury 1992; these previously unpublished images document the band's-eye view of the tented city that was theirs for the taking.

GLASTONBURY FESTIVAL
'93
of Contemporary Performing Arts

Exhibitions · Hot showers · Woodcarving · Theatre · Green Field · Hip Hop · Blind Springs · Permaculture · Workshops · Psychedelia · Domes · Markets · Story-telling · Fireworks · Stalls · Healing · World Music · Clowns · Exotica · Folk · Rides · Organics · Big Top · Pagans · Painting · Fire · Blues · Crafts · Bands · Playground · Alternative · Faceprinting · Stone Circle · Dragons · Lectures · Children · Non-conformists · Sculpture · Acrobats · Exhibitions

in aid of GREENPEACE

Those who have once been happy are for aye
Out of Destruction's reach
— John Masefield

Pyramid Stage *(running order)* – **Friday:** The Black Crowes • Robert Plant • Ian Dury & The Blockheads • Green on Red • The Tragically Hip • 4 of Us
Saturday: Red Hot Chili Peppers • Lenny Kravitz • Christy Moore • Hothouse Flowers • Saw Doctors • Alison Moyet & the Mothers of Good Intention • Barenaked Ladies
Sunday: Wynton Marsalis • The Kinks • PM Dawn • Van Morrison • Nanci Griffith and the Blue Moon Orchestra • Baaba Maal • Brontë Brothers • Glastonbury Town Brass Band

NME Stage – Suede • Stereo MCs • The Orb • Porno for Pyros • Belly • Digable Planets • Lemonheads • Ozric Tentacles • Spiritualized • Teenage Fan Club • American Music Club • Come • Jamiroquai • Mazzy Star • Mega City Four • Superchunk • Adorable • The Auteurs • Back to the Planet • Cholm Factory • Dr. Phibes • Eat • Fat Dinosaur • God Machine • Leatherface • The Rocking Birds • Ruff, Ruff & Ready • The Sea • Senser • Sunscreem • Ultramarine • Verve • The Wishplants

Acoustic Tent – The Black Velvet Band • Brontë Brothers • The Blues Band • Paul Brady • Christine Collister • The Coal Porters • Andy Davis • Donovan • Goats Don't Shave • Lindisfarne • Nanci Griffith • Christie Hennessy • Mouth Music • Christy Moore with Jimmy Faulkner • The Pale • Steve Phillips • John Prine • Eddi Reader • Sharon Shannon • Michelle Shocked • Darden Smith • The Ukrainians • The Wizards of Twiddly

Cabaret, Theatre, Mime and Dance – Arnold Brown • Attila the Stockbroker with John Otway and the Harlow Philharmonic Orchestra • Charlie Chuck • Compass Theatre Co. • Simon Day (aka Tommy Cockles) & John Thomson • Forkbeard Fantasy • Joolz • Malcolm Hardee • John Hegley • Roy Hutchins • Chris Lynam • Natural Theatre Co. • Parachute Theatre • Alan Parker – Urban Warrior • Frank Sidebottom • Mark Thomas • Gayle Tuesday • Woody Bop Muddy • Terry Alderton • Tony Allen • Boothby Grapho • Angela de Castro • Ian Cognito • Desperate Men • The Frigidaires • Grand Theatre of Lemmings • Steve Griven • Guns 'n' Moses • Charmian Hughes • Noel James • Jimeoin • Bob & Bob Jobbins • Jonathan Kay • Kevin McAleer • Rory Motion • Richard Moulton • Logan Murray • Original Mixture • Marian Pashley • Sean Percival • The Rapping Rabbi • Reaction Theatre • Rubber Bishops • Andy Smart – Vicious Boy • Linda Smith • Dave Thompson • The Whalley Range All Stars

Circus – Napthaline • Founambule • Chimaera • Foolhardy Folk • Fluke • The Flying Dutchmen • Lee Hayes • Le La Les • Ostrich Ostrich • The Pack • Rudi Wallenda • Stefan Cassini • The Count Spacey Orchestra • The Cuban Acrobats • Maggie Dick Gyroscope • Enigmatic Eve • The Famous Bramwells • Hercules • Ijs en Weder • Ian Jay's Sponge Plunge • Pete Madd • Jason Maverick • The Rhythm Doctors • Scarabeus • The Shock Brothers • William Shrew's Giant Robot Stilt Laser Show • Spiders in the Sky • Swamp Circus • John Teasdale • Trapeze Falco • The Vander Brothers • André Vincent • Wax & Wain • *plus Helter-Skelter, Raging Rodeo Bull, workshops in juggling, tight wire, trapeze and more*

Jazz World Stage – Aïrto Moreira, Flora Purim and Fourth World • Bheki Mseleku with Marvin 'Smitty' Smith • Baaba Maal • Keziah Jones • Omar • James Taylor Quartet • Varttina • Co-Creators • D. Influence • Donette Forte and the Revolutionary Dub Warriors • Emperor's New Clothes • FFF • Antonio Forcione • Fun-Da-Mental • The Inner Sense Percussion Orchestra • McCoy • Mistura • Moiré Music Drum Orchestra • Najma • Nitin Sawhney • Profusion • Protocol • Sound Advice • Trans-Global Underground with Natasha Atlas • Urban Species

Avalon Stage – Alan Stivell • Robin Williamson & John Renbourn • Afterhours • Mark Robson & Kangaroo Moon • Tim Wheater • Flying Pigs • Dominique Le Vack • Le Rue • The Morrigan • Asylum Beat • Big Mouth • Dolphin • D'Urberville Ramblers • Gordon Haskell • Graham Russell • Havana Fireflies • Hoodwink • Jess • Jimi Blue & Graham Clarke • Kangaroo Moon • K-Passa • Magoma • Show of Hands • Skin the Peeler • The Brew Band • The Emeralds

Film – Bladerunner (Director's cut) • Bram Stoker's Dracula • Last of the Mohicans • Lawnmower Man • The Punk (UK première) • Singles • Strictly Ballroom • Toys • The Jungle Book • Les Amants du Pont Neuf • Casablanca • Des by Temptation • Highway to Hell • Johnny Suede • Simple Men • Tetsu 2 • Une Époque Formidable • Wild West • Asterix and the Big Fight • Ferngully • La Petite Bande

... with more names to come, plus 60 acres of planet-friendly creative activities in the Green Field, and much much more…

Tickets £58 – advance only ☎ 0272 767868
– no tickets for sale on the gate

Price includes camping, car parking, V.A.T. and all on-site events. Children under 14 admitted free.

Information Hotline: 0839 66 88 99

For latest bookings, news and views. *Calls charged at 36p/min. cheap rate, 48p/min. at other times*

NME
VOX

1993

With the licensed attendance increased by 10,000, the Festival sold out two weeks before taking place. The Pyramid line-up included The Black Crowes, Christy Moore and Wynton Marsalis, and the international feel was developed further on the Jazz World Stage where Airto Moreira, Flora Purim, Nitin Sawhney, Transglobal Underground and a host of others brought world music into the mix. Cabaret, mime and dance were the focus in Theatre and Circus, and The Green Fields continued to expand, with debates in the Green Futures tent and plans for a permanent Permaculture Garden. Tent theft reached its highest recorded level and security again became an issue, with Michael deciding that a double fence would be erected for the next Festival.

The bulk of the proceeds of the Festival would be divided between Greenpeace, Oxfam and local charities.

The L.O.V.E. sign in the King's Meadow (top), a landmark of the early 1990s; Festival-goers in the Sacred Space (centre), complete with flares (seemingly inflation-proof at '£2 each, three for a fiver' for a whole decade); and the new father and daughter partnership in crew catering (left).

Clockwise from top left: Stereo MCs captured on film for *Glastonbury the Movie* in 1993; the Tor and full moon decorating a long drop; just one of the 100-plus smaller stages; and Baaba Maal and Mark E Smith on two of the bigger ones.

Caitlin Moran
Writer

I was a seasoned festival-goer by the time I went to Glastonbury. I knew all about festivals. After all, I'd been to Reading. Once. The year before, when I was seventeen, I'd seen Nirvana's already legendary 1992 headlining set, when Kurt Cobain was pushed onstage in a wheelchair, pretended to collapse, and then played the gig of his life. I stayed in a B&B in town, remembered my cystitis medicine, and left early on Sunday, as I was tired and wanted to be back in time for *Antiques Roadshow*. So I was no festival newbie. I was hardened and experienced. I had the whole thing on lock down.

Consequently, when I rocked up for Glastonbury in 1993 I was eighteen, working for *Melody Maker*, and totally prepared. When I stepped out of the van, into a blisteringly sunny day, I was wearing a floor-length black velvet dress, black velvet boots, a black velvet hat and black lace gloves. Everyone else around me was in shorts and T-shirts, and slathering themselves with sunblock in the manner most people lavishly creosote a fence.

'The Goth Van's arrived!' a cheerful security guard shouted, pointing at me. 'Anyone order a Goth?'

Twenty sweaty, velvety minutes later, I made the decision to spend all the money I'd brought for food on a new outfit. I hiked to a stall up a hill where I was decked out in a floor-length white cotton dress, a white straw hat and – having run out of money for sunblock – a waist-length white veil, which I draped over the hat and my face, to protect me from the glare. I returned triumphantly to my companions.

'Fucking hell – you've come as a Victorian beekeeper,' they exclaimed.

And so it was as a Victorian beekeeper that I attended my first Glastonbury. A few hours later, I was a Victorian beekeeper with only one functioning leg. Having had to abandon my velvet boots as they were too hot, I had subsequently trodden, barefoot, on a tent peg, and gashed my sole open. Mark Eitzel from American Music Club tended to the wound – pouring neat whisky on to sterilise it, and then binding the wound with a sock.

Over the next three days of hobbling around, the edges of the gaping wound took on a crisp, crunchy edge, while the rest of my foot went very pale, in shock.

'Look! My foot looks like Edvard Munch's *The Scream*!' I would announce cheerfully, holding up the mangled remnants to people I bumped into. Tanya Donelly from Belly did the most violent dry-heaving, but Brett Anderson from Suede looked the most purely revolted.

It's always good to have a talking point with rock stars, I thought to myself, as I thumped my infected foot down on various picnic rugs, to screams. Stops there being any awkward pauses!

In the early nineties – between acid house and Britpop – the British indie scene was small, based in London NW1, and closely knit. Consequently, Glastonbury felt like all of Camden on a mini-break to the countryside – like those episodes of *EastEnders* when the cast go on holiday to Spain, with hilarious results. Pale, wraith-like indie boys in dusty corduroy jackets – usually only seen in The Good Mixer, at night – looked like terribly misplaced objects in a sunny field in Somerset.

At first, they tried to replicate their natural pastimes and habitat – hunkering down in the backstage beer tent, in the gloom, and chain-smoking Silk Cut – but, after a couple of hours and pints, they were gradually coaxed out into nature. The backstage area – in 1993 simply a massive field with a beer tent in it – took on the air of a school playing field, as roadies turned up with footballs and urged everyone to join in. I would look up from sharing my foot wound with Porno for Pyros to see various members of Blur, Teenage Fanclub, Elastica and Suede cheerfully hoofing a ball around. Spiritualized and Mazzy Star would look on with disinterest. They were not football-playing bands.

Later in the day, as the sun went down, comedian Keith Allen – with a baby Lily Allen in tow – would begin the backstage karaoke. I would, by this point, be very drunk, so I can't remember what it was that Jarvis Cocker sang – I want to say 'Rhinestone Cowboy'? – but he gave it the full Jarvis, to an audience of maybe fifty people. Two years later, he gave one of the greatest-ever headlining sets at Glastonbury, after The Stone Roses pulled out at the last minute. I suspect half the reason his performance was so perfectly wired to the audience was that he knew what Glastonbury was like – he'd sat in those same fields, drinking cheap cherry brandy, getting dusty, sunburned and expansive. He knew how to plug into the Glastonbury Spirit – a much-mentioned thing for which I think the simplest explanation is 'forgetting there is anything, or anywhere, other than Glastonbury'. If you're doing it right, the concept of the outside world becomes increasingly distant and bizarre. Why would we invent places that aren't a city of fields with constant music, dancing, talking and joy? Who would have done that?

Since that first Glastonbury in 1993, I've not missed a Festival. I have gone from an eighteen-year-old apiarist to a 43-year-old mother of two, returning to the same place every year, save for the odd occasions when the selfish bastards prioritise the welfare of their cows above my need to spend five days floating around the Vale of Avalon, quiet and serene in the knowledge that there is nowhere more perfect than where I am right now.

It is a fixed point in the calendar that functions, culturally, like the part of the kitchen wall where you mark off your children's growth, year on year. I remember the introduction of mobile phones to this country for two reasons. The first because, for some reason, the mobile-phone company Orange used to have a tiny tent backstage from which they would hand out free mobile phones to accredited journalists, with unlimited free calls. Back then, it was presumed mobile phones would be a difficult sell to the public, and Orange wanted journalists to write about how great mobiles were so that they might 'catch on'. By the end of their first day of giveaways, the field was full of drunken journalists calling each other on their free mobiles, quoting *Beavis and Butt-Head* at full volume – 'I need TP! TP – for my BUNG HOLE!' – and then hanging up, laughing hysterically. No one wrote about the free mobile phones. Orange stopped supplying them shortly afterwards.

But despite the worst efforts of drunk, freeloading journalists, mobile phones did catch on. The second reason I remember the introduction of mobile phones to this country was when, in 1998, walking around the Festival site, I noted a glaring absence: no more drunken men, separated from their friends, walking around, exhausted, shouting, 'SIMON! SIMON! NEIL! ED! SIMON!' over and over again. This had, in years gone by, been a reliable and constant backing vocal to the general festival noise. 'SIMON! SIMON! NEIL! ED! SIIIIIIIIIMON!' Now it was gone for ever. Mobiles had arrived. Everyone was calling each other instead. 'I'm by the flag that says, "I LOVE SAUSAGES."'

Having gone to Glastonbury for so long, I've seen it go from being 'a thing someone is doing' to 'an institution'. In 2005 – now with my own, very small, children in tow – I was delighted when I noticed the jeep parking by our caravan, where I was putting the kids to bed, was driven by Joe Strummer and Chrissie Hynde. As I tucked my offspring in and prepared for an early night, I watched wistfully as Chrissie and Joe strode off into the night – clearly preparing for a good time.

The next morning, I was making the kids' breakfast when I heard sounds of confusion outside. Looking out the window, I saw Strummer and Hyde – clearly having had 'all the fun' – standing in an empty space where their jeep had been.

'It's gone!' Joe said.

'Someone's taken it!' Chrissie replied.

They looked at each other for a minute, then shrugged, lit fags and strode off, back towards the top fields like the rock 'n' roll legends they were.

They must have been heading towards what is now called Strummerville, the mini-village between the Stone Circle and The Park named after Strummer when he died, a few years later, in honour of his constant presence there.

Last year – my children now grown, allowing me to go out at night once more – I wandered through Strummerville at 3 a.m. A group of stoned young men were sitting around the perpetual campfire, earnestly discussing the history of the encampment.

'It was named after this guy who loved Glastonbury so much, he always used to come to here and light a fire,' one was explaining.

'Who was he?' the other asked.

'Jimmy Somerville. That's why it's called Somerville.'

And so it passes from incident to institution – and on, into myth. Wrong old amusing myth.

A couple of weeks ago, I was trying to explain to someone who'd never been to Glastonbury just what it is that gives it its magnetic edge – why it draws you back, year after year. It was difficult, because we didn't have two hours to spare. I vetoed nerdy marvelling over the infrastructure – that this is a temporary city, the size of Bath, that appears for only one weekend a year, with its own internal wholesale market for caterers, recycling project and welfare system. I thought it pointless to describe how beautiful it is – ponds lit by lanterns, sand-sculptures of dragons, fields of silk flags streaming against a blue sky – because, you know, it's on a farm in Somerset at midsummer. Of course it's gorgeous. It didn't seem necessary to go on about how exciting it is: surely everyone, by now, knows about the year a life-sized pirate ship drove around the site, filled with Goth girls in corsets dancing to 'No Diggity'; the recreation of a 1970s New York gay disco; or the gigantic metal spider that shoots flames into the sky. Or how wholeheartedly good it is: giving its profits to Oxfam and WaterAid; shunning advertising billboards; supporting the endangered steelworks in Port Talbot by ordering 250,000 reusable pint glasses, which were super-handsome to boot.

Instead, I decided the best thing was to explain how, when you're there, for three glorious days 'the news' stops being about the economy, war, sport and political tussles – and starts being about how artists seize a moment, have a revelation, lose their shit or opt to be very, very silly instead. At the end of every day, when you meet up with friends, you all download your headlines like doughty reporters in the midst of a cultural World Cup, where hundreds of bands vie to 'win' the Festival by simply being the most amazing/demented.

'Mary J. Blige was on her knees, in the rain, crying, during "No More Drama"!' 'Nick Cave leaned out into the audience and held this girl's hand – they just stared at each other, like someone had cast a spell on them.' 'Amy Winehouse punched someone!' 'Pulp premiered a new song called "Sorted for E's & Wizz"!' 'The Manic Street Peachers went tonto and said they wanted to build a bypass over the Festival site!' 'A naked man got onstage during Elastica!' 'A hundred thousand people came to watch Jeremy Corbyn!' 'Radiohead played a secret gig in The Park, and it was so muddy, people were skiing down the hill to get to them!' 'It's so flooded in Pennard Hill there are men in dinghies, sailing towards Ray Davies!' 'Jay-Z played "Wonderwall" just to annoy Noel Gallagher, who said rappers shouldn't play Glastonbury!' 'Keith from The Prodigy came onstage in a massive, see-through hamster ball!'

Really, what Glastonbury is – why thousands go back, year after year, me included – is because it is, for one weekend, a total immersion in how joyous, creative, unexpected, explosive and endlessly fascinating humans are. How we love to make each other giddy with excitement; how, at the right moment, we can make 100,000 people cry. Scientists have recently found that, at gigs, the heartbeats of the crowd gradually synchronise – until we all pulse to a single, universal, secret metronome. Anyone who's been to Glastonbury could have told them that decades ago.

Oppoosite: Visions from Glastonbury Festival's 'magnetic edge' — the Stone Circle by day (top), and the Pyramid field at dawn (bottom).

GLASTONBURY
24·25·26 JUNE 1994

In the height of summer, at the time of solstice – moon-mad, sun-begotten – we acclaim the glory of life with ungrudging senses.
—Llewelyn Powys

1000+ acts, 17 stages... performers include:–

Pyramid Stage: Peter Gabriel · Elvis Costello & the Attractions · The Levellers · Rage Against the Machine · Van Morrison · Paul Weller · The Spin Doctors · Nick Cave & the Bad Seeds · James · Johnny Cash · Jackson Browne · World Party · Dwight Yoakam · Galliano · Lucky Dube · Mary Black · Blind Melon · Ride · Grant Lee Buffalo · Jah Wobble & The Invaders of the Heart · Tindersticks · Ian McNabb with members of Crazy Horse · Little Axe

NME Stage: Björk · M People · Blur · Manic Street Preachers · The Pretenders · Apache Indian · Radiohead · Inspiral Carpets · Spiritualized · The Beastie Boys · The Boo Radleys · Orbital · Senser · African Head Charge · Chumbawamba · Credit to the Nation · Dub Syndicate · L7 · Me'Shell · Madder Rose · Tool · Trans Global Underground · Pulp · Ultramarine · Co-Creators · Deus · Echobelly · Honky · Green Apple Quickstep · Little Axe · Luscious Jackson · Oasis · Regeneration · Rub Ultra · Tiny Monroe · Wishplants · Burning Glass
+DJs John Peel · Paul Oakenfold · Mannasseh · Adrian Sherwood · Melting Pot

Cabaret: Attila The Stockbroker · Helen Austin · Boothby Graffoe · Brian · Charlie Chuck · Chris Cresswell · Ian Cognito · Corky and the Juice Pigs · Dreenagh Darrell · Dolly Dupree · Frank Chickens · The Frigidaires · Stephen Frost & the Wow Show · The Greatest Show on Legs · Steve Gribbin · Malcolm Hardee · Matthew Hardy · John Hegley · Harry Hill · Charmian Hughes · Joolz · Mandy Knight · Stewart Lee · Sean Lock · The Loreena Bobbett Fan Club · The Man with a Beard · Kevin McAleer · Rory Motion · Logan Murray · John Otway · Alan Parker – Urban Warrior · Peewee · Leelo Ross · The Rubber Bishops · Jack Russell · Andy Smart · Dave Thompson · John Thomson · Stu Who? · Woody Bop Muddy

Acoustic Stage: Mary Black · Bootleg Beatles · Brontë Bros · Cheapsuit O'Roonies · Andy Davis · Iris DeMent · Melissa Ferrick · John Hiatt · Horse · Gallagher & Lyle · Gorky's Zygotic Mynci · Man · Eleanor McEvoy · The Oyster Band · Penguin Café Orchestra · Pooka · Reconciliation · Sharon Shannon · Glenn Tilbrook · John Trudell · Trash Can Sinatras · Eleanor Shanley · Tom Robinson · Andy White · Bates Motel

Jazz World Stage: Lucky Dube · The Ash Band · Natacha Atlas · Batu · Bloco Acorda Povo · The Anita Carmichael Band · Co-Creators · D'Note · The French Funk Federation · Jah Wobble & The Invaders of the Heart · Joyce · Julian Joseph · Loop Guru · Rory McLeod · Me'Shell Ndege Ocello · Outside · Oui 3 · Pan · Paradesi Music Machine · Jason Rebello · Stan Rivera y su Coniunto · Sandals · Oumou Sangare · Sierra Maestra · Sunchilde · Suns of Arqa · Urban Species · US 3 · Weapons of Sound

Theatre: Footsbarn Theatre · Forkbeard Fantasy · Jonathan Kay · London Mime Theatre · Natural Theatre Company · Theatre of Fire · Trestle Theatre Company · Kevin Brooking's Zirk Cirque Theatre · Angela De Castro & Kim Tilbrook · Lady Christobel & Butler · Graham Duff · A Festival of Fools · Full House · Roy Hutchins · More Fool Us · Parachute Theatre · Raukus Mir · Herr & Frau Petersen · Peepolykus · Tash Wesp · Jonathan Acorn · Avanti Display · Ben Baddoo · Joe Bazouki · Bristol School of Samba · James Brommage · Co-ordinated Chaos · Cosmos · The Craic Society · Espiritu Flamenco · The Faceless Company · Rosie Gibb · The Jezabelles · Gotcha Kapanadze · Circus La Fong · Living Daylights · Anthony Livingspace · LOnger LAsting LIghtbulb · Tony Macaroni · Materfamilias · Ozzie Mclean · David Michelsen · Nathaniel of Wessex · Parsnip Kanker · Red Hot Theatre · Theatre Rotto · Scotty · Skidazzle · Stickleback Plasticus · Stretch People · Ultravision · Weapons of Sound · Word & Action · Xana B.

Avalon Stage: Afterhours · The Ash Band · Caribé · Carmina · Court of Miracles · Iona · Kangaroo Moon · K-Passa · Magoma · Dominique Le Vack · Robin Williamson & John Renbourn · Wolfstone · Ed Alleyne-Johnson · The Avalonian Free State Choir · Cheapsuit O'Roonies · Cosmic Charlies · The Dharmas · Dr Didj · Edward II · From The Hip · Havana Fireflies · Kora Colours · The Retreat · Shedding Skin · Show Of Hands · Sweet Soul Sisters · Tootin' Ska Moon · Uruk-Hai

Circus: Boulevard Lannes Company · High Tension · Higher than the Sun · Ian Jay's Sponge Plunge · Marin Magne · Naphtaline · No Fit State Circus · Las Piranhas · Skate Naked · Skinning the Cat · Swamp Circus · Têtes en l'Air · The Vander Brothers' Wheel of Death · Wax 'n' Wain · Bernie Bennett · Rex Boyd & David Cashell · Charlie Brown · Circo Berserko · Circus Space · Company Ubersee · Famos Bramwells · Ken Farquhar · Timothy Francis · The Gentlemen Jugglers · Get A Grip · The Great Dave · Lee Hayes · Tony Hunter · Inside Out · Marion Kenny & Rachel Henson · Kiss My Axe · Kwabana Lindsay · Adrian Love · Jason Maverick · Sarabian Knights · Sarah Slater · Joel Salom · Stretch People · Stompy · Taunton Community Circus · John Teasdale · Ashley Turk · Two Across · Rudi Wallenda · Windsor + Ferris Wheel, Trapeze and Circus Skills Workshops, Gyroscopes, Trampolines, Inflatables, Velcro Wall etc.

Cinema: In the Name of the Father · Baraka · Aladdin · Mrs. Doubtfire · Cool Runnings · The Northerners · Naked · The Secret Garden · Astérix in Britain · The Singing Ringing Tree · House of Angels · Les Visiteurs · A Leningrad Cowboy Goes to America · Orlando · Backbeat · In the Soup

Kidz Field: Michael Balfour · Circus Hazzard · Bodger & Badger · Circus Fiasco · Palfi · Goffee · The Fabulous Professor Panic · Juggletruck · Twist in the Tale Theatre Co. · Clown Jewels · Over the Top Puppet Co. · Big Peach Theatre Co. · Ian Fuller · Clownabout · Rose Theatre · Framework Children's Theatre · Bubble 'n' Squeak · Wozisname · Cirque du Pays de Galle · Dandelion Puppets · Martini's Magic · Foolhardy Folk · Circus Extraordinaire · Studio 3 Arts · Meynell Games · John Rowe · The Beetroots · Urban Strawberry Lunch · Combination Dance Education · Nick the Puppet · Bristol Playbus · Chairoplanes, Space Balls, Octopus, Astroslide, Airspace Inflatables, Swingboats etc.

Plus 60 idyllic acres of Green Field, and, as ever, much, much, much, more...
• NB: Sometimes unforeseen circumstances prevent advertised acts from appearing •

The event of the year in 1994!

in aid of GREENPEACE

Tickets £59 – advance only ☎ 0272 767868 · NO tickets available on the gate
Price includes camping, car parking, V.A.T. and all on-site events. Accompanied children under 14 are admitted free.

Information Hotline: 0839 66 88 99
For latest bookings, news and views. *Calls charged at 39p/min. cheap rate, 49p/min. at other times*

Three-day advance tickets *BY PHONE* – credit card sales: **0272 767 868** · *BY POST* – Glastonbury Festivals Ltd., PO Box 352, Bristol BS99 7FD.
Please **add £2 per ticket** to cover handling and p&p. Please make cheques payable to Glastonbury Festivals Ltd. Do not enclose a stamped addressed envelope.

Plans for the weekend were almost destroyed eleven days before the Festival when the Pyramid Stage burned down. A replacement was erected in time and was linked up to the Festival's first wind turbine, which supplied 150 kilowatts of power for performances from Peter Gabriel, Elvis Costello and The Attractions, Levellers, Dwight Yoakam, Johnny Cash and Rage Against the Machine, among others.

Channel 4 brought their cameras and crew down to Worthy Farm to broadcast the Festival live for the first time. Johnny Cash filled the Sunday afternoon slot and brought out his good friend the Bishop of Bath and Wells for a bit of spiritual refuelling during his set; he even edited out 'sonofabitch' in 'A Boy Named Sue', as he thought there might be kids watching the TV broadcast.

With Britpop in full force, Oasis, Blur, Radiohead and Pulp began their long relationship with the Festival. Under the guidance of Arabella Churchill, the Theatre and Circus fields continued to flourish, with walkabout performers adding to the anarchic atmosphere that permeated across several stages. This was also the first year that Orbital played at Glastonbury (returning in 1995, '99, 2002 and '04).

1994

CAPACITY: 80,000
TICKET PRICE: £59

Below: Glastonbury's Theatre and Circus fields play host to over 5,000 artists, performers and crew every single year.

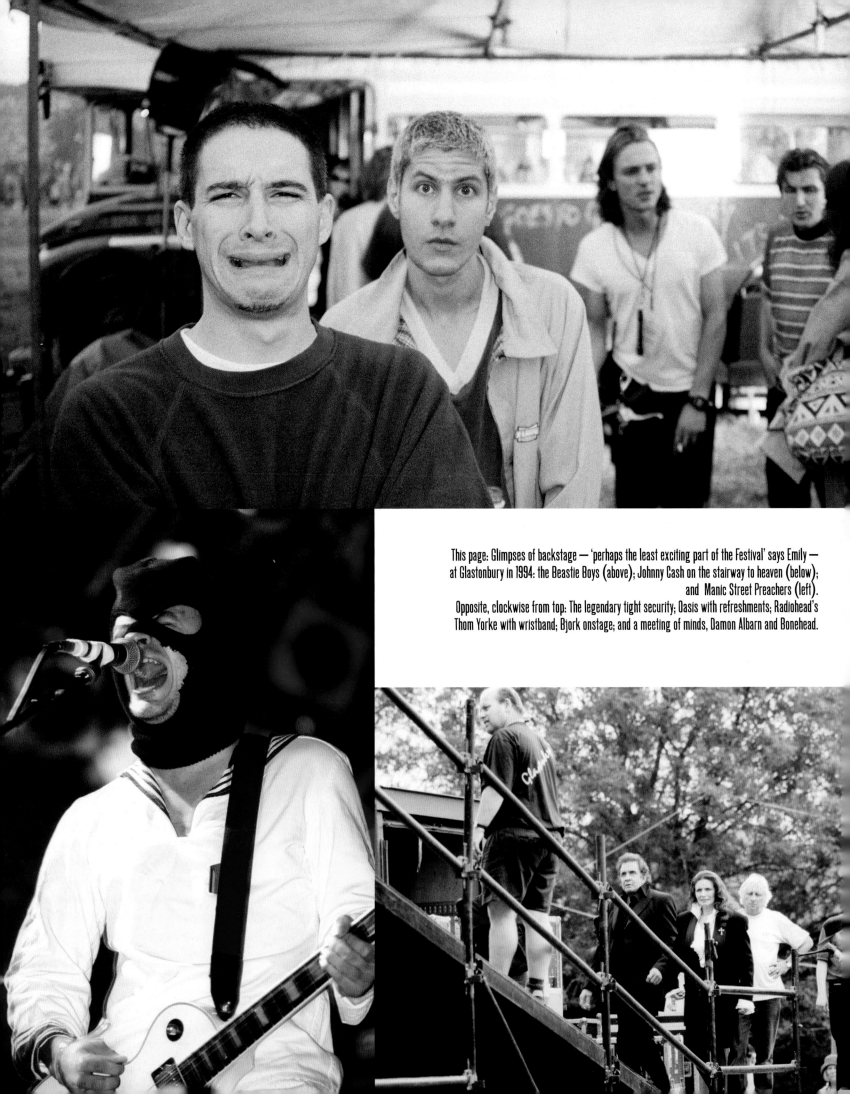

This page: Glimpses of backstage — 'perhaps the least exciting part of the Festival' says Emily — at Glastonbury in 1994: the Beastie Boys (above); Johnny Cash on the stairway to heaven (below); and Manic Street Preachers (left).
Opposite, clockwise from top: The legendary tight security; Oasis with refreshments; Radiohead's Thom Yorke with wristband; Bjork onstage; and a meeting of minds, Damon Albarn and Bonehead.

1994

NO LIGGERS

Jarvis Cocker

Pulp

The first time I came to Glastonbury was in 1982, and it was awful. A group of us decided to go to a load of festivals that summer, so we rented a van and just travelled around, sleeping in the van. But because it said Sheffield Auto Hire on the van it was obvious we weren't full-time travellers, so we didn't really fit in. We went to one festival in Wales, and we came back to the van and found some kids siphoning the petrol out of the tank.

Also, it turns out that when you try to sleep five people in the back of a Transit van with the door shut, you create a kind of weather system. You get all this condensation dripping off the roof, like it's raining in there. It was fucking horrible – I wouldn't recommend it to anyone.

Glastonbury was a particular low point of that summer, because it rained constantly and I was splitting up with my girlfriend at the time. We climbed over the fence to get in — sorry about that, but everyone was doing it then — and I just couldn't get on with the vibe at all. It was a very miserable experience, which was only lightened by seeing Jonathan Richman play somewhere in the afternoon. I'm sure the fault was with me, not the Festival, but after that year I decided that I never wanted to go again.

'It was quite a big gamble on everyone's part': Jarvis Cocker (opposite) reflects on THAT Glastonbury gig in 1995, and the ethos that kept him coming back.

Then, in 1994, we were offered a slot and I thought, Maybe it'll be different if we play. And it was. We played on the NME Stage in the afternoon and it was really good fun. I had a very tight tweed jacket on, and some sunglasses because we were playing in daylight. I don't usually agree with wearing sunglasses onstage, but I've never been a fan of daytime shows, so I decided to try to fool myself by putting some sunglasses on.

The weather was reasonable that year and we stuck around, wandering about and going to see some other people. I didn't see any of the headliners, but I discovered that year that Glastonbury's not about the headline acts. There's so much of the Festival that's not even got anything to do with music. I love that, and the fact that you can have your own unique experience there. It's not just one festival; everybody has their own Glastonbury. I definitely came away thinking, Yeah, Glastonbury's okay, actually.

The following year, 1995, The Stone Roses were meant to be headlining, but John Squire had a bicycle accident and they had to pull out. So we got the call asking us to step in. I've heard rumours that lots of people were called before us – someone said Rod Stewart was asked first. I tried to ask Michael Eavis once, but his answer was quite evasive.

Anyway, it doesn't really matter. I've since looked at the timeline of it and it's a bit flabbergasting, really. The thing that made it possible for us was that 'Common People' had been a hit, and that had only come out at the end of May 1995 and gone into the charts less than a month before the Festival. We hadn't even finished our album, *Different Class*, at that point; we were in the studio working on it when we got the call. But it was far too exciting an idea to turn down, so we all said, 'Yeah, let's do it.' It was quite a big gamble on everyone's part, though – Glastonbury's and ours. We weren't really sure how we were going to pull it off.

Because it was so near to the date of the Festival, our management couldn't find a hotel for us to stay in, so we sent someone out to Millets to buy some tents and we camped backstage. That was one of the most helpful things about the whole weekend: we turned up on the Friday, the night before our set, and we got to walk around the site and pick up on the atmosphere.

Oasis were playing that night, and I went to watch them. It was quite a windy evening, so the sound was blowing around and you couldn't really hear them, but people were still really into it. And I realised then that our performance was more about being part of the Festival and people's experience than it was about worrying about getting every single note right. That helped me to get out of my self-indulgent nervousness.

Before 'Common People', I think the highest we'd been in the charts was something like number twenty, and I suppose some people thought we were just one of those indie also-ran groups. And maybe we even started to think it too. So that show did feel like a very big deal. It was the culmination and validation of what we'd been trying to do since the band had started when I was at school in 1978. We didn't know if we'd get that chance again, so we didn't want to waste it.

I always get nervous before I perform, but that one was amplified because of the enormity of what it seemed we had to do. As it got closer and closer to showtime, I started to get really paranoid that I was going to fall over and break something. Maybe at the back of my mind I was thinking about the John Squire thing. So I decided to sit on this white plastic chair backstage, and once I'd sat on it, it felt dangerous to get up from it. I must've sat there for two hours. And then it was time to go onstage.

I can't remember much about the performance itself, but I do remember that during 'Common People', when I was singing the chorus, you could hear the audience singing as well. They seemed louder than me. That had never happened before. I remember thinking, Shit, I'd better not get the words wrong because they know them.

That concert will always be one of my favourites and, I suppose, one of the highlights of my life, because it was really an occasion. And that's what life is made out of. Those big moments like getting married and having kids. It was an occasion like that.

We came offstage knowing it had gone well. We had to make a connection and make people's evening exciting, and it felt like we'd managed to do that. I doubt we played perfectly, but it didn't really matter. It felt like the atmosphere had been right and that something had happened. It was good.

That show had a massive effect on the band. We'd played quite a few songs from *Different Class* at Glastonbury that we'd never played before, songs like 'Sorted for E's & Wizz', and we'd got away with it in front of all those people. We went back into the studio on the Monday after with such confidence to finish the record off.

I've been back to Glastonbury quite a lot since then. Pulp have played a couple more times, and I've done some solo shows and often deejayed in The Park. The bit I like most is still just wandering around and seeing what's happening. I love just stumbling upon a band in a tent where there are just twenty people watching, but they're all really into it.

I've played at a lot of festivals, and some have been good ones, but I still haven't come across one that's got the same atmosphere or the same amount of stuff going on as Glastonbury. Obviously it's changed a lot since I first came, but it has managed to keep what makes it special. It's more than just a music festival. The idea was always that it was an alternative thing, with its roots in the underground, making something away from the corporate structure. There may be cash machines and mobile phones now, but I think it's pretty amazing that it's maintained that original ethos.

I think there's a growing hunger for that now. As corporations have got bigger and stronger, people have realised that an alternative take on things is important. Glastonbury has always led the way with that. That's why I keep coming back. And it's why, even as its fiftieth anniversary approaches, Glastonbury still feels very current and, I think, more important than ever.

GLASTONBURY FESTIVAL

of Contemporary Performing Arts

23-24-25 June

1970-1995 · 25 YEARS ·

*And flowers and trees and beasts and men receive
comfort in morning, joy in the noonday.
And we are put on earth a little space,
that we may learn to bear the beams of love.*
—William Blake

in aid of GREENPEACE

Over 1,000 acts, at least 17 stages, performers include:–

Main Stage: *Friday–* Oasis • Black Crowes • Soul Asylum • War
Lightning Seeds • Ozric Tentacles • Senser • Spearhead
Saturday– The Stone Roses • P.J. Harvey • Guest Artists • Jamiroquai
Jeff Buckley • Everything but the Girl • Indigo Girls • Dave Matthews
Sunday– The Cure • Simple Minds • Guest Artists • Tanita Tikaram • Saw Doctors • Bootleg Beatles
Wincanton Town Band • Avalonian Free State Choir

NME Stage: Elastica • Belly • Galliano • Leftfield • The Prodigy • The Charlatans • Dodgy • Gene • Goldie • Offspring • Sleeper
Supergrass • Urge Overkill • Veruca Salt • Weezer • Ash • Flaming Lips • Dreadzone • Live • Marion • Menswear • Morphine
Soul Coughing • Skunk Anansie • These Animal Men • The Verve • 311 • Blameless • The Boredoms • Drugstore
The Mutton Birds • Scarfo • Strangelove • Die Totenhosen • Seven Day Diary • Zion Train

Dance Tent: The Massive Attack Sound System • Eat Static • Drum Club • Higher Intelligence Agency • Fluke • DJ Evolution
• Innersphere • Spooky • System 7 • Darren Emerson • David Holmes • Mixmaster Morris • Tribal Drift • The Aloof
Dreadzone • Kenny Larkin • Plastikman • Charlie Hall • Carl Cox

Acoustic Stage: Altan • Paul Brady • Billy Bragg • Cajunologie • Martin Carthy • Difford & Tilbrook • The Equation
G Love & Special Sauce • Keiran Kennedy • Les Negresses Vertes • Nick Lowe & The Impossible Birds • Mary Janes
Mike Scott • Gilbert O'Sullivan • John Otway Big Band • Prayerboat • Chuck Prophet • Rockingbirds
Seven Day Diary • Sharon Shannon • Al Stewart • Vulgar Boatmen • Zap Mama

Jazz World Stage: Tricky • War • Augustus Pablo, Junior Delgado & The Rockers Band • Gil Scott-Heron
Aïrto Moreira & Flora Purim • JTQ • Transglobal Underground • Incognito • Freak Power • Jhelisa • Diblo Dibala • The Roots
Spearhead • D-Influence • Jessica Lauren • G Love & Special Sauce • Trevor Watts & The Moiré Music Drum Orchestra •
The London Afro Bloc • The Rebirth Brass Band • Abdel Kabirr and the Gumbay Dance Band • Earthling
Ultrasound • The Federation • Bud Bongo • Tammy Payne • Brass Reality • John Perkins

Cabaret, Theatre & Circus: Helen Austin • Attila the Stockbroker • Avanti Display • Bob and Bob Jobbins • British Events
Brouhaha • Tommy Cockles • Ian Cognito • The Cottle Sisters Circus • Emergency Exit Arts • External Combustion • Ronnie Golden
Boothby Graffoe • Green Ginger • Malcolm Hardee • Haze v. The X Factor • Jonathan Kay • Kiss my Axe • Mandy Knight
Le La Les • Les Têtes en l'Air • Sean Lock and Bill Bailey • Marin Magne • Al Murray • Natural Theatre Company • Orchard Theatre
Alan Parker – Urban Warrior • Skate Naked • The Vander Brothers' Triple Wheel of Death • Andy Smart • Stickleback Plasticus
The Stopler Bangels • Theatre Schrikkel • Mark Thomas • Tout Fou To Fly • Woody Bop Muddy • Patience Agbabi • Terry Alderton
Avanti Display • Julian Barrett • Bastard Son of Tommy Cooper • Jo Bazuki • Stephen Bowditch • Ed Burn • David Cassel
Charmian Hughes • Circus Fudge • Miles Crawford • Dreenagh Darrell • Ivor Dembina • Louise Fransella • Dan Freedman
Ronnie Golden • Ricky Grover • Matthew Hardy • Kevin Hayes • Robb Johnson • Jugglestruck • Mandy Knight • Dino Lampa
Andrea Leigh • Chris Luby • Mark Maier • Tom Miles • Celia Milligan • Rory Motion • Logan Murray • Paul Nathan
Original Mixture • Nobby Shanks • Smiley • The Stick Man • Andy Robinson • Theatre Rotto • Dave Thomson • Murray Torkildsen
Ultravision • Wax 'n' Wain • Weapons of Sound • Matt Welcome • Wob • Bristol School of Samba • Clownabout
The Count Spacey Orchestra • Dynamix • Rosie Gibb • The Half Human Video Show • Parachute Theatre
Please Y'self • The Stennett Company • Taunton Community Circus • Dave Thomson • Rudy Wallenda
plus, Rodeo Bull, Helter Skelter, Big Wheel, Hall of Mirrors, etc.

Avalon Stage: Wolfstone • Edward II • Waulk Elektrik • The Dharmas • Banco De Gaia • Glaz • Rock, Salt & Nails
Iona • Steeleye Span 25th Anniversary Celebration • The Chase • Deep Blues Band • Dr Didg • Baka Beyond
Eden Burning • From The Hip • FOS Brothers • La Cucina • It's A Small World Band • Junction • Raka
Show of Hands • Vitamin X • Why • Zambula

Films: Pet Detective • Mask • Pulp Fiction • Startrek Generations • The Lion King • Forrest Gump
Reservoir Dogs • The Rocky Horror Picture Show • Baraka • Speed

Kidz: Bodger and Badger • Clown Jewels • Fiasco Fire Brigade • Goffee • Professor Panic • Il Calvone • PuppetCraft • Martiny's Magic
The Bright Red Circus Co. • Bazza Bizzare • Clownabout • Tin Drum • Openwide Theatre Co. • Tom Tom Troupe
Plymouth Puppet Theatre Co. • Mr Alexander's One Man Show • Tim Francis • Innuendo • Brolly Entertainers • Joake
The Beetroots • Stilt Affliction • Puppets Alive • Albion Kids Show • Ian Fuller • Street Heat • Over The Top Puppet Co.
Sylvester the Jester • Mr Bliss' Bizarre Bazaar • The Amazing Pee Jay • Nicada Puppets • Tippety Twig Entertainments
Otherworld Arts • Face Pack • Bristol Playbus • Airspace • Suffolk Playworks • Supertramps
Far & Wide Puppets • Michael Balfour • Packer the Incredible • Stagefright • Mrs Spoof and Hoodwink
Circus Desertus • Fools Jig • Norman Haddock • Steven John's Puppet Parade
plus Helter Skelter, chair-o-planes, swingboats, adventure playground etc.

Forty acres of Green Field, Markets, and, of course, much, much more...

• NB: Sometimes unforeseen circumstances prevent advertised acts from appearing •

Tickets £65 – advance only · NO tickets on the gate

Price includes camping, car parking, V.A.T. and all on-site events. Accompanied children under 14 are admitted free.

Caravans and Camper vans £20 extra

Information Hotline: 0839 66 88 99

For latest bookings, news and views. *Calls charged at 39p/min. cheap rate, 49p/min. at other times*

• Contrary to rumour, this is NOT the last Glastonbury Festival – see you next year!

1995

CAPACITY: 80,000
TICKET PRICE: £65

Celebrating the twenty-fifth anniversary of the Festival, two acts from its first year – Al Stewart and Keith Christmas – were invited back to play in a line-up that also included Oasis, The Cure and Pulp, the latter a late replacement for The Stone Roses, who pulled out the week before after John Squire was involved in a cycling accident. Cabaret, theatre and circus continued to stretch the imagination, with stand-up comedy and alternative poetry rubbing shoulders with chainsaw-juggling, sword-swallowing and traditional can-can. Long-standing on-site cinema, the Pilton Palais, offered Quentin Tarantino's *Pulp Fiction* and *Reservoir Dogs*, and by contrast the Kidzfield showed *Bodger & Badger*.

The Dance Tent was launched by Malcolm Haynes, a festival regular since 1989 who'd originally turned up with a sound system on the back of a truck. He had been pestering Michael for years about the new generation of dance music and his wish for a space of its own. The Dance Tent would eventually morph into the Dance Village, and more recently into the multi-stage experience that is Silver Hayes. Year one's line-up included Massive Attack, David Holmes, Carl Cox and System 7, and the ever-eclectic Jazz World Stage boasted Tricky, War, Jamaican dub-stylist Augustus Pablo and Gil Scott-Heron.

Greenpeace received £200,000, Oxfam £100,000, and a further £100,000 went to local charities. The decision was taken to rest the farm and the fields in 1996.

This page: Game-changers in 1995 — PJ Harvey onstage (top), and a boyband-less Robbie Williams gets a taste of a new life, courtesy of Oasis.

Overleaf: Chrissie Hynde introduces the late Jeff Buckley to the real 1990s Glastonbury (top left), where attractions included breached perimeter fencing put to creative use, flags from all nations, all-night entertainment and a dazzling array of temporary artistic installations.

Noel Gallagher

Oasis

Previous page: 'Glastonbury is whatever you want it to be' —
the 'city in the fields' from the air in 1997.
Above: Noel Gallagher prepares for the Pyramid Stage in 1995.
Opposite: A bootleg cassette with the setlist from that Oasis gig.

There are literally hundreds of festivals in the world, and I should know because I've played most if not all of them. The funny thing is, though, there's really only ONE festival in the world — in the truest sense of the word, anyway.

Glastonbury is more important than Christmas.

Glastonbury is more fun than New Year.

Glastonbury can be brutal.

Glastonbury can be magical.

The weather? Who gives a shit about the weather?

No one I know.

The music? Who gives a shit about the music?

No one I know.

Who's headlining? Who cares?

No one I know.

It's not about hippies or liberals or peace or love or politics.

Although all of the above do try to hijack it from time to time.

Glastonbury is whatever you want it to be.

Glastonbury will change your life . . .

and if it doesn't then I suggest

you get a fucking life!

Glastonbury 1995
ROCK
HARD

oasis
Live at Glastonbury

01 Spirits In The Sky
02 Some Might Say
03 Shaker Maker
04 Roll With It
05 Slide Away
06 It's Good To Be Free
07 Morning Glory
08 Cigarettes 'n' Alcohol
09 Don't Look Back In Anger
10 I Am The Walrus
11 Live Forever
12 I'm Rock 'n' Roll
13 Bring It On Down
14 Up In The Sky
15 Fade Away
16 Columbia

*   Bonus Tracks
The Metro, Chicago,
USA '95

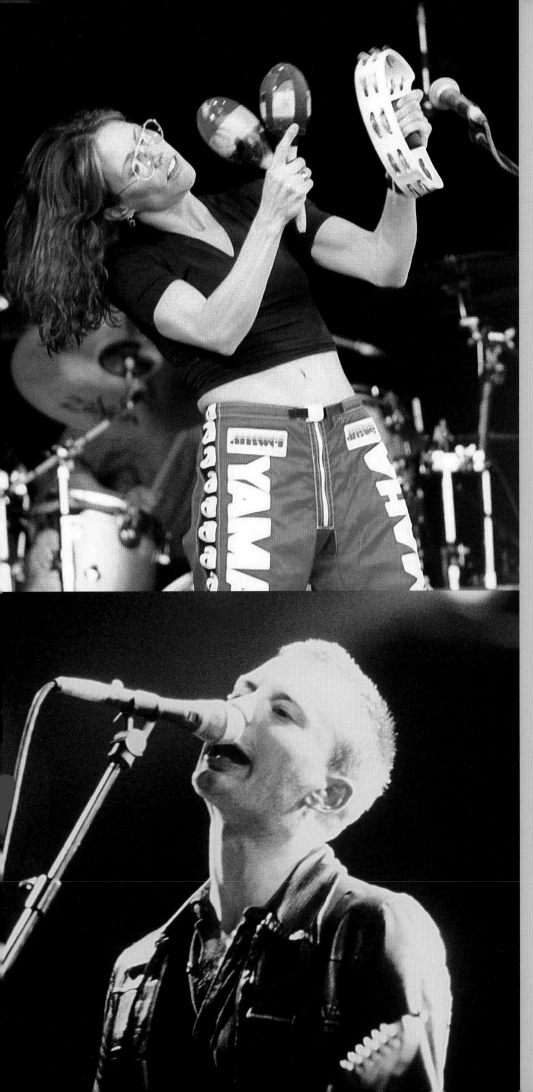

1997

CAPACITY: 90,000
TICKET PRICE: £75

Following negotiations during the fallow year in 1996, the BBC came to film Glastonbury live. A production crew of over 400, headed by Mark Cooper and Alison Howe, arrived after a solid week of rain, and the heavens continued to open as the weekend began. Amid the deluge, the rise of dance music was underlined, as The Prodigy headlined the Pyramid Stage, their bass frequencies literally making some of the backstage Portakabins move across the compound. On-site emergency measures were taken with waterproof bin bags, emergency crash tents and regular coaches to Castle Cary for those who had had enough. But even the site's muddy veneer couldn't detract from a host of new sculptures by Joe Rush, including Dubhenge, featuring upended VW Beetles and campervans.

The Festival footprint increased, with several neighbouring fields rented to cater for the 90,000 revellers, and additional areas like the Greenpeace Field, complete with a reconstruction of their *Rainbow Warrior* ship, enhanced its scale. Oxfam and Greenpeace were joined by WaterAid as official charities of the Festival.

The Smashing Pumpkins and Radiohead were the other Pyramid headliners, the latter producing one of the highlights of the weekend and one of the Festival's legendary sets. While The Chemical Brothers played The Other Stage, the Dance Tent line-up included Daft Punk, Aphex Twin, Armand van Helden and Primal Scream.

Above: Shake that thing: Sheryl Crow on the Pyramid in 1997. She returned in 2019.
Left: Thom Yorke during Radiohead's career-defining Glastonbury performance the same year.

1997

Clockwise from left: Greenpeace refashion the *Rainbow Warrior*, Glastonbury style; effective crowd management; Beck prays for rain; Keith Flint prays for fire; Neneh Cherry on point; and Nanci Griffith, one of the first country superstars to hit Worthy Farm.

GLASTONBURY FESTIVAL

26-27-28 JUNE 1998

> Rise up, my love, my fair one, and come away.
> For, lo, the winter is past, the rain is over and gone;
> The flowers appear on the earth; the time of the singing of birds is come,
> and the voice of the turtledove is heard in our land.
> —Song of Solomon, 2:10-

in aid of

GREENPEACE

TICKETS

£80

TICKETLINE: 0117 9 767 868

INFO LINE: 0839 668899

1998

CAPACITY: 100,500

TICKET PRICE: £80

With the official attendance now topping the 100,000 mark for the first time, and seventeen stages offering over a thousand acts, Glastonbury continued to grow. Here was not just a cross-section of music, but also insights into the politics and cultural influences informing the zeitgeist. For an alternative nation of that size, anything and everything began to make a story in the outside world, whether it be the Sunday afternoon slot with Tony Bennett, the mud-surfing, the half-a-million pounds that went to the Festival's three charities – Oxfam, WaterAid and Greenpeace – the improvement in loos, the arrival of an on-site bank, Fatboy Slim in the Dance Tent, the levels of recycling or the torrential rain as England played Colombia in the World Cup, screened on the main stage. Partly to reflect the changes, a venue was launched to focus on emerging talent, initially titled the New Stage.

Some 1,500 Christian Aid workers took to the site to help with the recycling effort, and in the fictional world of *The Archers*, the long-running BBC Radio 4 series, Kate Archer gave birth in The Green Fields. Tent thieves were apprehended at the perimeter fence, and festival-goers were asked from the main stage to 'go easy' on the water. Joe Strummer, one-time frontman of The Clash, created a sprawling encampment behind The Other Stage, the inspiration for the future Strummerville, recreated as a new area after Joe's tragically early death in 2002. Bob Dylan made his one and only appearance at Glastonbury.

Left: Suspended animation in the outdoor Circus Field.
Next page: Photographer Jill Furmanovsky was onstage to capture this classic thousand-yard stare from Bob Dylan's first and only Glastonbury Festival appearance.

This page: A passer-by snapped a hooded Bob Dylan greeting Nick Cave just before his gig, while 1998 also saw pioneering 'legend slot' appearances by Taj Mahal (right) and Tony Bennett (left). Opposite: Photographer Tim Walker's first major shoot for *Vogue* at a spectacularly muddy Glastonbury Festival in 1998. Model Trish Gough's clothes were carried around the site in black bin bags, the same ones used to line her wellies.

Skin

Skunk Anansie

If you want instant credibility, wherever you are in the world, then just tell someone you've headlined Glastonbury. It's still an amazing feeling to be able to say that I've done it. It really was the absolute pinnacle of our band's career.

It felt like a huge deal at the time, too. Particularly as there weren't that many women in bands, and I was aware that female festival headliners were few and far between. But we knew live performance was our strong point, and we put a lot of time and effort into making sure that we kicked arse at that show.

It was still really nerve-racking, though. The main thing was just praying that it wasn't going to rain. It really changes the mood of a show if it's pissing it down. You want people to jump up and down, but if it's raining and muddy that all falls to pieces. It did actually start to rain on the day that we played, too, but thankfully the sun came out during Lenny Kravitz's set and it stayed dry for us.

I've never been one to drink before I go onstage – we've always saved that for afterwards – which is maybe why I have such vivid memories of the show. I can remember practically every song and even what I was thinking as we went onstage. It was like I had a premonition that this was going to be our biggest gig. I was walking onto the Pyramid thinking, I wonder if we'll ever do this again?

We played really well, and the audience reaction was just phenomenal. There was a part of our set where everyone always jumped up and down, copying me, and it was unbelievable to see so many people doing it, stretching all the way back to the campsites. It was a complete ego trip being on that stage. It felt like the crowd loved me, and I certainly loved being there.

Our set was on the Sunday night, so we were the last band of the whole weekend. I think that slot is always quite a poignant one – the final hurrah of everyone's Glastonbury experience. It was also the year that Jean Eavis had passed away, and Michael was watching the gig from the side of the stage. We dedicated a song to him, and it was definitely an emotional moment.

That show wasn't just one of the biggest gigs we ever played; it was one of the best, too. When we came back on for an encore, I asked the crowd if they wanted one more song, and this huge roar of approval nearly knocked me off my feet.

I'm so proud to have had the experience. Even twenty years on, people still stop me in the street to talk about that show. Headlining Glastonbury is a heck of a notch to have on your bedpost.

Glastonbury Festival

25-26-27 JUNE

Pyramid Stage

REM • Manic Street Preachers • Beautiful South • Skunk Anansie • Hole • Underworld • Fun-Loving Criminals • Blondie • Texas • Lenny Kravitz • Bush • Ash • The Corrs • Barenaked Ladies • Joe Strummer & the Mescaleros • Al Green • Ian Dury & The Blockheads • Beth Orton • Delirious • Bjorn Again • Eliza Carthy • London Community Gospel Choir • Billy Bragg • Younger Younger 28's • Little Mothers

The Other Stage

Gomez • Cast • Mercury Rev • Pavement • Paul Oakenfold • Mogwai • Sebadoh • Super Furry Animals • Tindersticks • dEUS • Cardigans • Feeder • Elliot Smith • Travis • Delgadoes • Heather Nova • The Creatures • Dogstar • Smashmouth • Hurricane #1 • Electrasy • Everlast • Straw • Snowpony • Queens of the Stone Age • Mishka • Dr.Didg • Moke • Fungus • Toploader • Witness • Glastonbury Town Band

Acoustic Stage

Lonnie Donegan • Suzanne Vega • Marianne Faithfull • Mary Coughlan • Sharan Shannon • Glenn Tilbrook • Donal Lunny's Coolfin • Stackridge • Alisha's Attic • The London Community Gospel Choir • Henry McCullough • Tom Robinson • Grand Drive • Whistler • Christine Collister • Zebda • Mark Nevin • Nick Harper • Paddy Casey

Dance Tent

Chemical Brothers • Fatboy Slim • Gus Gus • Dave Angel • Lucid • Blueter • Binary Finary • Sharkey • Carl Cox • Praga Khan • Fabio & Grooverider • Breakbeat Era • Optical & Ed Rush • DJ Krust • Impulsion • Mateo & Matos • Indian Ropeman • DJs Dan & Jon Kahuna • Headrilliaz • Transglobal Underground • *Hip Hop Sensation:* Roots • DJ Cash Money • Jurassic 5 • DJ Noise & MC Supernatural • Dr Dooom • Scratcherverts • Slum Village • Jazz Fudge Co • Blak Twang • Rae & Christian

New Tent

Gay Dad • Wilco • Patti Smith • Kula Shaker • Cornelius • Dodgy • Built to Spill • Ultrasound • Dark Star • Death In Vegas • One ladyowner • Shack • Regular fries • TinStar • Dot Allison • Delakota • David Gray • Ooberman • Kitachi • NT • Annie Christian • Chicks • Muse • Sprung Monkey • Merz • Stroke • Nojahoda • Coldplay • Airbus • Venini • The Doves • Crazyface

Cabaret

Helen Austin • Kevin McAleer • Rory Motion • The Dustbin Dancers • Metal Bop Muddy • Jerry Sadowitz & Logan Murray • Windsor • Malcolm Hardee • Joolz • Attila the Stockbroker • John Otway • Les Bubb • Andy Smart • Charlie Chuck • Stewart Lee • Alan Parker – Urban Warrior • League against Tedium • Raymond and Mr Timpkins' Revue • Bastard Son of Tommy Cooper

Jazz World Stage

Afro Celt Sound System • Los Amigos Invisibles • Natasha Atlas • Baaba Maal • Baka Beyond • Waldemar Bastos • Black Star Liner • Burning Spear • CCQ • Junior Delgado • Dissidenten • The Egg • Faithless • Freestylers • Frederic Galliano • Groove Armada • The Herbaliser • Jazz Jamaica • Lamb • Pops Mohammed • Orbital • Eddie Palmieri • Courtney Pine • Rae & Christian • Ernest Ranglin • Jason Rebello • Sissi • Skinny • Urban Species

Avalon Stage

Roy Harper • System Seven • Peatbog Faeries • Headhunters • Banco De Gaia • Squarepusher • Bohinta • Back to base • The Bhagdaddies • Alabama 3 • Rhythmites • Marroon Town • Pops Mohammed • Kinsman • Flipside • Avalonian Free State Choir

...plus a Kids' area – a festival for children all on its own... 100 acres of Green Fields featuring everything from a solar-powered circus, to the Poets' tent, to sculpture, to healing... and so much more!

Theatre & Circus

over 300 shows every day, including: Los Excentricos • Jaleo • Jonathan Kay • Nola Rae • Weird Sisters • Heart & Soul • The Stephen Frost Impro All-Stars • Phenomena • Graeae • Heir of Insanity • Horse and Bamboo • Icarus • Kiss My Axe • The Natural Theatre Company • Arson About • La Compagnie Malabar

supporting **GREENPEACE**
WaterAid **OXFAM** *and worthwhile local causes*

£83

Ticketline: 01159 129 129
Info line: 09067 08 08 08*
*Calls charged at 50p per minute at all times

The Festival is grateful to our sponsors:– SELECT MAGAZINE The Guardian orange BBC RADIO 1 FM 97-99 BBC 2

After two years of rain, the organisers planned hard for the worst and spent £150,000 on precautions for the downpour, but the sunny weather was a welcome surprise for an event that continued to grow creatively. The Glastonbury website was launched, and the Festival gained an artist in residence for the first time – the Cornwall-based artist Kurt Jackson, who was seen on- and off stage, brushes in hand. The Glastonbury phonecard sold out before the first band had played a note, and in a bid to improve sound quality and visual harmony, the main stage was repositioned to point away from the village of Pilton and to be in line with Glastonbury Tor. Meanwhile, plans continued for the launch of the new steel Pyramid the following year.

Friday-night highlights included R.E.M., The Chemical Brothers and Fatboy Slim; Saturday delivered Manic Street Preachers, Underworld, Carl Cox, Lonnie Donegan and Patti Smith; and the Festival closed on Sunday with The Roots, System 7 and Skunk Anansie. More than a hundred acres of Green Fields featured a solar-powered circus, sculptures and The Healing Field.

The death of Michael's wife Jean, both inspiration and supportive rock from the very earliest days, was a tragic blow. Michael expressed hope that the event would continue past the millennium thanks to Jean's care and contribution: 'I would like this particular year to be dedicated to her memory as a tribute to Jean and her amazing life.' A two-minute silence was observed across the entire site at 11.30 on the Sunday morning.

1999

CAPACITY: 100,500
TICKET PRICE: £83

This page: Courtney Love (below left) and R.E.M.'s Michael Stipe.

Overleaf: (clockwise from top left) Starry-eyed surprises — the Dance Tent crowd in 1999; the Phoenix and fireworks in the King's Meadow; and Blondie's Debbie Harry on the Pyramid Stage.

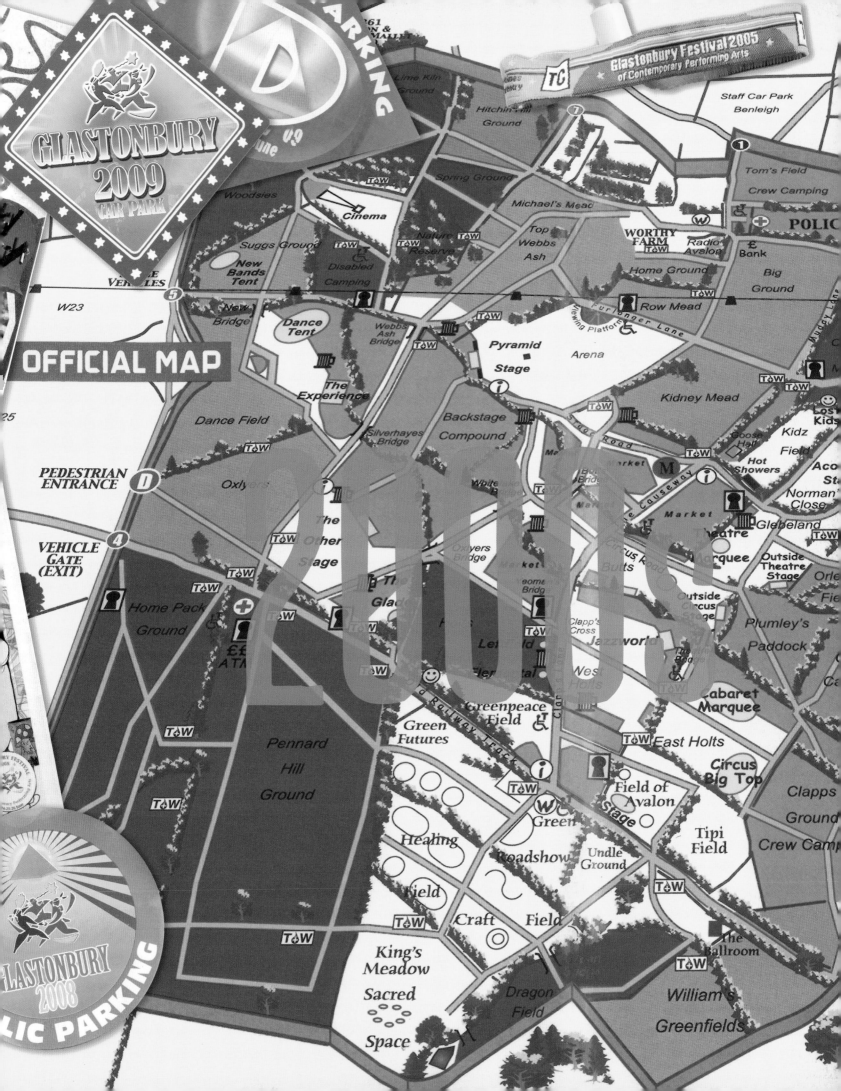

Michael

Jean and I had always intended to do the 2000 Festival and then stop. And although I did change my mind after she passed away and Emily came back from London, that first Festival of the new millennium did come alarmingly close to being our last event regardless.

A few weeks before the gates opened, we were really struggling to sell tickets. We were stuck at 80,000 sales and had to get to 100,000. Unlike the events run by big international companies, we don't have any reserve funding. If we don't sell enough tickets, we can't pay for the Festival.

One of the travellers, a guy called Roy Gurvitz, turned up at the farm and said he'd had an idea to do ballroom dancing in a marquee in the south-east corner of the site. He'd found an evening-wear hire company that had gone bust and bought all their dresses and suits. Roy had been doing his own little thing underneath the arches of the old railway line on the farm for years, but now he wanted a big tent for this. It sounded like a very good idea, so I said okay.

In those days I'd do a phone interview every week with the press in the build-up to the Festival, so I told them about the ballroom dancing. It became a big news story right across the world – suddenly I had journalists on the phone from America and Australia. We were really just known for having bands at that point, but this was the start of the whole late-night side of things at Glastonbury. Roy ended up running the Lost Vagueness field, which led to Shangri-La and all the other south-east corner areas that are such a big part of the Festival today. Back in 2000, I was just relieved that the ballroom-dancing tent drove so much interest in us. Within about three weeks of announcing it, we'd sold the remaining 20,000 tickets and reached our 100,000 capacity.

As it turned out, rather more than 100,000 people came to the Festival that year. The fence we had back then was a Mickey Mouse affair, and it completely came down on the opening day. Unfortunately, they publicised it on Radio 1, saying, 'It's virtually a free festival!' I was a bit fed up because thanks to that, along with the good weather we enjoyed that year, huge crowds of people turned up and just walked in. It was the most people we'd ever had on the site. I think there were probably 300,000 people there.

The traders certainly did well, but it was a much smaller site in 2000 so it was really packed, and a lot of bandits turned up. Despite the issues, it was a great Festival in many ways – we had David Bowie headlining – but there were more crimes, more drugs and, of course, more arrests. It did get a bit uncomfortable and embarrassing.

I knew it was going to go down seriously badly with the police and the council, so by the Monday morning I'd already started designing a new super-duper fence to make sure people couldn't get in without a ticket next time. I said to the police, 'This is not going to happen again, because I'm going to build this.' But they just replied, 'We don't believe you.'

Then, tragically, the very next weekend, nine people died in a crush at Roskilde Festival in Denmark while Pearl Jam performed on their main stage. Roskilde started on a farm in 1971, and we'd grown up together as festivals. My equivalent there, Leif Skov, was a lovely chap, and we used to compare and share bands. But there was talk of him going to prison after the deaths. He avoided that in the end, but he had to leave the event. I knew I wouldn't get a licence for 2001 after that. We had to take a year off.

The price of the new super-fence went up from about £300,000 to £1 million, but I knew I had to build it. In truth, I'd never minded whether people paid to get in or not, as long as we sold enough tickets to keep going. But it was clear we had to be able to control the numbers and keep it safe.

Unfortunately, when it came around to the 2002 licence, the police still said they were going to oppose it. We had a meeting and I showed them the plans for the new fence, and they said, 'But it's not

so much the fence, Michael. It's you. We know you're a nice chap, but you're not really an operational guy. You want to be popular. You want to be nice to everyone. You give all this money away. But you can't run this show.' After Roskilde, the police were worried that people were going to die at Glastonbury. They wanted change at the top or they weren't going to grant me the licence.

With only a couple of days to go until the licence hearing, I phoned Melvin Benn, one of the senior guys at Mean Fiddler, the company responsible for Reading Festival and most of the other big events at that time. I knew Melvin all through the 1980s, when he was working on the gates here. He was a very good operator: strict, tough and very straight. He got things done the way he wanted them to be done.

We agreed to meet the next morning in a café at Paddington Station. Melvin arrived with Vince Power, the founder of Mean Fiddler, and I explained our plight. Vince said, 'Why should we help you? You're our main opposition. We'd rather see you go down the pan.' But Melvin said, 'No, I think we ought to try to save Glastonbury.' Vince wasn't very happy about him taking my side. He said, 'If that's what you think, Melvin, I'm off.' And he shot up and stormed out of the café.

So the very next morning, Melvin, my solicitor and I met at eight o'clock at Gordano Services on the M5. We went straight to the police headquarters in Portishead, where Melvin had managed to get an appointment with the chief constable. They got on very well, and the chief constable thought Melvin was the real deal. The licence hearing with the council was the same day, at three o'clock. And the police said that, providing Melvin was in charge of operations, they'd support the licence.

There would have been other people who could have done that job, but I knew for sure that Melvin was right for it. And he did help to save the Festival. He sorted out all the structures and systems, and he put a good team in place. Melvin was with us for the next eleven years as Operations Director, until we eventually let him go and took back the running of the event ourselves. Coming in and making all those changes was always going to lead to some disharmony, and Melvin did unfortunately rub some of our long-time crew up the wrong way.

But he did a very important job for us, and he remains the Managing Director of Festival Republic (the new name for Mean Fiddler), which runs Reading, Wireless, Download and Latitude. We're still mates, too. We meet a couple of times a year for a meal in Basingstoke, halfway between London and Pilton. He respects me and I respect him. And I'm certainly grateful for what he did for us.

The super-fence completely did the job at the 2002 Festival. We did a lot of publicity telling people not to come without a ticket, which was the norm for a lot of people up until that point. Joe Strummer from The Clash helped with that, making a video saying Glastonbury is the most special, sacred event in the world. He said, 'Please can we all save it by not storming the fence?'

The campaign worked. In the end only about 200 people turned up without a ticket, and the fence held firm. Some people were organising cars at the top of the hill to roll down into the fence and smash it down, but the only things that broke were the cars. In fact, the fence almost worked too well, because those 200 who came without tickets were fairly unpleasant kids. When they couldn't get in, they went up to Pilton, where they got into people's gardens and caused a lot of trouble. They really scared some villagers who'd previously been onside, and it led to more big issues with getting the licence the following year. Thankfully Melvin was able to deal with all that too.

Inside the 2002 Festival, however, everything was hunky-dory. The fence made it safer and more secure, and while it did change the Festival – things were undoubtedly a bit less wild after that – there was simply no way we could have continued without it.

It was the first time Coldplay headlined, which came about because they helped me out of a hole in 2001 with the Pilton Party, the thank-you show we do at the end of the summer for the locals. Our big headliners pulled out with three days to go, so Emily said, 'Phone Chris Martin.'

Coldplay had broken through with their debut album, *Parachutes*, in 2000, and Emily had been on an Oxfam trip with Chris and got on really well with him, so she gave me his phone number. I called him up and said, 'Hi Chris, it's Emily's dad. I'm in a bit of a fix. We need a band for Friday.'

He said, 'Which Friday?'

And I said, 'The one in three days!'

They were doing something in Europe that day, but he said, 'Okay, I can get to Bristol airport by about eight o'clock.' I told him I'd pick him up from the airport and take him straight to the Pilton Party site.

So the plane landed and I was waiting with my hire van outside the glass doors. There was an old lady doing security, and she said, 'Mr Eavis, you can't park here.' I replied, 'This is a very important moment. I haven't got time to go to the car park.' I think I had to give her a tenner.

Chris and Coldplay's guitarist Jonny Buckland, who were doing the show as an acoustic gig, walked through the doors, and within seconds we were on our way. I was driving like mad through the lanes, while turning round to talk to them. 'This is fantastic,' I said. 'I cannot believe what you're doing for us. It's so important. You can headline at next year's Festival!'

'You're not serious?' Chris replied.

'I am,' I said. 'I've never been more serious in my whole life. You can headline the Friday.'

To which Chris replied, 'Michael, that's amazing – but please will you look at the road, otherwise we won't be playing anywhere!'

They were fantastic at the Pilton Party, but two or three days later Coldplay's agent called me to say, 'Michael, you think you've got Coldplay, but they can't headline yet.' He thought they simply weren't ready after only one album.

I just replied, 'I tell you, they are ready. And they've earned the slot. Chris did us an enormous favour.'

So then I got Phil Harvey, their manager, on the phone, and he said, 'Look, Michael, I know you owe them a favour, but quite honestly they're not ready.'

Again, I just replied, 'But they are, Phil!'

And he said, 'I just can't agree to it.'

Then Chris rang me and told me they'd do it. Although even then he did have another wobble a few months later. But eventually, of course, they took the slot. And with hindsight, that set was the making of them. They did it before they'd even released their second album, but they played an absolutely storming set. We've had

them back several times since – Chris even came to perform at my eightieth birthday party in 2015.

The 2003 Festival was the first to sell out really quickly – people obviously realised that with the new fence they couldn't get in without a ticket – and by 2004 the demand was incredible. People felt safer, and the BBC coverage was amazing publicity. Only a few years earlier we'd been desperately trying to sell tickets, but now everyone wanted to come, and all the bands wanted to play.

But you could still never take anything for granted. In 2005 we had an incredible amount of rain on the Friday morning, causing terrible flooding in the campsites. There were pictures of people canoeing around the tents. The Other Stage didn't open on time because of the flooding, and I was getting phone calls from the media asking if the Festival was cancelled. I had to do a live interview on Radio 1 to say we definitely hadn't cancelled, to stop people turning around on the motorway. I was on the line to the DJ trying to play it down, saying, 'It's fine. All this water will be in the sea in forty-five minutes.'

The DJ said, 'Oh, so it's not as bad as it sounds?'

I replied, 'No, it's fine!' as I watched a full-size settee float down the river.

The problem that year was that the old railway line was trapping the water and causing flooding. We had our fallow year in 2006 and spent a lot of that time improving the drainage around the site. We ended up having to put an enormous drainpipe underneath the railway line – big enough for someone to crawl through – just to get the water away. The drainage is much better now. People probably don't realise how much work we've done over the years to improve the site.

The fallow year was also when we put together the Glastonbury film with the director Julien Temple. It felt like a good time to get a real record of what we were doing. Emily and I were in London when it came out, and we went to see it in a cinema in Camden. We slipped in after the film had started and sat at the back. At the end of the film everybody clapped. I'd never seen that in a cinema before. It really did feel like people had started to appreciate us.

The following year, in 2007, Arabella Churchill died. I sat by her bedside with her towards the end. She'd put so much into the Festival over three decades. The whole theatre and kids offering at Glastonbury is down to her. We built Bella's Bridge on the site in her memory. She was one of the most important people in the Festival's history.

The Festival returned in 2007, of course, and its newfound popularity was why we brought in ticket registration. Having struggled to sell tickets for so many years, suddenly people were flogging them for £700. I hated that. I want every person who buys a ticket to come to this event. It's not something people should be trying to make money from.

We spoke to See Tickets, who we'd worked with since they were just a record shop in Nottingham doing coach packages, and they said it would only cost a couple of pence per ticket to put people's photos on them. So everyone who wanted a ticket had to register with their details and their photo. It stopped the ticket-reselling overnight. I actually got a letter from the Home Office congratulating me on solving the touting problem. A lot of people complain about touting, but few do anything about it.

Registration worked really well for us in 2007, but it was probably part of the problem when we had an awful time trying to sell tickets in 2008. We'd had a very wet Festival in 2007, which might have put people off, and people also had to register anew each year then (registrations last indefinitely now). A lot of people on our side wanted to abandon registration in 2008, but Emily said we had to stand firm – she got that one absolutely right.

In fact, she really held her nerve throughout the dramas of 2008. She was the one who suggested JAY-Z headline. Of course, we then had all the hoo-ha with Noel Gallagher saying Glastonbury shouldn't have a hip-hop headliner. I think Noel was caught unawares by a microphone on the way into a film premiere, and it was made into a huge thing.

Whatever the reasons, we really struggled to sell out that year, and I was really scared. With no reserve funding we have to sell all of our tickets. I couldn't sleep. I lost a lot of weight. At one point it looked like JAY-Z might even pull out. I was all for calling the Festival off. But Emily stayed really strong on that one too, and in the end it all worked out. We sold our final tickets on the gates the day they opened, and JAY-Z's set was an absolute triumph. It was such a turning point for him in the UK. He became huge after that.

That year was a turning point for Emily, too. She really came into her own. She'd had her own thing at the Festival since 2007, when she created The Park. That's the part of the site where my great-great-grandfather first farmed when he moved to Pilton in 1865, so there was a nice romantic connection. And she really succeeded with The Park. People love that area – it was proof that she could do it and her coming of age. She's got more and more involved ever since.

Emily and I get on really well – most of the time. She's got brains and she uses them. She's so on top of everything. She's taken to organising the Festival like a duck to water, and it's really lovely to see. Her mother was very keen that she should be on the farm, and I think Jean would be so happy that Emily loves the farmhouse and the Festival.

We haven't had a year like 2008, when it was a huge struggle to sell the tickets, since. People are wild about the Festival now, and the main complaint we get is from those who can't get a ticket. It's an amazing position to be in, but I'm still mindful of the possibility that we won't sell out. It was only a few years ago, and it could happen again. There's no magic formula to success. You have to work at it all the time. Even after all these years, I take nothing for granted.

Emily

When the new century came around I was only twenty, but to some extent I'd been involved in the Festival's organisation my whole life. You couldn't not be if you lived in the farmhouse – there really was no escape. We only had one phone line, which was in our sitting room, and any of us would answer it. It didn't matter whether it was something to do with a lost cow, the police or a headliner: you'd deal with it. I remember one time, when I was very young, Bob Dylan's agent called up and I answered the phone. He said, 'Can I speak to Michael?' But my dad was out milking so I said, 'No, but you can speak to the cat,' and put the phone down next to her. Not my finest hour! But you'd end up getting involved in all sorts of Festival business one way or another. And there was always a piece of paper on the fridge with potential bands scribbled on it. In fact, there still is. So now our kids are involved as well.

After my mum died in 1999, I moved back from London to the farm permanently to be with my dad, and I naturally started to get much more involved in the Festival. I think the only thing we could do after losing my mum was put everything into the Festival, so 2000 became a really important year for us. It was also the Festival's thirtieth birthday and the new millennium, and we had David Bowie coming back, so there was a lot of excitement about it. There were also lots of rumours that it was going to be the last Festival, which I think made even more people want to come. The crowds absolutely flooded in and the fence went down – it felt like anyone could just walk in without a ticket.

Watching The Chemical Brothers on the Friday night at the Pyramid, I've never seen a crowd like it. It was amazing, but from a safety perspective it was dangerous and we knew we couldn't go on like that. The word from the council was, 'Unless you sort it out, it's over,' and there were a few conversations along the lines of, 'Well, maybe it should be over.' But in a way it had become a lifeline to me and my dad, and it was also in tribute to my mum, who had been such a massive part of the Festival. We wanted to keep her memory alive through it. Without really planning it, I think we both knew

Michael and Emily at the Festival in 2007 (right), and Emily on the farm (opposite).

that we were going to keep it going somehow.

The following year, 2001, was always going to be a fallow one, but we had to make radical changes in time for 2002 or pull the whole thing. Melvin Benn returned to take on the operations and licence, and my dad designed the fence – or the 'super-fence' as people called it at the time. The fence was very controversial at first. I remember being out in Bristol one night and strangers were coming up to me to say we'd sold out and that the Festival was over. I could understand why people were worried about it – we were inevitably going to lose some of the edge that we'd had before – but we knew that we wouldn't be able to carry on without it.

So 2002 felt like the start of a new era. The fence did its job and the atmosphere was far less unpredictable, and we had great weather and some incredible performances. Coldplay did their first Pyramid headline set on the Friday, and that was such a moment for them and for the Festival. They'd only had one album at that point and really had to be convinced about headlining, but my dad and I just knew they would be great. Chris and I had visited Haiti on an Oxfam trip that year, which was a real eye-opener; it changed both our lives for ever, really. We both came back totally fired up about doing everything we could to help, and it has continued to inspire both of us in what we have done since.

I think that combination of the 2002 Festival going really well and people knowing they really did need a ticket to get in now meant that 2003 became the first year we sold all the tickets very quickly. I think they all went in twenty-four hours, which was just unheard of for us at that time. Selling all the tickets also meant that 2003 was the first year we were able to give a million pounds to our charities, which had always been at the heart of what we did but never on that level before. It was always such a struggle to make it work financially. For us it's all about putting on a fantastic show while doing some good. That ethos has come from my parents, and it's definitely filtered down to the crew. It couldn't exist in a purely commercial way because the whole thing is built on love and goodwill; if you took that away the entire thing would just fall apart.

The Festival is an enormous business now, and we spend as much money as we can on each area across the site. And we want to make it as good value as possible to everyone who comes, making sure that food and drink prices aren't inflated so it's affordable to people from all backgrounds. At other festivals they'll charge people around £20 for a programme to find out when the acts are playing, but we give everyone coming through the gate a programme for free. We give out free firewood and allow people to bring in their own food and alcohol. We don't charge early entry fees, like a lot of festivals do. We've never run the event with profit targets; our aim is to pay the charities as much as we can and put everything else back into the show. I really hope that's something people recognise.

The noughties became a decade of change for us. We really upped the game in terms of the food stalls, taking it from burger vans and a few vegetarian options to this incredible global festival of food that it is now. We also made a conscious decision to get rid of any sponsored venues and branding. People forget, but that had really sneaked in during the nineties. We had a Virgin tent and a Rizla tent and sponsored stages. It's funny when people say it's more corporate now, because that definitely peaked twenty years ago. We hadn't really policed the sponsorship, partly because it was all such a year-by-year thing then. The Festival was never seen as something that was going to be permanent, and in the eighties and nineties it was hanging on by a thread. It could have stopped at any minute. Now we have someone whose job is to actually stop branding appearing on site. And we spend half our time turning down offers from people wanting to cash in on the Glastonbury name in some way. We're very careful about not exploiting it, as I think it would take away from the magic.

After it became clear that the fence was working and the Festival was doing well, we started to really push it as far as we could in other ways, becoming much bolder with headliners. It was a real mission for me and my husband Nick [Dewey] when we started booking the Pyramid Stage together, though Nick came in with a totally fresh pair of eyes in terms of our bookings. I remember the day he said, 'I think we should try harder to get Dolly Parton.'

I just replied, 'Listen, babe, I've tried for Dolly for years.'

Above: Emily and Nick at the Festival in 2005. They were
married in Pilton in 2009.
Opposite: The Ribbon Tower in The Park.

And he said, 'Do you mind if I give it another go?' He spoke to a lot of people, sent all the right emails, made the right calls and then, lo and behold, she said yes for 2014.

Whereas before it was, 'Who have we been offered?', now it was, 'Who would be the greatest artist to headline and how can we get them?' When I said to my dad that we were going to try to get Bruce Springsteen, he just laughed and said, 'That is not going to happen.' The ultimate motivator! The agents had always told my dad that these mega-artists wouldn't play here because we didn't pay the right money. But if we could get Bowie, why not these people? And it really worked. We had Travis and Skunk Anansie headlining in 1999. Ten years later we had Springsteen and Neil Young. And that really opened the door for a lot of the superstar headliners we've had since, like The Rolling Stones, U2, Stevie Wonder and so on.

In the late nineties there really wasn't that much to do after hours. You'd get massive crowds of people raving in front of the wine bars and Joe Bananas stalls, as they seemed to be the only places playing dance music into the night. But the Travellers' Field was a bit of a best-kept secret and always had the most fun late-night parties. A guy called Roy Gurvitz used to come and put on an amazing show, which came out of the whole eighties convoy scene. And even though there was a lot of trouble around that time, my dad liked Roy and could see he was creating something special. So my dad brought him in at the very end of the nineties to do something inside the fence, and that became Lost Vagueness.

The nightlife down there was so exciting and totally unlike anything we'd had before. There was something magical about all these ragged characters coming out of the mud and dust and dressing up in gowns and black tie and entering the Ballroom. The music and the entertainment were just so different to anything else around. It was wild and totally hedonistic, but also really colourful and fun. It was a real Glastonbury kind of twist on burlesque, but all mixed up with ska and rock 'n' roll and rave energy. Suddenly the south-east corner became the centre for after-hours entertainment – partly because those fields, being right down in the valley in a low bowl, surrounded by thick hedges and trees, are best protected from Pilton, which means the sound doesn't bleed into the village. We still really had to earn the support of the village at that stage; there were people who would complain to the council about the noise, which we had to deal with.

Lost Vagueness eventually came to an end and new areas were seeded. Unfairground, Trash City, Shangri-La, Arcadia and The Common all created individual areas that had their own identities and ideas, together forming another world of late-night entertainment that had gone from one field to several over the span of a few years. It is now a big part of the late-night Glastonbury adventure. You get people who come to the Festival and don't go near the main stages all weekend. They'll spend the days in The Green Fields and Theatre and Circus, and the night in the south-east corner, and they'll have the most amazing time. The buzz from walking around those fields at night is like nothing else on earth. I think the evolution of the late-night areas since the nineties is probably one of the things that my dad and I are most proud of, and it's transformed what Glastonbury is about.

The other big change in the noughties was ticket registration. After 2003 we continued to sell out every year, and people were starting to get ripped off by ticket touts. The phone line was still in our house, and we were answering calls from all these kids who were heartbroken because they'd been conned by touts selling tickets that didn't even exist. It was awful. So we decided to crack down on it. We introduced the registration system to make sure that every person who's registered gets the opportunity to buy a ticket, and, if they get one, it can't be exchanged on some dodgy website. It was hugely controversial at the time. It brought up a lot of criticism and scepticism, but our intentions were always to protect the interests of the Festival-goers and to stop people being ripped off. There wasn't an ulterior motive.

We had a fallow year in 2006, which always gives us a great chance to come up with some new ideas that might take longer to develop. So that was the year Nick and I came up with the idea of The Park. I'd had a dream of having my own area for a while, and Nick and I had a plan to create a stage where we could put on a total mix of music — not focusing on a genre, but representing all of the music that isn't found elsewhere. We also wanted to create somewhere inspired by the Kidzfield and The Green Fields. When I was a kid I dreamed of building a tower. I always wanted to build something up high that would create a view from the sky. We had built as much as we could across the land and reached every hedgerow, so now it was time to go upwards. That's when the Ribbon Tower came in.

We also brought in Block9 in 2007. That area has obviously become a huge part of the Festival's late-night offering now, so it's almost quite hard to remember that back then gay culture wasn't well represented at British festivals at all. And I don't think it's an exaggeration to say that the NYC Downlow in Block9 has become one of the best gay destinations on the planet. I'm really proud of that. The venues that they build in a Somerset field — right up to the IICON structure in 2019 — are just mind-blowing.

Despite those amazing new additions, events seemed to conspire against us to get the 2007 Festival written off as a disaster. After a really positive few years, when everything seemed to work well — the fence improving security and registration winning the battle against touts — suddenly everyone was slagging us off. We had torrential rain and the conditions were pretty treacherous. The Killers' headline set had all kinds of sound troubles too. You could hear them perfectly in Shepton Mallet, but you couldn't hear them from just in front of the Pyramid. And with our newfound popularity we were attracting a different crowd, many of whom just didn't seem to want to be there. It seemed to have changed in front of our eyes and it needed a new lease of life. It felt like every time I turned on the radio or opened a paper there was someone talking about the demise of Glastonbury.

Left: Emily in Mozambique with WaterAid in 2006.
Opposite: Carnival time in Port-au-Prince, Haiti, 2001.
Overleaf: The city that never sleeps — a
Festival sunrise from the top of the King's Meadow.

Arcade Fire were very vocal in criticising the 2007 mud and conditions, and various other acts followed suit, saying they'd had the worst time of their lives. It was sad, and it was stressful. But it did give me a chance to go, okay, we're going to do something radical for 2008. I wanted to make it less predictable – to go in a direction we had never been before. Looking back, I don't think we had any idea how big a storm we were about to unleash.

I was very glad that I was with Nick by that point, because it would have been so much harder to get through that year without him. I met Nick in 2003, when he was part of the management team of an act I approached for an Oxfam fundraiser, and it was one of the luckiest things that's ever happened to me. He totally gets it and is very level. He's down to earth and doesn't like the limelight, but he really understands music and the industry around it. We're a real husband-and-wife team at a festival born out of a husband-and-wife partnership. There's no way my dad would have been able to do it without my mum, and Nick and I have become such a tight team too.

So, towards the end of 2007, I was at home with Nick and we were going through all the artists that could headline the following year, but they were either not available or people who'd played more recently. Then I said, 'What about JAY-Z?' We'd been listening to him a lot and we thought his show was exciting, really brilliant and energetic. It felt like something we had never touched on before. Even though he was a huge artist with a vast back catalogue, at that time he wasn't seen as being a festival headliner. In fact, the more obvious choice back then would have been Kanye, who was more on the festival circuit, but we just felt instinctively that we should go for JAY-Z. We got on the phone and, after quite a lot of persuasion, he said yes. My dad took a huge leap of faith, saying, 'I don't know who he is, but if you think it'll work it's fine by me.'

JAY-Z wasn't that big in the UK at the time – he hadn't yet had a top ten album here – but to a lot of people he was the don: the master rapper and the inspiration for so many who followed. I think we just assumed that everyone felt the same way and could see how

talented he was, so we really weren't expecting a negative response. We got that wrong.

From the minute we announced that JAY-Z was headlining it became this massive talking point. A lot of people were outraged that we were having a hip-hop headliner. And I suppose when Noel Gallagher chipped in it just blew the whole story up. One morning I turned on the car radio at about five o'clock, and this woman on Radio 2 was talking about the controversy over JAY-Z headlining. It was on *Newsnight* and all over the television and papers. It just took off like a forest fire – one that we were in the very centre of. It was frightening, as it felt like the whole Festival was under threat and I was personally responsible for that. It was the first time I had been under attack in the media like that, so it was tough to deal with, but it also gave Nick and me a bit of an us-against-the-world attitude, which was quite exciting and has stayed with us since. In hindsight, Noel stirring it up was the greatest thing that happened that year, because he turned a Pyramid headliner booking into a world event.

Several people in the industry were also putting the pressure on. I remember one saying, 'What have you done, Emily? This is a serious fuck-up. You're going to have a tiny crowd and it is going to be a disaster. Ring JAY-Z now, get him to bring on Chris Martin, get him to bring on Beyoncé, because if you don't make this work this is the end.'

I was worried he was right, because for the first time in years the tickets weren't selling. And we needed to sell out. This festival exists on very tight margins, and if we don't sell all our tickets we're in real trouble. My dad was saying, 'To be honest, we've done really well keeping it going this long; if we go out on this then so be it.' He was so stressed and worried, and I hated the feeling of causing him concern after all the years of struggle to get to this point. I was terrified that it would all come crashing down, but I was also determined to do everything we possibly could to avoid that and make a success of it. I remember hours and hours of crisis meetings and mad schemes to sell more tickets and avoid going bankrupt.

We scraped through by the skin of our teeth, selling the final

tickets on the gate on the Thursday, after we opened. And despite all the controversy, it turned out to be the most incredible Festival. The weather was good, the site looked great, the sound issues had been sorted and there was a fantastic energy all over the Festival. I remember looking out into the huge crowd with my dad before JAY-Z came on, and we were just so moved by the support for him. They were fully behind him, chanting his name. It was such an amazing atmosphere, and everyone was just so up for it.

That's the thing about the crowd who come to Glastonbury that a lot of people forget: they are open-minded music lovers who come to experience everything from The Healing Field to the Dance Tent, not just a concert by one artist with some support bands. And that's why it works. We have the best audience in the world – bands talk about it and it's true. After all the internet chat and news stories and pundits' opinions, if you put someone of the calibre of JAY-Z onstage then you know the crowd aren't going to let you down. And neither did JAY-Z – his show was just magnificent.

Directly before JAY-Z came on, he screened an amazing film he had made about the controversy, with the quotes from Noel in there, which just ramped up the hysteria. The crowd were going berserk before he'd even appeared. Then he came on with an acoustic guitar and started to sing 'Wonderwall'. It was absolute genius and it meant he had the whole field in his hands, singing along to every word. It was total joy. And then he launched straight into '99 Problems' and it just went off! It still gives me the shivers thinking about it. It was without doubt the best start to a show I've ever seen and one of the

greatest sets the Pyramid has witnessed. Someone had told us that JAY-Z always used to get up and sing 'Wonderwall' when he did karaoke in his local bar in New York, long before he was booked to play Glastonbury. So it was perfect – not just two fingers to the critics, but a genuine moment of celebrating that song along with a hundred thousand people in front of the Pyramid.

That year was a hard one to live through, but ultimately it reignited the Festival. It made it interesting again and gave us a new lease of life. We don't want to stick to the same formula every year. There are ancient parts of this festival that won't change, but there are other parts that have to move on in order to keep us relevant. That's crucial to us, and it's crucial to the spirit of Glastonbury.

Since 2008 we've sold all our tickets well in advance of the gates opening. And I think we've redefined what a great Glastonbury headliner can be, from Adele and Beyoncé to Metallica, Kanye, Ed Sheeran and Florence and the Machine. It's about great music whatever the genre, and supporting artists who are coming through, making them headliners, like Stormzy in 2019, who did what JAY-Z had to do and proved the critics wrong. It's amazing, really, the passion this thing inspires. But after 2008 I never take our success or popularity for granted. We're always on a cycle, and at some point people will have the knives out for us again. That drives us on to make it better and better every year.

BACK FROM THE BRINK

With a build-up dominated by slow ticket sales, mud and a hip-hop headline slot, Glastonbury faced its most difficult year ever. Here's how it played out

It is startling to think – given the military precision required in recent years to get in – that even as *NME* prepared to set off, a stack of unsold tickets for Glastonbury 2008 sat unloved somewhere deep in the Eavis farmhouse. Was it the thought of another weekend trudging through three feet of mud that dampened enthusiasm for the world's most famous festival? Or was it *really* the fact the coveted Saturday night headline slot was occupied not by rock titans, but a self-proclaimed "God MC"?

Truth is, sadly, a bit of both. Among other things, the memory of last year's hideous quagmire was still fresh in everyone's minds, while even the most open-minded or ardent Jay-Z aficionado would have questioned how his laconic flows would fare given the notoriously temperamental Pyramid Stage sound. Meanwhile, Kings Of Leon's bill-topping prowess, despite numerous great festival slots over the years, was unproven. And The Verve? Well, it wasn't even their only headline appearance of the weekend, let alone the summer. In fact, on looking at the line-up, there seemed to be few exclusives. Unless you counted Shakin' Stevens.

...ymns to decadence and ...ee love, the sojourns into ...oodly '70s rock territory... ...em barely having struck ...ield anywhere ever, it has ...n decided: MGMT *will* be ...tival Band.

...at everyone keeps telling ... Andrew VanWyngarden, as ...ner-in-prog Ben Goldwasser ...ir tourbus and into ...y, their first ever UK festival. ...ns they may be to all this, but ...nna have to learn fast. For as ...ir two sets on Worthy Farm,

Wars, 'The Youth' and of course 'Time To Pretend' are warmly rather than rapturously received, and in truth the show feels ever-so-slightly flat. We need

> "It's fucking true, this is the best music festival in the world!"
> ANDREW VANWYNGARDEN

FREE POSTER SECTION
TENT-SPOTTING AERIAL PHOTO

...L ISSUE!

NME

...CAL EXPRESS | 5 July 2008 | £2.20

They got 99 problems but Jay-Z ain't one...
GLASTONBURY REBORN!

Toilet humour: Banksy's monumental convenience

Glas 'not best fest'

GLASTONBURY has lost its crown as the UK's top music festival. Readers of music ma... NME instead voted f... the Carling Weekend Reading and Leeds ...dlined by the ...li Peppers.

METR...

Jay-Z h... at Glast...

Kapranos, happy that people turned up thanks to their hand-made flyer (inset)

FRANZ FERDINAND PARK STAGE 10PM TONIGHT!!! B.Y.O.B

Jack White (left)...

mily
avis

lastonbury

eeds

ay-Z

omment

age 27

Well, now you can't spend all your time in The Hawley Arms...
why not write to us about some other burning issues?

LETTER OF THE WEEK!

JAY-Z GLASTO HOVABULLOO

Respect to Michael Eavis for booking
Jay-Z. Glastonbury is supposed to be

More revie

I'm pretty awesome, Jay-Z assured us. And he was

Pop Pete Paphides

Glastonbury Festival
Worthy Farm, Glastonbury
★★★★☆

Until Jay-Z finally took to the stage
on Saturday night, it had been a
three-way split as to what the big
story of Glastonbury 2008 was going
to be: Amy Winehouse, the mud or
the possibility of Jay-Z being the first
headline act to be bottled off stage.
In the event, Jay-Z at Glastonbury
2008 proved to be the most thrilling

headline act for more than a decade.
We should have known that the
artist, who retired briefly from
making music in 2003 because there
was nothing new left to achieve,
would relish this sort of challenge.
A video montage chronicling the
furore that had led up to this most
controversial of bookings began with
Noel Gallagher piously proclaiming:
"Sorry, but Jay-Z, I'm not f***ing
having him at Glastonbury." Then
came Jay-Z, contemptuously miming
Wonderwall while strumming a
guitar. Finally, an explosion of

hip-hop beats heralded *99 Problems*.
With his biggest hit behind him, he
declared: "My name is Jay-Z and I'm
pretty f***ing awesome." He made
light work of proving it with the
elastic funk of *I Know What Girls Like*.
Flanked by a live band, Jay-Z
expanded *Blue Magic* to include a
verse about the Bush Administration's
reaction to Hurricane Katrina. The
"**** Bush" line elicited a seismic
cheer, as did the image of Barack
Obama that followed. For a second
you could have sworn that the world
had changed a little bit, just like it

did after Bob Dylan went electric at
Newport in 1965. Yes, it was really
that thrilling. And, truth to tell, it's
not as if we weren't warned by
people in the know. "That man's got
the b******s to come here," Amy
Winehouse had declared, halfway
through her Saturday set, in
customarily forthright fashion.
Winehouse's much-anticipated
arrival — as much for us to check
that she was still alive as for her
music — was another news event, as
she shared her delight that her
husband would soon be out of prison.
"I'm beyond happy," she screamed,

Rock report

Highs
Jay-Z
The high-risk, hig
that paid off and
Glastonbury's im

Elbow
Beautifully judge
deserve a prope
next year

Seasick Steve
No one can pla
one-stringed pl
the bearded

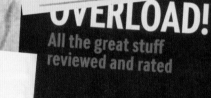

OVERLOAD!
All the great stuff
reviewed and rated

ONLY £3

BACKSTAGE

Glastonbury 2008: the eagle has landed.

After the hype and hysteria, the festival is
a virtual sell-out and – despite a bit of rain –
is living up to predictions of a vintage year.
Thousands of punters have been partying
since Wednesday – with or without the aid of
... and were treated to a supercharged
h kick-started
eakfast slot on the
ranz Ferdinand's
on the Park Stage was
iday. And you know

May 13th 2008

ack
tics

nticipated – and debated
ot in a decade hits Pilton
akes to the Pyramid
f the biggest star in hip-
tion ever since it was
uary 1.
e show is expected to be
s of the weekend. Over
der Mike
hink it's
s at every
to have
the only act
end."
ners were
ced by
booki
illion
ng
keepin
ge.

JAY-Z MAKES HISTORY
Glasto goes hip hop!

FREE!

The sounds of summer: Has Glastonbury lost its mojo?

Slow ticket sales, competition from groovy new 'boutique' events; and disqui
...at Britain's biggest music festival. Tim Wa
headline

NME
May 13th 2008

Jay-Z hits back at Noel Gallagher in Glasto row

NEHOUSE
, Saturday, 28/06/08

BY

d's gre
e's also
n ama
id. "We
ve him
ve that
ght act

s firml
go
tival sp
will be
ian
an
gr
nante
loo ould no
nt to pr
e
n

The real reason we invited Jay-Z to Glastonbury

EMILY EAVIS

When we booked Jay-Z as the
headliner for this year's Glastonbury Festival, we were delighted. He has not only become
one of the world's greatest hip-
hop stars, he is also an artist
who has an amazing live act. In

Since then, all sorts of things
have been said in print and online, most of which only go to
show that these critics fail to understand Glastonbury.
Some of the claims have been
wild. First, we were blown away
by selling 100,000 tickets on the
first day of sale, especially given
that it was a snowy Sunday in
April. Second, Jay-Z is far from
the first hip-hop artist to perform at Glastonbury, as one
might assume from some
strangely hysterical press reports. We have a long history of
attracting top rap artists, including De La Soul, Cypress Hill and
The Roots. Glastonbury has always managed to attract a diver-

simpler than that: we respect
Jay-Z as an amazing artist and
so, obviously, we want to see him
at the festival. There is no reason why we should not have the
greatest living hip-hop artist
at Glastonbury; in fact, he is exactly the sort of act we should
have performing.
The critics do not understand
the Glastonbury's audience. It is
a bunch of really open-minded
people, who come to the festival
to learn and experience new
things: new music, new food, new
people, new politics and a whole
range of new experiences. This
is what, I hope, makes our festival special – Glastonbury is about
more than just the

> One of hip-hop's
> biggest stars
> is exactly the sort
> of act we should
> be putting on

stinct to go back to base and play
safe. An innate conservatism, a
stifling reluctance to try something different.
This is not something that Glastonbury has ever embraced. And
there is also an interesting un-
dercurrent in the suggestion that
a black, US hip-hop artist should-
n't be playing in front of what
many perceive to be a white, middle-class audience. I'm not sure
what to call it, at least not in public, but this is something that causes me some disquiet.
In the end, this is nothing Glastonbury has not faced before. It
is just another chapter in Glas-

supporters, ready and willing to
listen to something out of their
normal music scene.
Perhaps this is why the hysteria in sections of the press has
not been matched by a similar
reaction from the

evolve and develop. With so ma
smaller music events croppi
up, it needs to keep moving an
trying new things, whether hi
hop, African music or just
amazing new indie group. This
is what has kept Glasto so popu
for so long.
In the end, the hot air sur
rounding Jay-Z's performance
will blow away. We are all con
fident that the best answer t
the critics will come in Ju
when Jay-Z strides on to th
stage. By the time he walks of
after perhaps the most eagerl
awaited performance in Gla

GLASTONBURY FESTIVAL

of Contemporary Performing Arts

23-24-25 June

2000

The ONE AND ONLY, with over 500 acts confirmed so far, many more than we could possibly mention here! Highlights include:

PYRAMID STAGE: Travis • David Bowie • Chemical Brothers • Pet Shop Boys • Ocean Colour Scene • Very Special Guest • Happy Mondays • Willie Nelson • Embrace • Counting Crows • Cypress Hill • Reef • Burt Bacharach • The Bluetones • Semisonic • Jools Holland • Live • Wyclef Jean • Asian Dub Foundation • Eagle Eye Cherry • Ladysmith Black Mambazo • Sharon Shannon • The Wailers • Gene

OTHER STAGE: Leftfield • Moby • Nine Inch Nails • Basement Jaxx • Death In Vegas • Beta Band • The The • Elastica • Muse • Idlewild • Feeder • Dandy Warhols • Bloodhound Gang • Wannadies • St.Etienne • Methods of Mayhem • David Gray • Dark Star • Fu Manchu • The For Carnation • Coldplay • A Perfect Circle • Toploader • Cay • Soulwax • Jack L • Rico • Wilt • Clinic The Blue Aeroplanes • Mo Solid Gold

JAZZ WORLD STAGE: Gil Scott-Heron • Reprazent • Morcheeba • Ozomatli • Groove Armada • Femi Anikulapo-Kuti & the Positive Force • Moloko • Terry Callier • Horace Andy • The Wailers • G-Love & Special Sauce • Ronny Jordan • Nitin Sawhney • Lynden David Hall • Andy Sheppard • Faze Action • Jazz Jamaica • Oil Experts • Ladysmith Black Mambazo • Erik Truffaz • Sidestepper

New in 2000 – **THE GLADE**, a natural amphitheatre for dance music set amongst the trees, featuring some very special acts – appearing on condition: that we don't publicise their names!

ACOUSTIC STAGE: The Waterboys • Hothouse Flowers • Suzanne Vega • G Love & Special Sauce • Paul Brady • Priory of Brion (feat. Robert Plant) • Paul Carrack • Sharon Shannon • Liam O'Maonlai • Eric Bibb • Kate Rusby • Jack Lukeman

DANCE TENT: Fatboy Slim • Kelis • Artful Dodger • MJ Cole • Bentley Rhythm Ace • Dave Clarke • Mickey Finn & Aphrodite & MC Fearless • Josh Winks • E-Z Rollers • Eat Static • DJ Krush • Nik Warren • Utah Saints • Justin Robertson • Gilles Peterson • Feat. MC Earl Zinger • Felix da Housecat • Rinoceres

CABARET: Attila the Stockbroker • Helen Austin • Les Bubb • Charlie Chuck • Ian Cognito • Boothby Graffoe • Greatest Show on Legs • Malcolm Hardee • League Against Tedium • Stewart Lee • Rory Motion • John Otway • Jim Tavare

AVALON STAGE: Gong • John Martyn • Shooglenifty • Bi-polar • Nick Harper • The Egg • Bhagdaddies • Rolf Harris • Kangaroo Moon • Arthur Brown

THEATRE, DANCE and more: The Cholmondeleys and the Featherstonhaughs • The English Shakespeare Company International • The Natural Theatre Company

Plus, as always, the New Tent; Circus with leading international performers; over 50 acres of Green Fields; Cinema; the Kidz Field – a mini-festival of its own for small folk; the Sacred Space with its stone circle; the Greenpeace stage; The Croissant-Neuf wind and solar-powered stage; 700 market stalls... and more... and more... and more...

supporting **GREENPEACE** **WaterAid** **OXFAM** *and worthwhile local causes*

TICKETLINE: 01159 129 129

www.tickets-online.co.uk

TICKETS £87 plus handling charge

Info line: 0906 708 0808*

Web: www.glastonburyfestivals.co.uk

*(Calls charged at 50p per minute at all times)

2000

CAPACITY: 100,000
TICKET PRICE: £87

The rebirth of the Pyramid Stage at Worthy Farm dominated headlines and pre-Festival publicity. The thirty-five-metre-high steel structure was designed for Michael by Bill Harkin, and built by Pilton village engineer Bill Burroughs. Four times larger than the second Pyramid (erected in 1981, then destroyed by fire in 1994) the new stage was made with over four kilometres of steel tubing, with a total weight of forty tonnes.

The Chemical Brothers headlined the Pyramid for the first time on the Friday night, while David Bowie's Sunday-night performance, his first appearance at Worthy Farm since his pre-dawn gig in 1971, is now recognised as one of the greatest festival gigs of all time.

Lost Vagueness, run by former travellers, celebrated the Festival's ever-increasing diversity, and created an area that included ballroom dancing.

The sold-out event attendance was swollen by a host of gate-crashers, with Michael subsequently fined for breaching licence conditions on both noise and numbers. Speaking to the press on the Sunday morning, he announced his plan to take a year off in 2001 and promised to return with a strategy that would finally put an end to fence-jumping and also secure the Festival's future.

This page: Fence jumpers swelled numbers to record levels in millennium year (top), yet The Green Fields remained an oasis of calm.
Previous page: Controversy over bookings, most notably for JAY-Z, overtook drugs and violence as the mainstay of newspaper coverage in the 2000s.
Overleaf, clockwise from top left: David Bowie on the Pyramid Stage in 2000, his coat a reproduction of the one he wore on the same stage in 1971; the Lost Vagueness can-can troupe onstage; rush hour on the road to the Stone Circle; and Pyramid stars Willie Nelson and Macy Gray.

Ed Simons
The Chemical Brothers

Michael Eavis has always said that when we headlined in 2000, it was the biggest crowd that's ever been in front of the Pyramid Stage. It was the year before the fence went up and it was a really sunny weekend, and those two things combined to make it a very busy Glastonbury. Legend has it there were 200,000 watching us. It certainly felt like a lot of people.

It was our first time on the Pyramid Stage and just being there was a big deal to us, let alone headlining. Tom and I absolutely loved Glastonbury from the very first time we went, and we'd been a lot by the millennium. We'd often deejayed there and we'd played on The Other Stage in 1997.

Glastonbury was — and still is — everything that we like in a festival: people there really enjoy music, the crowd is very diverse, there's so much to do and it's just a place for people to have fun. Some festivals you play around Europe feel like their main purpose is selling products to kids. Glastonbury isn't like that at all. It's still far and away the best festival that we play at, with the best spirit.

Glastonbury is also somewhere you can go and have any kind of weekend you choose. That's what makes it unique. But at the same time, I do think the headliners are important, because that's one of the few moments when the entire place comes together and the whole organism is doing the same thing.

Opposite: The Chemical Brothers on the Pyramid Stage in 2000 (top), and setting up camp at the Festival (bottom).

I love being in the crowd when there's a good headliner at Glastonbury. You get that feeling at dusk, when it's just starting to go dark and you can really feel that change in the vibe. The acts start to take on a different edge. They always programme it really well.

We were headlining on the Friday night in 2000. When we were given that slot, we were so excited about it, but when I turned up I remember feeling quite overawed by the experience. I don't really get nervous before we play, but I was watching Björk on the Pyramid, playing an early evening set, and I slowly started to think, God, we really are doing this. It was a good feeling, though, and there was definitely a fire in our bellies before the show. We really wanted it to be good, because we were just so proud to be doing it. And you could tell there was an extra spring in the step of our managers and crew because it was such a big deal.

We felt we had to do something to mark the occasion production-wise – especially because it's such a big space – so we stepped up the whole visual aspect. We hired tons of extra gear, which we set off at opportune moments. I've always liked those big sky-cannon searchlights since I went to raves in 1989, so we got two of those, which needed their own lorries. They lit up the sky behind us while we were playing. We couldn't see them, of course, but it was good to know they were there.

I think it was the perfect time for us to play, right at the start of the whole weekend. And the reaction to our set was just crazy. People really went for it. It was an amazing sight, to be standing there in front of all those people, with all the flags at the front and the campfires in the distance at the top of the hill.

As I stood on the stage I can remember thinking that, apart from concentrating on making music, I must remember how this feels – I should store this somehow. I haven't really been able to do that, but it will always be a good feeling to know we played to Glastonbury's biggest-ever crowd – and that we really pulled it off.

Banksy

Artist

I've made a bunch of work at Glastonbury over the years — I don't think the country has a better art gallery.

There are lots of things to love about the Festival, but I especially enjoy how it throws mud in the eye of common sense and market forces. It shouldn't really exist, never mind succeed. It's a glorious five-day rebuttal of corporatism – none of the big entertainment companies can pull off anything close. You simply cannot replicate its workforce with money – they will only work for love.

The Festival is an event that nobody asked for, or made easy. For years the authorities and neighbours tried to close it down. It's an object lesson in the wilful pursuit of a dream in the face of so many enemies – a fable you can dance to.

2010

2005

2009

2004

2005

2005

2007

14

GLASTONBURY
2002

The greatest festival in Europe is back!

28-29-30 June

supporting
GREENPEACE ⊗ **Oxfam** **WaterAid** and worthwhile local causes

Tickets £97
Subject to booking fee
CAR PARKING £5 PER VEHICLE

By phone:
☎ **01159 129 129** ☎

By post:
**Glastonbury Ticket Unit, The Hollows,
St. James St. Nottingham NG1 6FW**
Cheques/POs only. Please add £3/ticket booking fee

and in person from usual outlets

We are grateful to the following for their considerable help:

Q *The***Guardian** orange™ **BBC** RADIO 1 97-99 FM **2** BBC

2002

CAPACITY: 140,000
TICKET PRICE: £97

The Festival returned with a steel fence around the entire perimeter of the site. The 'super-fence' stood fourteen feet high and surrounded the whole site at a cost of over £1 million. Allied to the hugely successful 'No Ticket, No Show' campaign launched nationwide in January, it secured both the site and the future of the Festival. Attempts to gain access continued but on a much smaller scale. Two hundred fake tickets were seized outside, and travellers were thwarted by police when they tried to demolish a section of the fencing with cars and lorries.

The licensed attendance increased to 140,000, including 5,000 Sunday tickets made available to locals for the first time, and the Festival sold out within four weeks of its launch in February.

Coldplay headlined the Pyramid for the first time on the Friday night, with Stereophonics also headlining on the Saturday. On the closing day, Rod Stewart topped a Pyramid bill which contained a number of all-time music legends, with Roger Waters, Isaac Hayes and Manu Chao also delivering memorable sets on the Festival's main stage that day.

This page: Roger Waters (centre) played the Pyramid in 2002. Meanwhile, in the Theatre and Circus fields, dance took many different forms.
Overleaf, clockwise from top left: Daytime Lost Vagueness, 2002; a scene from the crowd in the same year; Joe Strummer (centre, in hat) sits alongside The Stone Roses' Ian Brown and friends at the campfire which led to the creation of Strummerville; and The White Stripes on the Pyramid.

Chris Martin
Coldplay

I grew up very close to Worthy Farm. I was at boarding school about fifteen miles away and by the time I became aware of the Festival — which would've been when I saw some of it on TV — I knew that music was what I wanted to do. So Glastonbury became my Mecca. A trillion miles away, but just up the road.

The first time we played, in 1999, the whole thing felt a bit like Charlie visiting the Chocolate Factory. And I still feel that way about it. Glastonbury fills me with wonder, because it's such a peaceful place where all kinds of different people with different tastes just get along and accept each other. You don't even have to watch any music if you don't want to. It's always seemed to me like this dream city that just appears and disappears.

We played again in 2000, just before our first album came out. We were on the second stage in the midday slot and it was good. Then, the following year, I was sitting in Soho Square and my mobile phone rang. It was Michael Eavis, and I was a little bit starstruck. He said, 'Chris, I've got a problem. This other band's let me down, can you come and play the Pilton Party?', which is the show they put on as a village fundraiser in September.

Opposite: Chris Martin onstage with Coldplay in 2002.

So I called up our manager and we figured out that Jonny and myself could do it if we flew into Bristol airport from wherever we were going to be on that day. Michael then came to pick us up from the airport in his Land Rover. We were so excited to hang out with him, and on the way down I asked who was going to headline the next Festival. Michael replied, 'Well, we're thinking of this band for Saturday, and this band for Sunday, and we thought maybe you'd want to do the Friday?' I nearly fell out of the car.

The fact that Michael and Emily were able to offer that gift of belief at that time – when we'd only released our first album – was very powerful for me and something that I'll never forget. We owe a lot to that moment. We could've said we weren't ready (I did think the idea was just completely crazy), but we agreed to do it and make ourselves ready for it.

Then, at some point over the next year, I decided we weren't up to it, and we pulled out. It felt awful to have to do that, but I just didn't think we were ready. But then, not long afterwards, I woke in a cold sweat one morning, thinking, 'No, you've got to do it. You've got to accept that challenge.' So we asked if the offer was still there, and luckily for us it was.

By that time we were well into recording *A Rush of Blood to the Head,* our second album. We wrote the song 'Politik' specifically for Glastonbury. We knew we'd be very nervous and that we'd just want to bash things very hard, so we wrote a bashy song. Glastonbury is actually still the place that I always visualise when I'm trying to write in the middle of the night. Whenever I close my eyes and think of a place where a song might sound good, it's that triangle you see when you look out from the Pyramid Stage.

So we headlined in 2002, before the second album was even released. It felt like it was the moment of our lives which, if we got right, would mean we'd go one way, but if we got it wrong, we'd go another. Fucking it up just wasn't an option. It was a huge gamble, on our part and theirs, but it paid off. It really was life-changing for us, and I'm so happy that we did it.

The fact our 2002 set worked is testament to the Glastonbury audience too. They're very giving, but also open-minded. That audience can listen to Dolly Parton one minute and Metallica the next. They're just into good music and it's very non-judgemental. One of the benefits of having headlined is that you can tell other artists what it's like. I'll say, 'Even if you don't think it's your kind of audience, you're great and it is going to go well.'

Glastonbury really gives me such hope. It's an amazing microcosm of what the human spirit is able to put together. It's also a testament to people's resilience. It's a lot of people living very, very close to each other in not entirely comfortable conditions, and no one really gives each other a hard time.

Another thing that makes it very special is that it's so organic. It's grown from a little seed into this huge oak tree. You couldn't have just popped it there four years ago and made it up. It had to develop from this one idea from this one guy.

I've known Emily since she was twenty, and the thing that she shares with her dad is that they both love music and they both love the Festival. You can't really substitute anything for passion and drive. They're not in it for the money, and they're not in it for the accolades. They're in it to make the Festival great and for people to have a good time. They don't slag off any other festivals, they don't bad-mouth anybody. The whole thing is very open-minded and big-hearted, and that comes from Michael and Emily.

I try to go to the Festival every year, even if we're not playing. And I like to visit the farm in the winter, just to be in those fields and feel that spirit. I'll climb the Pyramid Stage and dream things up. So much of what we do around the world is created when we're putting together a Glastonbury show.

It's hard to express how much Glastonbury means to me without sounding very cheesy, but it's the closest thing that we have to a home gig and it just amazes me that the whole thing exists. There are so many places in the world where it couldn't happen, for all kinds of reasons. It's a privilege to have been a part of it.

2003 2003

GLASTONBURY FESTIVAL 👉

of Performing Arts &c., at Worthy Farm, Pilton, Glastonbury, Somerset.
Being Three days & Nights of Unparalled Spectacular Surprise, Wonder &c. The festival in
Increasing Demand, Hailed by Thousands, an Immense Attraction & triumphant Success!
New Songs & Dances! Crowded Every night! Shouts of Laughter & applause!

AMONG ACTS DIVERSE & WONDROUS:—

REM   **RADIOHEAD**   **MOBY**

MANIC STREET PREACHERS

FLAMING LIPS   DAVID GRAY   FEEDER

PRIMAL SCREAM   SUPER FURRY ANIMALS   DOVES

SUPERGRASS   TURIN BRAKES   SUEDE

IDLEWILD   THE CORAL

SIGUR ROS   GRANDADDY   RÖYKSOPP

THE POLYPHONIC SPREE   ZWAN

WITH **MORE & MORE & MORE ACTS!**

Glastonbury has ever been the Home of Men & Women who have Seen Visions.
The Veil is thin here, and the Unseen comes very Near to Earth.   HIC SEPVLTUS IACIT ARTVRIUS

Stanle

2003

CAPACITY: 150,000
TICKET PRICE: £105

Despite the great strides made at the 2002 Festival, the annual battle to obtain a licence continued. Chris Martin of Coldplay, who had visited Oxfam aid projects in Haiti with Emily Eavis the previous year, wrote to Mendip District Council to insist that 'the loss of this extraordinary event would be a tragedy'.

The Festival rolled on with Stanley Donwood (Radiohead's sleeve designer) producing the programme cover and attendees revelling in the heat and enjoying R.E.M., Moby and Radiohead.

A memorial stone was laid for Festival regular, the late Joe Strummer, in what would become Strummerville.

Oxfam launched the Make Trade Fair campaign and over a million pounds was eventually donated to Greenpeace, WaterAid, Oxfam and many local charities. The Jazz World Stage hosted the Skatalites, Yes and the Grammy Award-winning Buena Vista Social Club.

This page: Thom Yorke returns to headline the Pyramid Stage with Radiohead (top); and geodesic airborne art in The Green Fields.
Overleaf: Freaks, flares and campfires in Glastonbury 2003's canvas city.

Glastonbury Festival

of Contemporary Performing Arts

25 · 26 · 27 June 2004

It is an easy thing
To see a god on every wind and a blessing on every blast...
Thus could I sing and thus rejoice, but it is not so with me.
I will arise Explore these dens and find that deep pulsation.
Perhaps this is the night of Prophecy...
When thought is closed in Caves, Then love shall shew
its root even in deepest Hell   —William Blake

supporting

GREENPEACE Oxfam WaterAid

and worthwhile local causes

Tickets £112

plus £3 booking fee and postage

CAR PARKING PASS, PURCHASED WITH TICKET, £5 PER VEHICLE

ON SALE FROM 8PM, APRIL 1ST

Ticketline:

☎ 0870 830 2003 ☎

DEBIT CARD, POSTAL ORDER & CHEQUE ONLY

www.glastonburyfestivals.co.uk

we are grateful to the following for their considerable help

The weather in the lead-up to the Festival was poor, making the build difficult, but new infrastructure and drainage meant that the site survived better than in previous years.

Paul McCartney, who headlined on the Saturday night, became the first Beatle to appear at Glastonbury, while politics and activism were given a home at the Festival with Left Field launched next to a seventy-foot-tall revolving tower representing the workers' struggle (it was renamed the Tony Benn Tower after Benn's death in 2014). The Unsigned Performers Competition – later retitled the Emerging Talent Competition – brought a host of new acts onto the main stages, while the Pyramid Stage also saw a performance by the English National Opera, who delivered Act III of Wagner's *The Valkyrie*.

Future headliners The Killers played the New Stage, in a year when the number of acts performing across the site over five days topped the thousand mark for the first time. Crime rates dropped by 43 per cent, while charitable donations again topped £1.2 million.

2004

CAPACITY: 150,000
TICKET PRICE: £112

An advert for the 2004 Festival (opposite), designed by Alister Sieghart. Soul legend James Brown made his only Glastonbury appearance on the Pyramid (below), while Sir Paul McCartney (right) took the Saturday-night headline slot and Matt Bellamy of Muse made the first of three headline appearances to date.

2004

Clockwise from top left: Crowd
surfing; the Lost Vagueness Chapel
of Love and Loathe; 2004's entrance
to the Kidzfield; and an early
morning pilgrimage to the Stone Circle.

2005

CAPACITY: 153,000
TICKET PRICE: £125

Fork lightning and torrential rain on Friday morning – two months' worth in several hours – stalled the start of proceedings, with car parks and camping areas flooded and entry to the site temporarily halted. The Glastonbury team rose to the challenge and managed to resume normal service, with only a few acts missing out on their slots.

The Festival's firmly established partner charities – Oxfam, Greenpeace and WaterAid – introduced the official programme, asking that, along with ending poverty, we should also 'make clean energy our future'.

The event donated £1.35 million to charities and other local causes, and waste recycling topped 50 per cent for the first time. Full weekend tickets had sold out in under three hours, setting a new record. The Dance Tent became a Dance Village, with eight venues, including the first Silent Disco. In memory of another departed Festival legend, the New Tent became the John Peel Stage.

This page: Brian Wilson salutes the crowd from the Pyramid Stage (top); a big crowd for The Chemical Brothers' DJ set in the East Coast venue in the new Dance Village (centre), and the lightning strike that signalled the heaviest and most prolonged rain in the Festival's history.
Overleaf: Figures in a landscape — from a thronged Stone Circle to the ever-present Wicker Women (bottom right), Glastonbury in the noughties celebrated atmosphere over commercialisation.

GLASTONBURY FESTIVAL

of contemporary performing arts

22-23-24 June 2007

> *On with the dance! let joy be unconfined;*
> *No sleep till morn, when Youth and Pleasure meet*
> *To chase the glowing hours with flying feet.*
>
> **–Byron**

Glastonbury Festival is back this year with a midsummer feast of music, theatre, dance, explosive ideas and magical moments...
...and a thousand and one surprises

As a consequence of the new anti-touting measures, **ticket purchasers will now be able to buy up to four tickets** (though all ticket holders will have to be pre-registered – see below).

As well as allowing everyone to come with their friends, this should also encourage people to come in full cars – it's likely to reduce car numbers by 7,000.

Please note, all potential ticket-holders will have to pre-register before 28 February, either online at www.glastonburyfestivals.co.uk or using a form available from Millets, the high street camping store.

supporting **GREENPEACE** Oxfam **WaterAid** and worthwhile local causes

we are grateful to the following for their considerable help:– Q orange **theguardian** BBC TWO BBC RADIO 1

2007

CAPACITY: 177,500
TICKET PRICE: £150

After a year off, a new system of pre-registration with photo ID was introduced making touting tickets nearly impossible. Emily Eavis launched The Park, an area that included new venues including The Rabbit Hole, Stonebridge Bar and a stage that featured Africa Express, Spiritualized and Gruff Rhys among others.

Theatre and Circus increased its late-night activity, launching Trash City, a Mutoid Waste Company concept. The late-night excess in the south-east corner of the site was further developed with the birth of Block9 and their NYC Downlow venue. Celebrating the drag clubs of late seventies New York, it quickly became a late-night favourite. The Green Fields featured the legendary Banksy art installation Portaloo Sunset.

Michael Eavis was awarded the CBE for services to music in the Queen's Birthday Honours list.

This page: Shirley Bassey on the Pyramid Stage (top), Norman 'Fatboy Slim' Cook dressed as a tutu-wearing bumble bee (centre), and Tinariwen on the Pyramid (bottom).
Overleaf: Africa Express on the new Park Stage in 2007 (left), the year when Iggy Pop and The Stooges (top centre) and the Arctic Monkeys (bottom) also made their Glastonbury debuts.

GLASTONBURY
27-28-29 June 2008

Pyramid Stage:

Friday	*Saturday*	*Sunday*
Kings of Leon • The Fratellis	Jay-Z • Amy Winehouse	The Verve • Leonard Cohen
Editors • Gossip	Manu Chao • The Raconteurs	Goldfrapp • Neil Diamond
The Feeling • KT Tunstall	James Blunt • Crowded House	John Mayer
Get Cape. Wear Cape. Fly	Seasick Steve • Martha Wainwright	Brian Jonestown Massacre
The Subways • Kate Nash	Shakin' Stevens	Gilbert O'Sullivan
		Martina Topley Bird

Other Stage:

Panic at the Disco • The Enemy	Massive Attack • Hot Chip	Groove Armada • The Zutons
We are Scientists • Foals • The Hoosiers	Elbow • Duffy • The Wombats	The Pigeon Detectives • Mark Ronson
Ben Folds • Vampire Weekend	Neon Neon • Black Kids	Scouting For Girls • Jack Penate
Joe Lean and the Jing Jang Jong	One Night Only • Los Campesinos!	Newton Faulkner • Black Mountain
The Rascals • Hilltop Hoods	The Golden Silvers • The Travelling Band	The Hoodoo Gurus • Black Cherry

Jazz World:

Jimmy Cliff • Estelle	Ethiopiques • Buddy Guy	Manu Chao • King Solomon Burke
Fun Lovin' Criminals	Imagined Village • Joan Armatrading	Eddy Grant • Dub Colossus
Lupe Fiasco • Candi Staton	Eric Bibb • Massukos	Billy Cobham & Asere
Alabama 3 • Soha	The Blessing • Neil Cowley Trio	Balkan Beat Box • Almasäla
Phantom Limb • Mankala	Bedouin Jerry Can Band	Portico Quartet • Sense of Sound

Acoustic Stage:

Seasick Steve • Sinéad O'Connor	Gilbert O'Sullivan	Joan Baez • Suzanne Vega
The Blockheads • Luka Bloom	The Swell Season	London Community Gospel Choir
Arno Carstens • Eddi Reader	Glenn Tilbrook & the Fluffers	Stackridge • Tom Baxter
Camille O'Sullivan	Seth Lakeman • Andy Fairweather Low	Tift Merritt • Athena
Eleanor McAvoy • Devon Sproule	Thea Gilmore • The Coal Porters	Blues Club w Grainne Duffy
Blues Club w Grainne Duffy	Emily Maguire	Amsterdam • Lazenby

Dance Village (8 venues, 280 acts):

Fatboy Slim • Róisin Murphy	Simian Mobile Disco • Dave Seaman	UNKLE • Appleblim • Sam Sparro
Hercules & Love Affair • Ozomatli	A Trak • Nicky Holloway & Trevor Fung	System 7 • Hexstatic • Jape • Don Letts
Charanga Habanera • Booka Shade	Audio Bullys • Natty • Rumba Caliente	Derrick May • The Moody Boyz
James Zabiela • DJ Yoda	Cadence Weapon • Cantankerous	Midnight Juggernauts • Manteca • Ladyhawke
Cuban Brothers • Addictive TV • N Dubz	Trojan Sound System • Phil K	Quiet Village • Loungeclash • Pnau
Stanton Warriors • Utah Saints	Roland The Bastard • Ben Westbeech	Kissy Sell Out • The Presets

The Park:

Pete Doherty • Dizzee Rascal • John Cale	CSS • Battles • MGMT	My Morning Jacket • Tunng Vetiver • Caribou
Special Guest • Edwyn Collins • The Duke Spirit	Special Guest • Shlomo	Laura Marling • The Mystery Jets
Operator Please • Sons & Daughters	Kool Keith & Kutmaster Kurt	Kathryn Williams & Neill MacColl
Santogold • Beggars • Magic Wands	Cerys Matthews • Alphabeat	Alberta Cross • Mumford & Sons
Eugene Macguinness • Island Line	Team Waterpolo • Lykke Li	Alan Tyler & the Lost Sons
	St Vincent	Redbridge Brass Band

John Peel Stage:

The Cribs • Reverend & the Makers	Biffy Clyro • The Futureheads • Band of Horses	The National • Spiritualized
MGMT • The Kills • The Ting Tings	Black Lips • Vampire Weekend	Crystal Castles • The Long Blondes
The Young Knives • Lightspeed Champion	The Courteeners • British Sea Power	Stars • Rocket Summer
Make Model • Glasvegas	Holy Fuck • The Teenagers • Hilltop Hoods	Friendly Fires • The Whip
Patrick Watson • Royworld	Emmy the Great • Dogtanion	Yeasayer

Avalon Stage: Alabama 3 unplugged • Bacalao • The Baghdaddies Big Band • Blazin' Fiddles • The Family Mahone • Frank Turner • The Handsome Family • Hazel O'Connor • Hobo Jones & the Junkyard Dogs • John Tams & Barry Coope • Justin Adams & Juldeh Camara • Katie Melua • Kissmet • Malarchy • Blackskywhite • Brendon Burns • Bruce Airhead • Cascade • Cholmondeleys & Featherstonehaughs • Coreo Hazzard • Dare • Dino Lampa • Ed Tudor-Pole • Fidget Feet • Flameoz • Fraser Hooper •

Glen Wool • Guy Pratt • Half Human Video • Hard Shoulder • Ian Cognito • Jeff Green • Jonathan Kay • Joolz & the NYAAA • Josie Long • Keth • Kevin Eldon • Mike Raffone • Missfitz • Mitch Benn • Nick Wilty • Nina Conti • Norbi • The Others • Ole • Robin Ince • Rod Laver • Rory Motion • Russell Howard • Shep Huntley • Sierra Maestra • Siyaya • Starfiz • Stargazing • The Stephen Frost Improv Allstars • Steve Gribbin • Twisted Cabaret • Yvette Du Sol

The Glade: Aliji vs. Cassette Boy & DJ Rubbish • The Charles Hazlewood All Stars • Clive Craske • Danny Howells • DJ Donna Summer • Dr Meaker • Dreadzone • Eat Static • DJ Flip Flop • Freefall Collective • Lucas • Mark Broom • Massonix • Matt & Ans • Nick Warren • Pathaan • Radioactive Man • Regan • Rob Hall • Robert Logan • Sian Evans & Simon Kingman • Simon Atkinson & the Ben Marcato Trio • Six By Seven • Squarepusher • Steve Hillage's Mirror System • Symmetrik • Tayo • Tristan • Vexkiddy • ZubZub

Leftfield Stage: Beans On Toast • The Beat • Billy Bragg • David Ford • Dirty Pretty Things • Don Letts & Dub Cartel • Elle S'Appelle • Get Up Stand Up • John Byrne • The Krak • The King Blues • Lazy Habits • The Levellers • The Mentalists • Mungos Hi Fi • Neville Staple • The New York Fund • Pama International • Phil Jupitus • The Pietasters • The Seal Cub Clubbing Club • The Slackers • The Thirst • Tony Benn • Up The Poles

Shangri La: 12 Stone Toddler • 40 Thieves Orkestar • Amigos • Babyhead • Bearlesque • Black Twang • Blackblock • Brothers Bab • Cut A Shine • The Don Bradmans • Dub FX • Dynamos Rhythm Aces • Gaz Mayall • Gypsy Delica • Hayseed Dixie • The Holloways • J-Star & McHoney Brown • Kartel Records • Kid Harpoon • Last Man Standing Saloon • Mud Sun • Natty Florence and the Machine • Neville Staple • Orb Benga & Skream • Pronghorn • Robyn Hitchcock • Shantel and the Bucovina Club • Stranger Than Paradise Club • Tofu Love Frogs • Vagabond Boogaloo • Vjamm Allstars

Croissant Neuf: 3 Daft Monkeys • Avalonian Free State Choir • Bad Science • Banco De Gaia • Biggles Wartime Band • Billy – Undercover Hippy • Boat Band & Rory McCleod • Dubblehead • East of Ealing • Elephant Talk • FOS Bros • Global Village Trucking Co. • Jerry Cahill • Johnny Action Finger • Mark Levin • Martha Tilston • Mik Artistik • Nizlopi • Rainie & the Dust • Samsara • Sheelanagig • Soul Immigrants • Sufira • These United States • Tumbleweed Jim • The Weavils • The Weirdstrings • Vandeveer • Yoav • Your Dad

Theatre & Circus: The 2 Ladies • 3cubed • 4 Poofs and a Piano • Airealism • Andi Neate • Andrew Maxwell • Andy Parsons • Angie Mackman • Attila the Stockbroker • Black Eagles •

Nuala & the Alchemy Quartet • One String Loose • Prison Love • The Proclaimers • Rachel Unthank & the Winterset • Räfven • Ron Sexmith • Sharon Shannon & Big Band • The Wurzels • Will Young • Xavier Rudd

Kidz Field: Bell & Bullock • Black Cat Theatre • Bodger & Badger • Chris Woz & Picklelily • Christine Willison & Mitzi • Coreo Hazzard • DNA • Eventuality • Foolhardy Folk • Goffee • John Row • Mainbrace Theatre • Monkey Shine Theatre • Mr Mike & Mr Maynard • No Strings Puppets • Noisy Oyster • Norbi • Parasole Productions • Prof. Panic • Seikou Susso • Sirkus on Foot • Strawberry the Clown • Tallulah Swirls

...and even this isn't all: for further info and more complete listings please visit www.glastonburyfestivals.co.uk

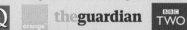

The announcement of JAY-Z as Saturday-night headliner sparked a lively international debate, which rumbled on until the hip-hop star silenced the doubters by walking out onto the Pyramid Stage with an acoustic version of 'Wonderwall', immediately followed by '99 Problems'.

Arabella Churchill, who made the Theatre and Circus area such a huge success after she arrived with Andrew Kerr in 1971, sadly died in late 2007. Her role was picked up by her husband Haggis, who has continued to grow the area's reputation ever since. Arabella is remembered with Bella's Bridge, over the Windlake River in the Theatre Fields, built from recycled oak lock gates donated to the Festival by British Waterways.

Shangri-La and Arcadia made their debut this year, the latter bringing its lightning show to Trash City.

This page: Amy Winehouse and Leonard Cohen both played the Pyramid Stage in 2008.
Overleaf, left-hand page: Dizzee Rascal, The Verve's Richard Ashcroft, Neil Diamond, Lily Allen, Mark Ronson (clockwise from top left), and (bottom) Kings of Leon on the main stages in 2007.
Overleaf, right-hand page: After-hours entertainment courtesy of Trash City (top) and the first incarnation of a pre-Spider Arcadia in Clapps Ground.

Headlining Glastonbury was a special moment. I remember coming over the hill when we arrived and seeing all those tents. It felt like we were invading a large country with twenty people. It was yet another win for hip-hop, facing insurmountable odds. It was long overdue.

Truthfully, with the controversy there was ahead of the show, I thought about not coming. Who wants to perform in a place where you're not welcome? I spoke to my friends, including Chris Martin. We came to the conclusion that it was bigger than myself and a chance to break down barriers. The attitude that hip-hop is somehow any less than any genre of music was an old way of thinking. It was close-minded to the impact it was having on the global community. Here was the perfect moment to showcase this very fact.

Before the show, I remember talking and laughing with Amy [Winehouse] and Jack White backstage. It was a relaxed environment. Nobody was tripping on what type of music was what. We were just all part of the same community of musicians.

Then the idea struck me to mimic the chords of 'Wonderwall'. The irony of it being the song of the biggest critic of my headline slot. Plus the fact that his biggest song was a simple (and GREAT) four chords that I learned in twenty minutes. It was the type of tongue-in-cheek humour that I'd come to love of the English in particular. It was just a perfect moment. I knew right after that moment we were in for a special night.

Opposite: JAY-Z owns the Pyramid Stage in 2008.

*'In the height of summer, at the time of solstice, moon mad, sun begotten —
we acclaim the glory of life with ungrudging senses' —Llewelyn Powys*

Glastonbury '09
26-27-28 June

THE FESTIVAL HAS SOLD OUT, AND WE ARE VERY GRATEFUL FOR YOUR CONTINUOUS SUPPORT. ONCE AGAIN, GLASTONBURY BRINGS YOU ALL THE VERY BEST, WITH THOUSANDS OF PERFORMANCES IN OVER 100 VENUES. ACTS SO FAR INCLUDE:–

PYRAMID STAGE: BRUCE SPRINGSTEEN & THE E STREET BAND · NEIL YOUNG · BLUR · KASABIAN · THE SPECIALS · NICK CAVE & THE BAD SEEDS · CROSBY, STILLS & NASH · LILY ALLEN · MADNESS · DIZZEE RASCAL · FLEET FOXES · TOM JONES · SPINAL TAP · AMADOU & MARIAM · TINARIWEN · REGINA SPEKTOR · TONY CHRISTIE · EAGLES OF DEATH METAL · GABRIELLE CILMI · STATUS QUO · VV BROWN · BJORN AGAIN · EASY ALL STARS

OTHER STAGE: FRANZ FERDINAND · BLOC PARTY · PRODIGY · PENDULUM · TING TINGS · GLASVEGAS · MAXIMO PARK · BON IVER · YEAH YEAH YEAHS · PAOLO NUTINI · LADY GAGA · BAT FOR LASHES · PETER DOHERTY · WHITE LIES · THE VIEW · THE SCRIPT · FRIENDLY FIRES · ENTER SHIKARI · THE MACCABEES · PETER, BJORN & JOHN · MR HUDSON · IN CASE OF FIRE

JAZZ WORLD STAGE: Q TIP · BLACK EYED PEAS · PLAYING FOR CHANGE · BAABA MAAL · THE STREETS · MANU DIBANGO · LONNIE LISTON SMITH · STEEL PULSE · ROOTS MANUVA · JAMIE CULLUM · LAMB · KHALED · ROKIA TRAORE · HOT 8 BRASS BAND · ORQUESTA ARAGON · ERIK TRUFFAZ · STEPHANIE MCKAY · LINDA LEWIS · ROLF HARRIS · SPEED CARAVAN

ACOUSTIC STAGE: RAY DAVIES · GEORGIE FAME · TINDERSTICKS · FAIRPORT CONVENTION · ROGER MCGUINN · NEWTON FAULKNER · JASON MRAZ · SHARON CORR · LISA HANNIGAN · SCOTT MATTHEWS · KILFENORCA CEILI BAND · LONDON COMMUNITY GOSPEL CHOIR · GARY LOURIS & MARK OLSON · NO CROWS · BETH ROWLEY · LUNASA · HUGH CORNWALL · IMELDA MAY · BAP KENNEDY · BEN TAYLOR · PENGUIN CAFÉ ORCHESTRA

DANCE VILLAGE: CALVIN HARRIS · DAVID GUETTA · 2 MANY DJs · ALEX WILSON'S SALSA CON SOUL · ANNIE MAC · CHASE & STATUS · CHIP MUNK · CRAIG CHARLES · CROOKERS · DANNY HOWELLS · DAVE SEAMAN · DEADMAU5 · DJ YODA · THE EGG · LA EXCELENCIA · ERIC PRYDZ · EROL ALKAN · FREELAND (LIVE) · IRONIK · JOSH WINK · KISSY SELLOUT · LA ROUX · MR SCRUFF · PEACHES · PETE TONG · THE QEMISTS · RYE RYE · TIMO MAAS · TINCHY STRIDER · TOM MIDDLETON · WILEY · THE EMPEROR MACHINE

THE PARK: ANIMAL COLLECTIVE · BON IVER · SEUN KUTI & FELA'S EGYPT 80 · M WARD · THE HORRORS · COLD WAR KIDS · EMILIANA TORRINI · TUNNG & TINARIWEN · NOAH AND THE WHALE · ALELA DIANE · HORACE ANDY · TERRY REID · THE ROCKINGBIRDS · THE MEMORY BAND · ALBERTA CROSS · GOLDEN SILVERS · CHIEF · THE LOW ANTHEM · MICACHU & THE SHAPES · VERY SPECIAL GUESTS

JOHN PEEL STAGE: JARVIS COCKER · DOVES · ECHO & THE BUNNYMEN · JAMIE T · LITTLE BOOTS · LADYHAWKE · GASLIGHT ANTHEM · THE WOMBATS · FLORENCE & THE MACHINE · JACK PENATE · NOISETTES · PASSION PIT · METRONOMY · THE SOFT PACK · HOCKEY · JUST JACK · TEMPER TRAP · THE VIRGINS · EMMY THE GREAT · ESSER · F*D UP · TWISTED WHEEL · BIG PINK · RUMBLE STRIPS · WE HAVE BAND

AVALON STAGE: WILL YOUNG · BRITISH SEA POWER · THE WONDER STUFF · SETH LAKEMAN · BADLY DRAWN BOY · THE BLOCKHEADS · ELIZA CARTHY · THE PUPPINI SISTERS · DODGY · PEATBOG FAERIES · TEDDY THOMPSON · MICHAEL MCGOLDRICK · IAN FLETCHER & ANDY DINAN · EDWARD II · THE KING BLUES · SOLAS · ORKESTRA DEL SOL · THE MUMMERS · 3 DAFT MONKEYS · THE DESTROYERS · THE LANCASHIRE HOTPOTS · 6 DAY RIOT · BASKERY · THE MARTIN HARLEY BAND · WHEELER STREET · STORNOWAY · THE MANDIBLES

THEATRE & CIRCUS: PHILL JUPITUS, ANDRE VINCENT, MARCUS BRIGSTOCKE & CARRIE QUINLAN · BLACKSKYWHITE · TONY BENN · MARK THOMAS · FIRE TUSK PAIN PROOF CIRCUS · ARTHUR SMITH · ROBERT LLEWELLYN · THE FROST IMPRO ALLSTARS · RHYTHM WAVE · ED BYRNE · INCANDESCENCE · JONATHAN KAY · CARNIVAL COLLECTIVE · BONGO BOLERO · JAIPUR KAWA BRASS BAND · RUMBA CALIENTE · TAIKO MEANTIME · EMPRESS STAH · TWISTED CABARET · PRONGHORN · FULCRUM · ROBIN INCE · SHARPWIRE · ELETRICAT · LEO & YAM · NOEL BRITTEN · MIMBRE · INKO DANCERS · HAGGIS & CHARLIE · 4 POOFS AND A PIANO · THE MAGNETS · ESCAPE · THE OTHERS · HERBIE TREEHEAD DISASTER BAND · SPYMONKEY · CHRIS LYNHAM · LES OOH LA LAS · STARFIZ · BILL FERGUSON · JON HICKS · JOHN OTWAY · RIOT SHOWGRRRLS · STEWART PEMBERTON · SPACE COWBOY · MUNDO JAZZ · BETTY BRAWN · ATTILA THE STOCKBROKER · JOOLZ DENBY

THE GLADE: STEREO MCS · TIMO MAAS · GONG · STANTON WARRIORS · TOM REAL · STEVE HILLAGE · DJ FRESH · BEARDYMAN WITH THE BAYS · EATSTATIC · DUB PISTOLS · JAMES MONRO · DON LETTS · RICHARD "KID" STRANGE & THE PARTY · PATHAAN · BANCO DE GAIA · 2ND CLASS CITIZEN · DR MEAKER · BACK TO THE PLANET · TAYO · OUTMODE · RUSKO · 3 DAFT MONKEYS · CLIVE CRASKE · SANCHO PANZA · HYBRID CINEMATIC SET · RED SNAPPER · HOWARD MARKS · NAIROBI · CLIVE CRASKE · JINX · MIM SULEIMAN · CLIVE CRASKE · JOHHNY MARS BAND

TRASH CITY & ARCADIA: LUCIFIRE AND FANCY CHANCE · EBONY BONES · ZION TRAIN · DUB FX · EDDIE TEMPLE MORRIS · NIK DIEZEL · NIGHT OF THE DAY OF THE DAWN OF THE… · KITTY BANG BANG AND ROXY VELVET · MISS PINK · SELFISH CUNT · EMPRESS STAH · URBAN VOODOO MACHINE · MY TOYS LIKE ME · HOOLIGAN NIGHT · STEVE BEDLAM · WARLORDS OF PEZ · COPPERDOLLAR · LAST MAN STANDING · FREEFALL COLLECTIVE · EVIL NINE · JAZZSTEPPA

SHANGRI-LA: AFRICA EXPRESS DJ SPECIAL · THE DYNAMICS · POLKA MADRE · HYPNOTIC BRASS ENSEMBLE · THE DELEGATORS · LES FANFARE PETARD · DJ HEAD GARDENER · ORKESTRA DEL SOL · NO. 1 STATION · WARLORDS OF PEZ · TRANS SIBERIAN MARCH · KILLA DILLA · BLACKBERRY WOOD · LE VAGABOND BOOGALOO CLUB · PEYOTI FOR PRESIDENT · THE PYRAMID AUDIO · DJ TOFOWSKI · HEAVY LOAD · LAZY HABIT

KIDZ FIELD: SEIKOU SUSSO · HEAD ABOVE WATER PRODUCTIONS · THE BROTHERS DIMM · STRAWBERRY THE CLOWN · NORBI THE CIRCUS BOY · ONEWHEELSAM · COREO HAZZARD · NIK ROBSON-KING'S · RAINBOW THEATRE PRODUCTIONS · MR MIKE & MR MAYNARD · ANDY DAY FROM CBEEBIES · DNA · BODGER & BADGER · FUNTASTIC · STEVE TASANE · THE FOOLHARDY FOLK · PROF. PANIC · NICADA PUNCH AND JUDY · NO STRINGS PUPPET THEATRE

CROISSANT-NEUF: THE COMMUNICATORS · TEN BEARS · THE CHEW LIPS · MR B THE GENTLEMAN RHYMER · THE DESTROYERS · THE CORRESPONDANTS · THE CHRIS JAGGER BAND · THE TRAVELLING BAND · BOWJANGLES · THE STAVES · STEVE KNIGHTLEY · THE MANDIBLES & MANDIBLETTES · BIGGLES · THE BOAT BAND · MANKALA · JOHN ASHTON THOMAS & IAN RITCHIE · KING SIZE 5

QUEEN'S HEAD: JASON MRAZ · ROBYN HITCHCOCK · MAXIMO PARK · THE BIG PINK · THE ALIENS · THE RAKES · DAN BLACK · BOMBAY BICYCLE CLUB · RUMBLE STRIPS · THE KING BLUES · JOE GIDEON & THE SHARK · THE VIRGINS · THE SHORTWAVE SET · VAGABOND · DAN LE SAC VS SCROOBIUS PIP · THE WOMBATS · FIGHT LIKE APES · TOMMY SPARKS

PLUS OVER 40 ACRES OF THE UNIQUE AND WONDERFUL GREEN FIELDS, WITH GREEN CRAFTS, HEALING AREA, THE STONE CIRCLE, GREEN FUTURES AND MUCH MORE…

…AND EVEN THIS ISN'T ALL: FOR FURTHER MYSTERIES AND MAGIC, AND MORE COMPLETE LISTINGS, SEE WWW.GLASTONBURYFESTIVALS.CO.UK

  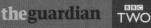

2009

CAPACITY: 177,500
TICKET PRICE: £175

With mass online registration and a new ticket-deposit system, the Festival sold out its 135,000 weekend tickets two months in advance. The year 2009 saw Neil Young and Bruce Springsteen's only Glastonbury appearances to date, plus the return of Blur who headlined the Pyramid Stage on Sunday night.

Arcadia was given its own field and Shangri-La created an enthralling retro-futurist virtual world of snaking corridors and fake hotels with neon-gilded surprises, and also hosted a secret Lady Gaga gig in Club Dada.

By the end of the decade, annual donations to the Festival's chosen causes and charities were approaching the £2 million mark. And the temporary population arriving at Worthy Farm meant Glastonbury Festival had become recognised internationally as a true 'city in the fields'.

This page: Neil Young (top), and Bruce Springsteen singing in the crowd (left), both headlined in 2009. Overleaf: Lady Gaga onstage (left), and (opposite) Glastonbury's fabled late-night zone above the railway line, where Gaga also played a secret gig at Club Dada.

Lauren Laverne
Writer & Broadcaster

I have long considered Glastonbury to be the Christmas of music. The two sit opposite one another in the cycle of the year in perfect counterpoint: one an explosion of colour and joy to celebrate summer's headiest heights, the other a glittering feast to warm winter's darkest depths. There are other festivals, other holidays, but these non-identical twins are a unique pair. I know what you're going to say. 'Is this about beards, Lauren? Just because two iconic annual feasts are synonymous with their own benign father figure who sports signature facial hair does not mean they are connected in any way. Michael Eavis and Father Christmas are quite different. Okay, so they've both dedicated their long lives to bringing people together in a joyful celebration of our better natures, but *one has a herd of reindeer and the other a herd of cows.* What kind of false equivalence are you trying to draw here?'

You're right. Of course it's not about beards (although I must confess I find the coincidence pleasing). No. Glastonbury and Christmas resemble one another because they share the same ingredients. There's music, culture (or, if you prefer, counterculture), tradition, the opportunity to try living a different way, and lastly (and perhaps most importantly) the chance to connect with people — those you know and those you don't.

Previous page: Photographer Liam Bailey captures late night at Trash City.

Left: Glastonbury performer-turned-presenter Lauren Laverne.

Like most people, music was what took me to the Festival at first. In 1997 I was a teenager in a band that was due to play. Our gig fell foul of the weather (it rained so much that the stage we were booked to play actually sank). My knowledge of performance fabrics was sorely lacking, so when my charity-shop outfit was exposed to the weather and a few rock 'n' roll adventures, it promptly disintegrated. (Like the rest of the band and our tour manager – a hardcore punk called Geoff – I drove back to London in my pants and a dress made of bin bags.)

As festival baptisms go it was – ironically, considering the conditions – a fiery one. But something must have clicked, because I've been going ever since. At first I went along as a fan. By 2002 I had fallen into presenting on TV and radio, and was offered the chance to join the BBC Glastonbury team. In the early days (before social media, live streaming and multi-channel on-demand coverage) the job involved disappearing off into a field for as long as you possibly could, before arriving back at an appointed time to sit on the floor and talk about what you'd seen – for hours and hours – live on TV. I was simultaneously completely out of my depth and in hog heaven.

At the time I was only really presenting for shoe money. I had no notion of what broadcasting was really about, or how much fun it could be. I certainly didn't think I was good at it. I decided to stick with it because John Peel leaned over to me during our first show together and whispered, 'You're made for this shit, aren't you?' And as always, I simply assumed he knew what he was talking about. Now that I'm older I realise the statement could just as easily have been a gentle joke about the silliness of showbusiness. Luckily I missed that at the time and just took it as the closest thing I was going to get to official approval to keep cracking on (there's a lesson in there somewhere).

Presenting the Glastonbury coverage was the first chance I got to talk about the music I loved for a living. Until that point I was doing what you might describe as light sidekick work – the kind of gig where three blokes would have a meeting about whether you could be trusted to read out a phone number. Now here I was, expected to know stuff! Asked my opinion! Enthusing was not just permitted but actively encouraged! It was addictive. Imagine it being your actual job to spaff on about things you find fascinating and wonderful – things you'd be spaffing on about any-way. Who would have known such a career existed? Not my careers advisor, who was so out of ideas she told me to become a careers advisor.

I have seen some of the best gigs of my life at Glastonbury. Mercury Rev singing up a luminous moonrise on The Other Stage in 1999. The Flaming Lips' psychedelic lunchtime utopia of 2002, which introduced many of the now-ubiquitous visual signatures of contemporary festivals – fancy dress, glitter, insane props, group performances (they had twenty-odd friends join them dressed as everything from Father Christmas to the sun). The pinch-yourself-repeatedly 2004 bill with two of pop's greatest geniuses – James Brown and Sir Paul McCartney. The almost-religious fervour when Brian Wilson played the following year. (I had been sent up in a helicopter to report over aerial shots of the site and saw the entire place empty as everyone gathered at the Pyramid Stage. We landed as the set concluded and everyone I spoke to was crying.) Speaking of which, Blur's triumphant headline set in 2009: so good it brought the always-composed and often caustic Damon Albarn to tears – a contrast to Candi Staton (and the euphoric Park crowd) singing 'You Got the Love' as the sun melted into the horizon the year before. I surprised myself by getting choked up when David Crosby played 'Guinnevere' in 2009, but couldn't stop smiling at the joyful genius of Stevie Wonder in 2010. Beyoncé's tour de force performance in 2011 felt like it recalibrated Glastonbury – and pop music – for a new decade. Year on year I watch The Chemical Brothers play and am surprised by how surprised I am that they just keep getting better. Glastonbury feels like their natural home.

Sometimes the best thing about seeing an artist come onstage to play is watching their reaction to the experience. In 2013 Nick Cave climbed out into the crowd and spotted a fan on someone's shoulders. She was wearing a long white dress and her red hair loose. He took her hand and directed the rest of his electric performance of 'Stagger Lee' entirely to her. I have no idea what Pharrell was anticipating when he walked out there in 2015, but it was obvious from the look on his face that the reality far exceeded his expectations.

There was a similar moment during Barry Gibb's Pyramid performance in 2017. Gibb had made no secret of the fact that it was going to be a little strange for him to play such a huge show without his brothers. He started his Sunday afternoon 'legends' slot (an unofficial headline spot with a crowd to match) steadily. After a while his attention was drawn by three lads dressed as the Bee Gees who had managed to get to the front of the crowd. One of them, buoyed on his mates' shoulders, floated stage-wards. He removed his ridiculous, tiny, spangly gold jacket and proffered it. Barry (in a sombre black turtleneck at this point) looked down and smiled.

Below: Lauren Laverne with Kenickie at Glastonbury in 1997.
Opposite: The Stone Circle in 2009 (top); on-site procession with Mutoid
vehicles and fire (bottom left) and Damon Albarn headlining the Pyramid
with Blur in 2009 (bottom right).
Overleaf: Photographer Matt Cardy's view across the valley from the
entrance of what is now Strummerville.

He seemed to relax. He put it on. And honestly? He looked amazing in it. Then he did 'Stayin' Alive', and the security team at the front of the stage burst into a synchronised dance routine that they had worked up in secret. I thought he might just about cry.

Some bands wait their entire career for their Glastonbury moment. Lars Ulrich told me that after a show in Antarctica, Metallica had played every continent on earth and ticked off every item on their bucket list – except one. Like all old-school heavy-metal fans, the band are diehard Anglophiles, and Lars in particular has an encyclopaedic knowledge of Glastonbury culture. It was a thrill to see them embrace the weekend (and to discover that he spent every hour he wasn't onstage exploring the deepest recesses of the Festival site). There was a sense of destiny about their gig – their arrival on site was even marked by a huge clap of thunder. 'There's your metal soundbite,' Lars remarked, looking up at a rather foreboding sky. 'Metallica bring the thunder to Glastonbury.'

The culture and traditions of any celebration are part of what makes it a rich experience. Those traditions might be shared by many (decorating your Christmas tree) or unique to you and yours (decorating it with enjoyably hideous baubles only you and your loved ones appreciate). It's a cliché to say that everyone who comes to Glastonbury experiences a different Festival, but it's true. Every regular attendee I know has their own individual set of rituals, and chooses the communal moments – like watching the sun rise at the Stone Circle or taking a trip to the Underground Piano Bar – that matter to them. There's so much to choose from, and almost all of it is experimental, innovative and alternative.

No matter how big the headliners, however many viewers the coverage reaches (20 million in 2019), Glastonbury remains inherently countercultural. It's built that way from the ground up – from the organisers' insistence on donating to good causes to the ecologically attuned site infrastructure and the Festival's ongoing commitment to inviting people with alternative ideas (political or practical) to participate. It's also countercultural in the broadest possible sense – a weekend when the prevailing social values we all live with are inverted, when the things we are often told are unimportant or ephemeral (especially music and the arts) take their rightful place centre stage.

Just like Christmas, Glastonbury is a necessary moment in the year when life's usual script gets flipped, when we leave whatever the day-to-day is for us behind and try on another way of being. We smile a little easier, we cheer a little more. For a couple of hours out of the whole year, we are the people that we always hoped we would be. Yes, I am quoting Frank Cross's conversion speech from *Scrooged,* thanks for noticing. Like Frank Cross (and Ebenezer Scrooge before him) some people enjoy who they become at Glastonbury so much that they decide to keep living that way the rest of the year. You'll most often find them in the Green Futures area of the Festival. Despite its name, Green Futures is the part of the farm that most closely resembles Glastonbury's early days. A visit there always feels like you're following the Festival spirit upstream to its original source.

Being part of the BBC team is the most fantastic ex-cuse to get out into the Festival and find out what has brought people there. Their reasons aren't always what you would expect. Over the years I have talked politics with the drag artists of Block9, environmental issues with an astronaut (NASA's Mike Massimino) and heard from Usher syndrome sufferer Jo Milne, whose recently fitted cochlear implants were enabling her to hear live music for the first time. I met the Motörhead fan who had carved the band's War-Pig mascot out of a tree with a chainsaw in the hope of meeting Lemmy, just months before he died. I even spoke to a young man about his estranged father – whom he was about to meet for the first time. The Festival seemed like the perfect place to get acquainted.

Spending time with people who matter is an essential part of the magic of Glastonbury. Choosing whom to share the experience with is a serious business, very much like deciding where to spend Christmas. Yet both celebrations share a curious contradiction; they are a combination of private and public experience, an opportunity to bond with the people you love and a chance to share something with a group of like-minded strangers. Both of these are hugely powerful and highly pleasurable experiences. For me they are at the heart of the Glastonbury magic. Where else can you have your arms around your best mate as you sing your song to each other one second, and then realise a second later that you are surrounded by 30,000 strangers who are also singing along and own that song every bit as much as you do for reasons you don't know but completely understand?

Fellowship – a friendly association with people who share one's interests – is a gloriously old-fashioned word, but I like it. There's something humble about it, and I think it describes Glastonbury, where the spirit is one of assumed similarity and cooperation, very well. Like Christmas, the Festival is a chance to find out who we are outside of the daily grind. It's a chance to meet other people on those terms, too.

Until next summer, then, in fellowship: here's to a Merry Glastonbury 2020 and many more to come.

PUBLIC PARKING

CAMPERVAN

Glastonbury
festival of contemporary
performing arts
21-25 June

the guardian
guide

Glastonbury 20
Truly Ep

BLUE ROUTE

2010s

7

Hill

Michael's
Mead

Hawkwell

Top Webbs Ash

TW

TW TW

W Worthy FM
ATM
PROTECTION
TENT TW
Big Ground

Row Mead

Cockmill
Meadow
Family
Camping
only

Big Lickle

Arena

PYRAMID

Kidney
Mead

LOST
KIDS
TW ACOUSTIC

KIDZ
FIELD

Barren Ground
Staff short stay parking

MEETING
POINT TW
TW

Little
Lickle

CINEMA
TW

TW E23

E24

CinemaBandstand

i
The Meeting
Point Bar
Bourbon St

GLEBELAND

Phone
Recharge

LABE

Blazing
Paddles
Stage

Phone
Recharge
vers Bridge

Yeoman's Bridge

BIG
TOP

CIRCUS
FIELD

SOUTHEAST
VENUE AREA
ACCESS POINT
2300-0400hrs

C

E25

E24

E25

LEFTFIELD

Cubana
Salsa

£
ATM
TW

WEST HOLTS
STAGE

Outside
Circus
Stage

Orchard
Gate

THE 'G'
STAGE

Holts

Elemental

SPIRIT of '71
STAGE

LOST
RIOS

Green
kids

Greenpeace
Stage

Mandala
Stage

Speakers
Forum

i

Green Futures

Small World
Stage

TW

CABARET
MARQUEE

Sensation
Seekers
Stage

BELLA'S
FIELD

Avalon cafe

Poetry &
Words

Cockm

Glastonbury 2017

Tadpole
stage

W TW

B'stand
Stage

FIELD OF
AVALON

Arcadia Stage

Cockmill
Farm

Healing
Field

TW

Croissant
Neuf
Stage

THE
COMMON
Bassline

ARCADIA

Bez's Acid
House
T
UN
GR

Chai
Wallahs

BLOCK 9

Craft
Field

TW

Shangri
merville
Camp

EPO

PEO

Sacred Space

Dragon TW
GLASTONBURY FEST
PERFORMING ARTS 20
MID-FRI

Glastonbury Festi
of Contem 2

Michael

The first Festival of the new decade was our fortieth anniversary, which I suppose was quite a big deal. That year, with only twenty minutes' notice, I ended up onstage with Stevie Wonder – who was headlining on the Sunday night – to sing 'Happy Birthday'. It was the first time I'd ever performed on the Pyramid Stage, and it felt quite surreal to be standing up there with a music legend, looking out at the sea of faces and flags.

Unfortunately it did not go very well. The problem was that Stevie sang a different 'Happy Birthday' to me. He did his version, while I sang the traditional one. I couldn't hear what was going on and we were miles apart. It was my worst performance ever. But he did tell his band to change key halfway through to try to get to my level, which was very nice of him.

I felt quite ashamed about the whole thing, but Stevie was very kind about it. Afterwards, he gave me a top-of-the-range mouth organ as a present. Apparently only three of them had been made, and he gave the others to President Obama and Paul McCartney!

Despite that episode, I did sing on the Pyramid Stage again in 2016 with Coldplay, and thankfully it went much better, mainly because I was prepared. Chris Martin heard me singing 'My Way' at my eightieth birthday party the year before and said, 'You've got to sing that at the Festival next year.'

'I don't think so,' I replied, but he made it seem almost an ultimatum, like he wouldn't come if I didn't do it.

I put the idea to bed and hoped he'd forgotten about it, but then about three weeks before the 2016 Festival he phoned me and said, 'You are going to sing that song, aren't you?' So I started practising and learning the words. On the Sunday of the Festival, the day Coldplay were headlining, I did a full rehearsal with the band in the dressing room. I was much happier with the performance and I enjoyed the experience this time around. I was still quite nervous beforehand, but people said it went really well. It definitely helped to be singing the right song.

Since then I've sung a number of times at the Festival, which I've really enjoyed. I'd been doing a song or two in the Avalon Café on the Thursday each year, but for 2019 we stepped it up to a proper seven-song set with a live band. We did a full weekly band practice

Opposite: Michael on the Pyramid Stage with Coldplay in 2016, performing 'My Way'. Right (from left to right): Dolly Parton, Michael, Emily and Noah, and Nick Dewey and George on the Dolly tour bus backstage at Glastonbury 2014.

for a couple of months leading up to it. I'm a lot more confident now, and I've found that nettle tea really helps with my voice. I think the full set went rather well, and I even persuaded Emily to come and do a duet with me. The *NME* gave us a glowing review, and the *Bristol Post* said I'd come a long way since that duet with Stevie Wonder.

It looked like we'd finally booked U2, alongside Stevie, for the 2010 Festival. I'd been trying to get them to perform since I prematurely put them on the poster in 1982, when I was misled by the doorman at the Portobello Hotel who said he knew them really well and could book them, which, of course, turned out to be wishful thinking.

Then, at the beginning of 2010, I got a call from Paul McGuinness, U2's manager, saying, 'Michael, the band want to do it this year. Will they get paid anything?' I told him that of course they would. When he asked how much and I told him, he just laughed and said, 'Okay, that'll do, they're not really bothered about the money.'

But then, a few weeks before the show, Bono injured his back very badly while the band were preparing for their tour and they had to cancel. He phoned me himself from his hospital bed to say how sorry he was, after all the expectation and excitement, which was good of him.

U2 did come and play the following year, though. Unfortunately it rained right through their performance and I don't think U2 were very pleased with it. The expectations were so high, and I don't think they felt they did themselves justice, for whatever reason. But I loved their show, and I hope they come back and do it again one day.

We had a fallow year in 2012, which everyone said was because the London Olympics needed all the portable loos. That wasn't the case at all. We were always due to have our year off then, but I did say in an interview that not having to compete with the Olympics for the equipment would make it easier for us. That's where the story came from.

I've had to get used to the fact that anything I say can become a news story. It does add a bit of pressure when I do an interview or a talk somewhere, but it doesn't really put me off. I still say what I need to say.

A good example is when I had a chat with Glastonbury FM, the local independent radio station in the town, at the beginning of 2017. During the interview I mentioned that we were considering doing another event, called Variety Bazaar, about a hundred miles away from Pilton. It quickly became a huge worldwide story.

Doing an event away from Worthy Farm was a very real consideration for us. The Festival site covers twenty-two farms now, which means I'm dealing with twenty-two farmers. And those farmers can get a bit demanding because they're in such a strong position. They can see that the Festival is a good earner.

I don't like that, obviously, although I suppose you can't blame them. But if they're looking for more money, then it makes the Festival less likely to work financially. So I'd have to look for a cheaper site, preferably with only one landowner.

We really would have moved. We did seriously consider several locations, and I think it would have worked. I asked Peter Paphides from *The Times* about it, and he said, 'As long as your team are running the show, it won't make a difference where it is,' and I think a lot of people felt that way.

I was excited by the challenge of a new event in a new location, but I also knew it would be very hard to replicate the site we have now, with all the work we've done to it. The landowners got the message, though, because I've got twelve-year deals from all of them now. That should see me through.

I haven't thought about retiring since Jean passed away. I've got no idea what would make me stop. Ill health, I suppose. But I'm definitely not bored of it. There aren't many people my age who can still go to a gig and have young kids coming up to them, saying nice things and asking for selfies. It's a wonderful position to be in, and the thought of giving it all up and sitting in a deckchair in Weymouth all day long eating doughnuts is not really a runner.

I'm very different to the 35-year-old who started the Festival. I didn't have any real self-confidence then. I didn't know what I was doing. The idea was good and the site was good, but it was all held together by string. It wasn't until after 1979 that I first stopped feeling like an imposter. Arabella Churchill and Bill Harkin were squabbling about me interfering, and I said, 'Yes, but I'm the only one who can make this happen.'

Arabella looked at me and said, 'You know what, Michael? You're probably right.'

I think I'm a better husband now, too. I married Liz, my third wife, in 2001. She was a midwife for over thirty years and is quite an exceptional woman. I'm sure it helps that I'm happier, which is a lot easier when you're no longer short of money and don't have all this risk hanging over you.

Emily and I run the Festival together now, of course, but I'm still out there every day, working on it. I am lucky to have Emily – we complement each other incredibly well. She's very intelligent, and she'd never do anything to upset me. My relationship with her is the key to the success of the event now.

I've got a really good relationship with Emily's kids too. I put them on the school bus every morning, and they always want to come to my house. I spend a lot of time with them. I suppose I'm making up for the time I didn't spend with my own kids when they were young, because everything back then was such a struggle, with the Festival and the farm, and I was so obsessed with making the Festival a success.

I'm not as hands-on with the farm now, but it does still keep me busy, and I was very happy indeed in 2014 when we won the Gold Cup, given to the best dairy farm in the whole of the UK. We've been farming on this land for centuries, and it was the first time we'd ever won that award. These cows have been my life, my history. I think my ancestors would be so proud of that achievement.

My mother never really came round to the farm very much, or the Festival, but she was very proud of the social housing I've been building in Pilton since 1990 – she was a bit of a leftie when she was young. Before she died, she said, 'Michael, this social housing is the best thing you've ever done in your whole life,' and I'd probably agree with that.

After Maggie Thatcher sold off all the council houses, there were none left in this village, so the working-class people who were working here on the farm, or on the one next door, had nowhere to live. To have a home they'd have to be saddled with a mortgage they couldn't really afford, and risked losing their home if they couldn't pay it.

I felt it was my mission to replace those social houses in Pilton. That's why we've put millions into this project. The first ten houses opened in 2010, and we'll be up to fifty of them by 2020, all built on my land using stone quarried from the farm, and with a very reasonable rent. The people living in them are all very proud because they're nice houses. It gives them a sense of worth. And they'll never be sold, because they're on my land and they are owned and run by a reputable housing association. That's a hell of a legacy for the village.

Jeremy Corbyn came down to Pilton to open the latest batch of social houses in 2017, a few months after speaking to an enormous crowd at the Pyramid at that year's Festival, which, again, became international news. It's an incredible thing that we were able to give the Labour leader such a massive boost. And it's really important that we still have that political side to the Festival, something that stretches right back to the CND campaigning. The Festival has changed enormously since then, of course, but we'll always hang onto those core values. And people seem to appreciate that more than ever.

I've certainly come a long way from the days when people would regularly shout unpleasant things at me in the street and tease my kids at school. These days it's more likely to be, 'Legend!', which always makes me smile. It's an amazing turnaround. Great Western Railway even named a train after me. I'd never have thought all this was possible when I was getting all that flak in the eighties and nineties.

There were so many times that the Festival could have fallen apart, but it feels strong now. And we've got the money to do amazing things, like the pier we built in 2019, which was incredible. I think the only reason we would stop it now is if we chose to. But I don't see that happening. I love it more than ever. The people, the ideas – I love the whole thing. And I just want to keep going and make sure that we're doing the best possible show in the world. It's a marvellous life for an 84-year-old. What a privilege.

Emily

One evening towards the end of 2013, I was walking up the hill from the farmhouse with my husband, Nick, when we got the email we had been waiting for. I can remember exactly where I was when we read it, looking out over the valley below. The email said that Prince had confirmed to headline Glastonbury. We walked the rest of the way in a kind of ecstatic daze, as we'd been trying to get him to play for as long as I could remember, but it had never looked like it was going to happen. Until now!

Prince's promoter in the UK had even told us in a very direct manner that Prince would never play our festival. But we never gave up on it because we knew how incredible it would be. We just thought, if we can get Paul McCartney and Stevie Wonder, then why not Prince? And finally we had him! The funny thing was that evening there was an incredible sunset, and the sky was completely purple. It felt like a sign from Prince!

But only a few days later we got a message to say that Prince had changed his mind. One of the reasons was that, not for the first time, a newspaper had decided to run a story saying that he was playing Glastonbury, which they used to do pretty much every year, along with the Led Zeppelin and Pink Floyd rumours. His lawyers thought we'd given the story to the press to promote ourselves and help sell tickets, which we would never do. Nor was it in our interests to: we'd already sold all of that year's tickets. We deliberately don't announce acts before the tickets go on sale. We want people to come because they want to be here to experience the Festival for everything it has to offer, not because one particular act is playing. Music is fundamental to this festival, but there is so much going on here beyond that.

The great thing about not announcing the line-up before the ticket sale is that people will discover acts that they wouldn't normally go and see. There were definitely people who saw Metallica in 2014

who wouldn't have described themselves as fans, but who came away thinking that show was fantastic. And I think that was definitely the case for Stormzy in 2019, too. When we announced he was playing there was a lot of outrage about him not being suitable or ready for it, but I think you would struggle to find anyone saying that now after seeing his show.

I'd say Stormzy's performance was one of the greatest sets we've ever had on the Pyramid, because it felt like things shifted culturally. It was so high-profile and intense – from the moment he came onstage in that Banksy flak jacket he just never let up – and it reached an audience way beyond the Festival. I've spoken to people who had never heard Stormzy's music before but came down to check him out and ended up staying for the whole show, totally blown away. Likewise, people who are big fans of his but have never been to Glastonbury before watched it on the telly and are going to come along to the Festival in the future. It felt like it really opened things up in such a positive way, and all because Stormzy just gave it his all and delivered an unbelievable show. I feel so strongly that there are moments when you can almost feel the evolution of the Festival taking place – almost touch it – and that happened when Stormzy was onstage. After all the drama and conflict there had been in the run-up to him headlining, there was nothing better than seeing him smash it on that Friday night and walk offstage a superstar.

Headlining Glastonbury is a curveball for some of the more established artists too. You have massive acts like U2, Beyoncé or The Rolling Stones, who don't usually play outside of their own huge shows filled with people who've specifically come because they're fans. Suddenly they're playing as part of a festival bill that wasn't announced when the tickets were sold. It makes it quite nerve-racking for them. When Paul McCartney played here it was probably the first time he'd played to a non-partisan crowd like that since Hamburg! I've heard acts talking about the jeopardy of a big Glastonbury set: they really don't know who's going to be out there in front of the stage and what the response will be. They have to come out, pumped up like a prize fighter, and work extra hard to put on a great show and win over the crowd. I think that's a big part of what makes so many Glastonbury sets so memorable. They have a real edge.

I think the whole JAY-Z furore in 2008 probably took that to a new level, and it hasn't really stopped since. We had it all over again in 2015 with Kanye West. As soon as we announced he was playing, a petition sprang up – started by someone who, it turned out, had never actually been to Glastonbury – saying Kanye shouldn't play because he wasn't right for us. The media jumped right on it. I suppose that kind of negative story will always get clicks and attention, but the coverage becomes self-fulfilling too. That petition quickly gathered momentum and became worldwide news. Again, we had to reassure

Opposite: Emily, George and Noah in front of Sam 3's murals for Greenpeace.
Above: Emily with newborn Nelly and bunting in The Park, 2016.

the people around the artist that it was all going to work, that these stories don't reflect the attitude of people coming to the Festival – or in the UK, for that matter. It's just a load of hot air.

The criticism we got that year was pretty extreme. And a lot of it was quite personal towards me, as people knew that I was booking the acts. I was an obvious target. I think as the child of a founder of something, you're always going to get criticism because you're perceived as doing things differently to how it was done before. I've had to get used to that and try to develop a bit of a thick skin about it all, as it can get pretty unpleasant on social media. You can't please everyone, and the haters tend to be the ones shouting the loudest a lot of the time. But it's the same for anyone in the public eye these days, sadly.

I actually had death threats in 2015, which seemed a little harsh. Especially given that we had booked what we considered to be one of the most exciting and innovative artists of his generation. But it worked out for Kanye in the end, despite the drama. It was a lively night and exciting from start to finish – he arrived in a whirlwind with the Kardashians, and he had these plans to go up in a huge cherry-picker crane during his set. The idea was to get it into the pit at the front of the stage for him to climb into, which was quite an operation. But even five minutes before he was due to go on, he hadn't decided whether he was actually going to use it. I was waiting at the side of the stage for their final call. It all felt very unpredictable and I had no idea what to expect. Then, during his show, he had a stage invader – we still don't know how that guy made it past Kanye's security.

I'm so glad we had Kanye that year, but it was probably one of the most divisive gigs we've had here. Some people thought it was absolutely brilliant and others thought it was overindulgent. And although it didn't fully connect with everyone, I loved that it was totally uncompromising and original and bold; it was quite unlike any other show we've had here. He did end up using the cherry picker too. I'm not sure how well that came across on TV, but in the field, with Kanye rapping from this huge crane above the crowd, it was awesome. If you've ever been up in one of those things you'll know that it's enough of a challenge just to stand there and hold on for dear life, let alone rap to a hundred thousand people all that way below. He's incredibly ballsy.

Kanye's set also led directly to Adele agreeing to headline the following year. I'd been trying to persuade her to play here, but I think she was quite unsure. She didn't really need to do it as such; she was already playing stadiums in her own right, and with her it almost seems like the less she does, the bigger she gets. But I think deep down in her heart she knew she wanted to, as she'd been coming to Glastonbury since she was a little kid.

I walked her onto the platform next to the stage just before Kanye came on, and we looked out at this huge crowd chanting Kanye's name. I said, 'Are you ready for it? Come on. Next year?' And she just looked at me with a twinkle in her eye and said, 'I'm gonna do it.' It was such a brilliant moment.

The 2015 Festival involved perhaps the most extreme couple of days I've ever had at Glastonbury. On the Friday morning our little boy Noah fractured his leg coming down a slide in the Kidzfield, which was awful. But the medical-tent crew were amazing, and within a couple of hours he'd been X-rayed and was hobbling about in a cast. Then we got back to the office and had to plan the arrival of Kanye and the Dalai Lama – it was quite surreal.

I felt very honoured to have the Dalai Lama come and visit. Nick and I had been planning it for two years by then. When he came onstage with Patti Smith it was just one of those very special moments. It meant so much to have him here, and Patti has a long history of

Opposite: Trailer ride during the site build in 2015.
Right: Emily with Stormzy in his dressing room
after his Friday-night headline show in 2019.

campaigning on his behalf, so it was very powerful.

Part of the excitement of creating the Festival year on year is the fact that we don't quite know how long it will go on for. In many ways it's like walking a tightrope, trying to keep everyone happy: the crew, the local community, the neighbouring farmers, the council and the emergency services. A lot of our time is spent managing the incredible team of people who help us make the Festival happen. Some years, depending on the weather or other issues, it can be a very hard thing for people to work on. It really takes its toll physically and emotionally.

In 2016, when we had the relentless rain and mud, I'd say it was one of the most challenging years we've ever had. The conditions in the parking fields were treacherous and, although the public had a brilliant time, we were really struggling to get all the vehicles off the road and onto the site, which was causing massive traffic issues for miles around. I can remember having a conference call with the authorities at 3 a.m. on the Wednesday, and some people were suggesting we should close the Festival. It's really hard to make clear-headed decisions in situations like that, especially when everyone's working incredibly hard and not getting any sleep. But we managed to convince them we were definitely going ahead, even if it did feel quite touch and go for a few hours.

I actually had that 3 a.m. conference call while I was in bed breastfeeding my third child, Nelly, who'd been born just a few weeks earlier. The 2010s have been a rollercoaster for me and Nick, with all of our kids born in this decade – Nelly in 2016, Noah in 2013 and George in 2011 – and all three were born just before the Festival. I hope they'll grow up to love it as much as I have; it brings so many interesting people and so much energy into their lives. I can't help but feel that they're lucky to be surrounded by it all. The world comes to them once a year, and I can see it opening up their minds!

The 2016 Festival also saw the EU referendum result on the Friday. It was a really emotional year. There was an opinion poll done on site, which found that 83 per cent of people at the Festival had voted remain – including me and my dad – and a lot of people felt quite broken when the result came through. It was like they needed Adele and Glastonbury to help them through. And she gave us one of the most heart-wrenching performances I've ever seen in the headline slot. She had such a connection with the audience that it felt like she was out there in the crowd herself. And before that, Christine and the Queens played on the afternoon of the referendum result and just seemed to capture something very wonderful and European amid the doom and gloom. She was fantastic, and the whole set was totally joyous and uplifting.

I think a lot of people actually stayed on site longer that year, to postpone going back to the real world. Or maybe it was just because their cars were stuck in the mud! Coldplay headlined to one of the biggest Sunday-night crowds we'd ever seen, and it was wonderful. They put so much into that show and brought an incredible sense of warmth, colour, optimism and togetherness. Their tribute to the young band Viola Beach, who'd died so tragically a few months earlier, was an unbelievably touching moment. And then they brought my dad on for 'My Way'. It was such a great way to round off what had been a hard year.

It took a few months for a lot of our crew to recover from 2016. Everyone who works here pours a vast amount of energy into creating such a spectacular show, and when conditions are hard it definitely takes longer to come back down to earth afterwards. The Festival completely takes over my life and the lives of my kids; there are so many reminders of how it was for me when I see it through their eyes. It can take over your whole body and soul.

I feel incredibly lucky to be able to do what I do. In many ways it really is the best thing in the world to be a part of – the creation of a magical city that never sleeps and exists for five days and then disappears without a trace. To be able to bring people this much joy and to work with such incredible, enthusiastic, creative individuals is just the best. The energy of the people who come to the Festival really keeps us going too. They bring such excitement and love to this farm.

I felt that in waves when we opened the gates on the Wednesday morning in 2019. It's an experience I never tire of. Obviously, I'm involved with it all year round – it's my life – but Glastonbury Festival is definitely still capable of blowing my mind. And the last Festival did that all over again for me; it was just so positive and vibrant from start to finish. I really can't remember a better one.

I've ended up taking on more and more responsibility as the years have gone on, initially with the music and then gradually with all areas of the Festival. We've really focused on improving the site, the green initiatives, the production levels, the art and the installations, the markets and bars, and just generally creating a space that is more colourful and creative throughout. It's all developed quite gradually, but if you compare the Festival now to how it was back in the nineties, there's been such a transformation. Even down to getting rid of the branding that had crept in. The only logos you will see on site now are our three main charities, or partners that provide a service, like the BBC and the *Guardian*.

A lot of the hard work that takes the most time is not always noticed, but I'm so proud of what we achieved in 2019 with the ban on sales of single-use plastic drinks bottles. It was the culmination of many years' work, gradually bringing in the steel bottles and reducing plastic wherever we could. More than a million plastic bottles were sold at the 2017 Festival, so it's wonderful to know that the planet has a million fewer to deal with now. The 200,000 people at the Festival demonstrated that refilling a reusable bottle with free tap water is the right way forward. These ideas can seem very straightforward on paper, but actually making them happen can be incredibly complicated and involve overcoming a lot of obstacles. Green issues have always been at the heart of the Festival, and we need to keep fighting to bring new initiatives on board. We will always face resistance, but I feel so strongly that it's our responsibility to demonstrate what's possible to the rest of the world – and we are getting more ambitious!

I don't think my dad ever had a conscious plan for there to be a transition to me. It's not really like that. We've got a really good relationship and we're very close. We each have our areas and we work really well together as a team. He's been happy to let me get on with it. I think we're both very respectful and trustful of each other. And I do love working with him – he brings so much enthusiasm to everything. And now we find ourselves in this phenomenal position of planning for our fiftieth anniversary, having been through so much and somehow surviving it all.

I honestly can't imagine what the future holds for us after 2020. I think our history has proven that it's impossible to predict what will happen next, though I don't think Glastonbury is still hanging on by a thread quite like it was. We will always enjoy each year as if it's the last, however, as you never know what's around the corner. There had been some talk of us trying an event in another location at some point, but that's still quite hard to imagine. I think we're already in the perfect place. We're just really enjoying and relishing these moments, because it's so hard to say where the Festival will be in ten years. I definitely hope it will still be going, though. I would love for my kids to experience it as they get older.

I'm also proud that, throughout all the changes and the dramas, we've stuck to our principles. We've had so many speakers and campaigners over the years championing the messages of equality, fairness, sustainability and caring for each other. Our roots are totally on the left. We've never been quiet or embarrassed about that. Throughout the eighties we campaigned like mad, with a CND logo on top of the Pyramid Stage. And that campaigning has continued right up to today, whether it's speaking out against Brexit or pushing environmental campaigns.

Millions of people were made aware of our green initiatives and plastic bottles ban, and it's had a genuine wider impact, particularly thanks to Sir David Attenborough talking about the ban from the Pyramid Stage on the Sunday afternoon. We've already seen other organisations and events around the world being pressured into following suit, with the words, 'Well, if Glastonbury can do it …' We've always wanted to use Glastonbury to make changes for the good of the planet, and it feels like we really managed it in 2019 – on a grand scale.

Who knows what lies ahead and which new paths we will take with the Festival, but whatever happens our ethos will remain true to what it has always been. As we head into the next chapter of Glastonbury Festival, we want to keep moving forward with sustainability at the heart of it all, creating an alternative universe for five days in which you can be whoever you want to be.

Surely there's nowhere better on earth.

Above: Emily and family in The Park on the opening day of the 2019 Festival.

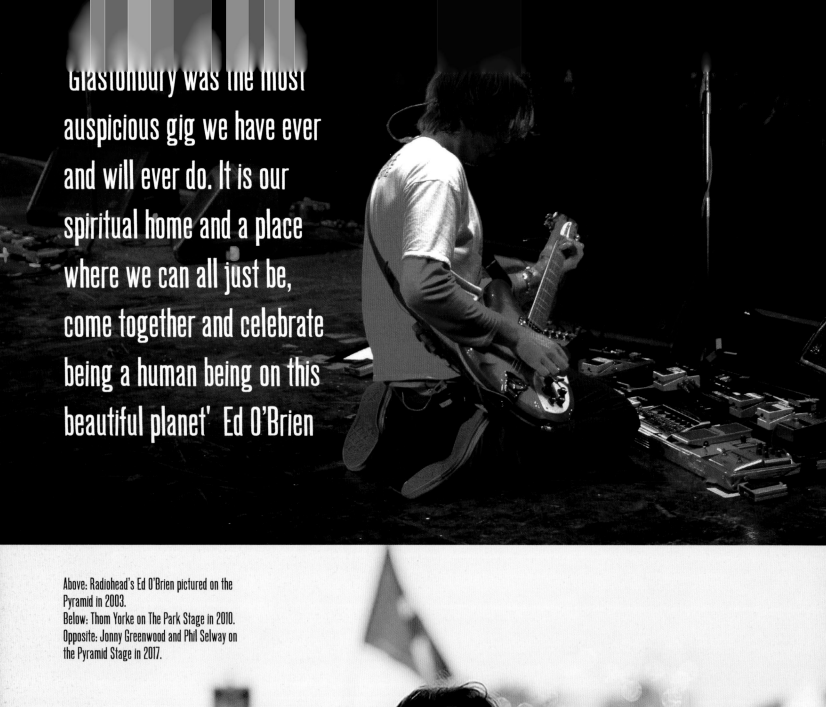

'Glastonbury was the most auspicious gig we have ever and will ever do. It is our spiritual home and a place where we can all just be, come together and celebrate being a human being on this beautiful planet' Ed O'Brien

Above: Radiohead's Ed O'Brien pictured on the Pyramid in 2003.
Below: Thom Yorke on The Park Stage in 2010.
Opposite: Jonny Greenwood and Phil Selway on the Pyramid Stage in 2017.

Radiohead

Glastonbury Festival of Contemporary Performing Arts

1970–2020

How sweet, to such a place, on such a night,
From halls with beauty and festival a-glare,
To come distract and, stretched on the cool turf,
Yield to some fond, improbable delight
—Alan Seeger, 1888-1917

Pyramid Stage:

Friday	Saturday	Sunday
Gorillaz • Dizzee Rascal • Vampire Weekend Snoop Dogg • Willie Nelson Corinne Bailey Rae • Femi Kuti Rolf Harris	Muse • Scissor Sisters • Shakira The Dead Weather Seasick Steve • Jackson Browne The Lightning Seeds • Tinchy Stryder	Stevie Wonder • Faithless Jack Johnson • Ray Davies Slash • Norah Jones Paloma Faith Yeovil Town Band

Other Stage:

The Flaming Lips • Hot Chip • Florence and The Machine • La Roux Phoenix • The Courteeners The Stranglers • Joshua Radin The Magic Numbers	Pet Shop Boys • Editors The Cribs • The National Kate Nash • Imogen Heap Coheed and Cambria • Reef Two Door Cinema Club	Orbital • LCD soundsystem • MGMT We Are Scientists • Grizzly Bear The Temper Trap • The Hold Steady Frightened Rabbit The Joy Formidable

West Holts Stage:

Femi Kuti • Mos Def Nouvelle Vague & Guests Breakestra with Chali 2na Bonobo • Mariachi El Bronx tUnE-yArDs Matthew Herbert Big Band	George Clinton with P-Funk Jerry Dammers Spatial AKA Orchestra Os Mutantes • Devendra Banhart Bassekou Kouyate & Ngoni Ba The Phenomenal Handclap Band Brother Ali • Troy Ellis & The Longshots	Rodrigo y Gabriela Toots & the Maytals Quantic & his Combo Barbaro Staff Benda Bilili Dr John & the Lower 911 • Tunng The Bees • Dizraeli and the Small Gods

John Peel Stage:

Groove Armada • The Black Keys Mumford & Sons • Ellie Goulding Kele • Bombay Bicycle Club Tegan and Sara • Miike Snow De Staat • Detroit Social Club	Jamie T • The XX • Foals Marina & The Diamonds • Delphic Wild Beasts • Field Music Cymbals Eat Guitars • Sophie Hunger Let's Buy Happiness	Ash • Julian Casablancas Broken Social Scene • Gang of Four The Drums • Holy F*** These New Puritans • Everything Everything Black Cherry • Dan Mangan

The Park:

The XX • Broken Bells • Special Guests The Big Pink • Local Natives Steve Mason • Hypnotic Brass Ensemble Beth Jeans Houghton • Lissie Peggy Sue • Steel Harmony	Midlake • Laura Marling • Candi Staton Special Guests • Stornoway • Beach House Strange Boys • Frankie & the Heart Strings The Ballad of Britain • Here We Go Magic I Blame Coco	Empire Of The Sun • Dirty Projectors Tony Allen • Archie Bronson Outfit Beak • Portico Quartet • Fionn Regan Avi Buffalo • Villagers • The Travelling Band

Acoustic Stage:

Bootleg Beatles • Alan Price Set McIntosh Ross • Turin Brakes • Brian Kennedy Danny and the Champions of the World Megan Henwood • Cory Chisel Julie Feeney	Christy Moore with Declan Sinnott • Nick Lowe Imelda May • Al Stewart Michael Eavis in conversation • Gandalf Murphy & The Slambovian Circus • The Leisure Society Ellen & The Escapades • Jon Allen & Band	Jackson Browne with David Lindley Richard Thompson • Loudon Wainwright III Blues Band • London Community Gospel Choir • Joel Rafael • Robinson Fisherman's Friend • Mayhew

Avalon Stage:

New Model Army • Transglobal Underground Newton Faulkner • The Woodentops • Lou Rhodes Goldheart Assembly • Gabby Young & Other Animal Hobo Jones & The Junkyard Dogs	The Lightning Seeds • Alabama 3 • Charlie Winston Steve Harley & Cockney Rebel • The Unthank The Avett Brothers • The Wurzels • Nick Harper Tom Williams & The Boat	Gomez • The Saw Doctors • Imelda May Judy Collins • Keane • Teddy Thompson Adrian Edmondson & The Bad Shepherds Kirsty Almeida • Ellen & The Escapades

The Glade: Sub Focus • Sasha • The Levellers • Freq Nasty • Quivver • Alabama 3 • Dreadzone • Hybrid • Arthur Brown • Don Letts • Way Out West • Quintessence • The Orb • Afrobeta • System 7 • Head Charge • Husky Rescue • FA~RM (Ans & Allaby) • Tony Thorpe • Nneka • Cassette Boy Feat DJ Rubbish • ON u Sound/Sherwood • Charles Hazelwood Allstars • Inverse Gravity Vehicle • Nero • The Widowmaker • Suns of Arqa • Statement Code • City Calls

Dance East: N-Dubz • Fatboy Slim •

Above & Beyond • Chipmunk • Chase and Status • Crystal Castles • Kelis • Zane Lowe • Filthy Dukes • MistaJam • Plan B • Professor Green • Roll Deep • Rob da Bank • Yasmin • Tinie Tempah • Example • Naive New Beaters • Giggs • Roger Sanchez • Crystal Fighters • Chiddybang • O Children • We Have Band • McClean • Bunny Come • Primary 1 • Bashy • Inko Dancers • Donaeo • Skepta • Scorcher • Ras Kwame

Dance West: Dubfire • Boys Noize • Magnetic Man • Nick Warren •

Simian Mobile Disco DJ Set • Jack Beats • Mixhell • Delphic • Stanton Warriors • Sander Kleinenberg • Fake Blood • Adam F • Banco de Gaia • Rusko • Blasted Mechanism • Riva Starr • Chromeo • Toddla T • Neville Staple • Aeroplane • Alex Metric Live • Dub Pistols • Boy 8-Bit • South Central • Parker • Hannah Holland • Jaguar Skills • Foreign Beggars • A1 Bassline • Killaflaw • Virus Syndicate

Leftfield Stage: Billy Bragg • Carl Barat • Paul Heaton • Frank Turner • Reverend & the Makers • Lucky Soul •

Thea Gilmore • Get Cape, Wear Cape, Fly • Get Up, Stand Up • Bill's Big Round-Up

Croissant Neuf: The Beat • Movits • RSVP • Kissmet • MrB. The Gentleman Rhymer • 6ixtoys • The Baghdaddies • Curved Air • Hot Feat • The Boat Band • Zen Elephants • The Kevin Brown Trio • Julien Tulk Band • Prof Nohair & the Wig Lifters • The Vagaband • Undercover Hippy Band • Corinne Bailey-Rae • Dizraeli & The Small Gods • Seth Lakeman • The Strumpettes • Biggles Wartime Band • The People's String Foundation • Posh Boy

Plus Tadpole/Green Futures • Small World Stage • Mandala Stage • Speakers Forum • Avalon Café • Glade Lounge • NYC Downlow • Block 9 • Arcadia • Lunar Sea Lounge • Cubana • Igloo • Bez's Acid House • Bassline Circus • Wow! • Pussy Parlure • **and a lot more!**

supporting
 GREENPEACE • WaterAid • Oxfam and other worthwhile causes

we are grateful to the following for their considerable help
Q • orange • theguardian • BBC TWO •  BBC RADIO • 6music

2010

CAPACITY: 177,500
TICKET PRICE: £185

Crucial site improvements in the off-season included the building of a second reservoir, holding two million litres of drinking water, essential for a tented city whose June population had overtaken both Oxford and Bath.

The long-standing Jazz World Stage was reborn as West Holts, and the south-east corner now became the official name of the late-night entertainment area featuring The Common, Arcadia, Block9, Shangri-La and The Unfairground. Prince Charles made an historic first visit to the Festival, taking in the Pilton social-housing project and the Greenpeace Field.

This page: Stevie Wonder (top) on the Pyramid in 2010, the Festival's fortieth anniversary year. Snoop Dogg (left) during his afternoon show on the Pyramid in 2010; he also joined Gorillaz onstage later that night.
Overleaf, clockwise from top left: Rinky Dink's pedal-powered sound system in the King's Meadow; art in The Green Fields; pole position — a view from the top of the Pyramid field; Gorillaz headlining the Pyramid; MGMT before their Other Stage performance in 2010.

GLASTONBURY FESTIVAL 2011
24-25-26 JUNE

For everything that lives is holy,
life delights in life,
Because the soul of sweet delight
can never be defil'd
—William Blake

PYRAMID STAGE: U2 △ COLDPLAY △ BEYONCÉ
ELBOW △ MORRISSEY △ PENDULUM △ PAUL SIMON △ BB KING △ BIFFY CLYRO
PAOLO NUTINI △ PLAN B △ TINIE TEMPAH △ LAURA MARLING △ WU-TANG CLAN
TWO DOOR CINEMA CLUB △ RUMER △ METRONOMY △ THE GASLIGHT ANTHEM △ TAME IMPALA △ DON MCLEAN
THE LOW ANTHEM △ STORNOWAY △ FISHERMAN'S FRIENDS △ THE MASTER MUSICIANS OF JOUJOUKA

OTHER STAGE: PRIMAL SCREAM △ THE CHEMICAL BROTHERS △ QUEENS OF THE STONE AGE
MUMFORD & SONS △ FLEET FOXES △ KAISER CHIEFS △ FRIENDLY FIRES △ BRIGHT EYES △ WHITE LIES
TV ON THE RADIO △ EELS △ JESSIE J △ THE VACCINES △ WOMBATS △ JIMMY EAT WORLD
BOMBAY BICYCLE CLUB △ THE NAKED & FAMOUS △ TWILIGHT SINGERS △ NOISETTES △ COLD WAR KIDS

WEST HOLTS STAGE: CEE LO GREEN △ BIG BOI △ KOOL & THE GANG △ CHASE AND STATUS
JANELLE MONÁE △ DR JIMMY CLIFF △ HERCULES & LOVE AFFAIR △ DUANE EDDY △ THE HELIOCENTRICS
ALOE BLACC △ FOOLS GOLD △ DENGUE FEVER △ THE GO! TEAM △ GONJASUFI
JAH WOBBLE & THE NIPPON DUB ENSEMBLE △ JAMIE WOON △ LITTLE DRAGON △ NICOLAS JAAR
BELLOWHEAD △ OMAR SOULEYMAN △ THE BRANDT BRAUER FRICK ENSEMBLE

JOHN PEEL STAGE: DJ SHADOW △ GLASVEGAS △ THE STREETS △ NOAH & THE WHALE △ BATTLES
THE HORRORS △ ANNA CALVI △ ROBYN △ THE CORAL △ EXAMPLE △ WARPAINT △ THE VACCINES △ HURTS
EVERYTHING EVERYTHING △ THE JOY FORMIDABLE △ DARWIN DEEZ △ MILES KANE △ YUCK △ MONA
DRY THE RIVER △ FOSTER THE PEOPLE

THE PARK STAGE: CRYSTAL CASTLES △ WILD BEASTS △ GRUFF RHYS △ CARIBOU △ JAMES BLAKE
LYKKE LI △ BIG AUDIO DYNAMITE △ WARPAINT △ TAME IMPALA △ JOHN GRANT △ THE BEES
THE WALKMEN △ JAMES VINCENT MCMORROW △ GRAHAM COXON △ JENNY & JOHNNY △ CAITLIN ROSE
THOSE DANCING DAYS △ DYLAN LEBLANC △ GROUPLOVE △ ABOUT GROUP △ SEA OF BEES △ THE PIERCES

DANCE VILLAGE: CARL COX △ FATBOY SLIM △ SKREAM & BENGA △ KATY B △ PROFESSOR GREEN
ANNIE MAC △ LABRINTH △ KESHA △ PETE TONG △ EROL ALKAN △ PHOTEK △ DEVLIN △ JOHN DIGWEED △ NENEH CHERRY
CLAUDE VONSTROKE △ SKEPTA △ THE MIDNIGHT BEAST △ WRETCH 32 △ SUBFOCUS & ID △ THE JAPANESE POPSTARS
SANDER KLEINENBERG — 5K LIVE FEATURING DEV △ STEVE LAWLER △ YOUSEF △ JAMES HOLDEN △ DJ FRESH △ ZINC △ JAMIE XX
CASPA FEAT MC ROD AZLAN △ JAH SHAKA △ MS DYNAMITE

ACOUSTIC TENT: BRIT FLOYD △ DEACON BLUE △ SUZANNE VEGA △ RAUL MALO FROM THE MAVERICKS
NICK LOWE △ IMELDA MAY △ ERIC BIBB △ PENTANGLE △ JOHN COOPER CLARKE △ HOTHOUSE FLOWERS △ THEA GILMORE
WINE WOMEN & SONG FEATURING MATRACA BERG △ SUZY BOGGUSS △ GRETCHEN PETERS △ NEWTON FAULKNER
THE WEBB SISTERS △ LONDON COMMUNITY GOSPEL CHOIR

SPIRIT OF '71: TERRY REID △ MELANIE △ SYSTEM 7 △ LINDA LEWIS △ THE CRAZY WORLD OF ARTHUR BROWN
NIK TURNER'S SPACE RITUAL △ BJ COLE AND EMILY BURRIDGE △ EDGAR BROUGHTON △ ROBYN HITCHCOCK △ NICK LOWE
MARSUPILAMI △ MURRAY LACHLAN YOUNG △ AVALONIAN FREE STATE CHOIR

AVALON STAGE: BARENAKED LADIES △ C.W. STONEKING △ CHUMBAWAMBA △ CITY AND COLOUR △ DEVOTCHKA
FLOGGING MOLLY △ GUILLEMOTS ACOUSTIC SET △ KT TUNSTALL △ LAU △ NEWTON FAULKNER △ RON SEXSMITH △ SHOOGLENIFTY
SHOW OF HANDS △ THE LOW ANTHEM △ THE WOMBLES

THEATRE & CIRCUS: NOFIT STATE CIRCUS △ THE POWDER PUFF GIRLZ △ MARCUS BRIGSTOCKE △ MITCH BENN
CIRCOLOMBIA △ KEVIN CRUISE △ MARK THOMAS △ INSECT CIRCUS △ BLACKSKYWHITE △ STEVEN FROST'S IMPRO ALLSTARS △ DIRTY FRED
CIRCOMEDIA △ MURRAY LACHLAN YOUNG △ AVANTI DISPLAY △ THE BLACK EAGLES △ JONATHAN KAY △ THE DREAM ENGINE
NORMAN LOVETT △ AREA 51 △ BABYHEAD △ SONIC FOREST △ MIMBRE △ SHAPPI KHORSANDIE △ HAGGIS AND CHARLIE

KIDZFIELD: RASTAMOUSE & DA EASY CREW △ THE GRUFFALO △ THE ZINGZILLAS △ CBEEBIES CREW △ TUCKEDIN △ TIM & LIGHT
BELL & BULLOCK △ MAGIC KEV △ SEIKOU SUSSO △ MISS LOULOU △ OBJECT DART △ CLOWN ZAZ △ CECIL SASSOON'S SILLY CINEMA

GREEN FIELDS: TONY BENN △ HEALING FIELD MUSIC SPACE △ RESIDENT EARTH MUSICIANS △ MEDITATION GARDEN
HEARTFELT PERFORMANCE △ PARTICIPATORY LISTENING △ HANDS ON CRAFTS AND SELF-SUFFICIENT SKILL-LEARNING
HIROSHIMA PEACE FLAME (BURNING SINCE 1946)

G STAGE △ GREENPEACE FIELD △ LEFTFIELD △ THE HEALING FIELD △ SHANGRI-LA △ UNFAIRGROUND
THE COMMON △ BLOCK 9 △ GREEN FUTURES △ BELLA'S FIELD △ STRUMMERVILLE △ WALL OF DEATH
THE RABBIT HOLE △ ZONA BASSLINE △ CLUB DADA △ THE FREE UNIVERSITY OF GLASTONBURY
CUBANA SALSA TENT △ MAVERICKS LATE NIGHT CABARET △ ARCADIA △ STONEBRIDGE BAR △ CLIMATE CAMP TRIPOD STAGE
CROISSANT NEUF △ HMS SWEET CHARITY △ BOURBON STREET △ 'BABYLON UPRISING' MARKET SOUND SYSTEM △ WOW! △ THE BANDSTAND
HURLY BURLY △ THE DRAGON FIELD UNDERGROUND PIANO BAR △ GREEN KIDS △ THE TREEHOUSE CAFÉ △ MAGIC BUBBLES △ THE CIDER BUS
WHITE RIBBON ALLIANCE TATTOO PARLOUR △ THE TIPI FIELD △ CAFÉ AVALON △ THE CROW'S NEST △ CUBEHENGE △ THE PILTON PALAIS CINEMA TENT
THE BIMBLE INN △ CAROLINE LUCAS MP △ THE WORTHY FARM SOLAR ARRAY △ GLASTONBURY FM △ WORTHY FM △ 24/7 COVERAGE BY 6MUSIC
SOUND ARTIST MARIA MARZAIOLI △ SSH DISCO △ SILENT DISCO...

AND INTRODUCING... CAMPO PEQUENO △ LOS ARTISTAS BOHEMIOS △ CARNIVAL SIDESHOWS
TWISTED VOODOO PARLOURS △ OXLYERS ON WEST △ THE GLASTONBURY FIRELIGHTER DAILY NEWSPAPER
AND MUCH, MUCH MORE!

supporting
GREENPEACE ◌ **WaterAid** ☉ **Oxfam**
and other worthwhile causes

2011

CAPACITY: 177,500
TICKET PRICE: £195

U2 finally made it to Worthy Farm, headlining a rain-soaked Pyramid on the Friday night. Coldplay's third headline slot followed a day later, with Beyoncé triumphantly closing proceedings on Sunday. Radiohead and Pulp played unannounced gigs on The Park Stage, and the Festival celebrated forty years of the Pyramid with a Spirit of '71 Stage featuring many of the pioneering legends, including Melanie, Arthur Brown, Steve Hillage, Terry Reid, Nick Lowe and Hawkwind's Nik Turner.

Newcomer Ed Sheeran played an early-afternoon set in the solar-powered Croissant Neuf Stage and was referred to as 'hotly tipped folky hip-hop' in the programme. The Festival donated over £2 million to WaterAid, Greenpeace, Oxfam and other local good causes.

Previous page: Sunset overlooking The Park, 2010.
This page: Beyoncé during her Sunday
Pyramid headline show in 2011 (top); U2 (left) finally
took the Friday headline slot the same year.
Overleaf, clockwise from top left: Jarvis Cocker onstage
with Pulp in The Park; The Common; Shangri-La; dressing
rooms for the NYC Downlow in Block9.

Guy Garvey
Elbow

The show Elbow played on the Pyramid Stage at Glastonbury 2011, just before Coldplay, wasn't just the best gig we've ever done, it was one of the best days of my life. And it still marks the pinnacle of our entire career. If you're a band, festivals are the best part of your job. And if you're from this country, Glastonbury is the festival you want to play. To perform on the main stage at sunset with a really joyful crowd is as good as it gets. It was just magic. People still stop me in the street all the time to say they were there.

Glastonbury was always something I was aware of growing up, but I think the first year I really took notice was 1998. The TV coverage was just picking up then, and I saw Nick Cave doing his legendary performance from The Other Stage. I remember thinking, Fuck, I've got to go there — it looks amazing.

Fast-forward just a few years and I found myself sitting around the Worthy Farm kitchen table with Michael and Emily, doing an interview with them for a magazine. I became firm friends with Emily that day. And we're still really good mates, because we only ever see each other under ridiculous, joyous circumstances. If it's not at some family wingding, then it's at the Festival.

Guy Garvey with Emily in the King's Meadow in 2004 (above), and taking a bow on the Pyramid Stage with Elbow in 2011.

I remember Emily walking me round the site that day, and sitting with her on the hand-painted litter bins piled up at the end of a field. I asked her what it was like as a kid growing up with the Festival. What really came across was her family's extraordinary warmth. I got a real sense that this thing was, and still is, an enormous labour of love for Michael and Emily. The highs and lows of the Festival have been the highs and lows of their personal lives.

The Great British public do this thing where if you say, 'I'm gonna do something new,' they say, 'Well, it'll never work.' Then you do it and it works, and they go, 'Well, that's ours now. You can't change it.' And Glastonbury is no exception. Every time they try something new, it happens. When they tried a hip-hop headliner in 2008, with JAY-Z, the press were merciless in their criticism. It was all, 'The Festival's forgotten who it is,' and all that typical *Daily Mail* bullshit. And of course it was an absolute raging success. One of the all-time great performances at the Festival.

The best thing people could do for Glastonbury would be to trust Michael and Emily to throw the party the way they see fit. They're never fucking wrong. Year in, year out, they throw the best party in the world. People should just trust them to do it.

Michael and Emily's endless warmth and generosity of spirit are right at the heart of the whole thing. They still treat every single person who comes onto their land for that festival like a member of their family. Whether you're on a train or in a restaurant, I always think you can tell if the boss is cool by the way the staff are. Because cool people hire cool people, who hire cool people. And when you're at Glastonbury there's simply no better experience of your fellow man.

I make it a mission of mine to go, whether we're playing or not. I like to take a flask full of whisky and just go for a wander across the site, letting the Festival take me with it. I've had some incredible experiences doing that.

For months before we played that 2011 show, I'd been saying to the band, 'Lads, it might not get any bigger than this, let's keep it together.' We knew we'd be at the Festival for two days before we played, and I said that we had to make sure we didn't overdo it, so we were in good shape for the show.

But then, the evening before, at about seven o'clock, I reached saturation point with my own worry, and completely flew in the face of my own advice. I totally got on it, and I was absolutely fucked in no time whatsoever.

I woke up the next day in a tipi and had a moment of panic that I'd slept through our show. Luckily, it was only 8 a.m. That's a relatively quiet time at Glastonbury, and I wandered out into the camping field. The only person awake was a spinal surgeon, who I think was a mate of Radiohead's. I found a wine sack that had fallen out of its cardboard box due to the rain, and a couple of grubby goblets, and offered him a glass of Glastonbury wine.

We sat there chatting, and then this other fella wandered up the field, still flying from the night before, and started reciting the entire script from an episode of *Fawlty Towers*. The three of us – three complete strangers – stood in a field, with rained-on wine, laughing our heads off. It was the essence of being at Glastonbury, and it was the perfect way to start the day.

Then, after I'd watched The Walkmen on The Park Stage play one of the best performances I've ever witnessed, I had to go and get ready to play. Just before I changed, I thought, I don't want people to think I've been helicoptered in. I'm wearing my fucking muddy trousers. If you watch the footage, I look like I've got legs made of mud.

Before we went onstage, the DJ very cheekily played 'Hey Jude', which shares some chords with our biggest hit – our only hit, in fact – 'One Day Like This'. And the crowd started singing 'One Day Like This' over it. So before we'd even set foot onstage, we were having a great gig.

We all agree that it was the best show we ever did. It was just amazing. You don't really expect gold-medal moments when you're a musician, but playing to 90,000 very, very happy people was definitely one. I can't even describe what a good time we had.

You never feel that safe or welcome in a crowd that size anywhere else in the world. When you're at Glastonbury, if it's rained, you've been through it together. If the sun's come out, there's absolutely no doubt in your mind that it's come out for you.

Everybody helps one another out, and all the staff are lovely. That beautiful, generous spirit of 'come and sit in our field' reigns. People go to Glastonbury and don't have another holiday all year because it's their favourite thing to do. We'd certainly play it every year if we could.

I've said it many times before: Glastonbury tops up your faith in humanity for the year. I'd like to see what would happen if they ever tried to stop it. I think you'd have a very peaceful but overwhelming national uprising.

GLASTONBURY 2013

Festival of Contemporary Performing Arts • 28-29-30 June

PYRAMID STAGE Arctic Monkeys ★ The Rolling Stones ★ Mumford & Sons ★ Dizzee Rascal ★ Primal Scream ★ Nick Cave & The Bad Seeds ★ Vampire Weekend ★ The Vaccines ★ Elvis Costello & The Imposters ★ Kenny Rogers ★ Ben Howard ★ Rita Ora ★ Rufus Wainwright ★ Jake Bugg ★ Professor Green ★ Laura Mvula ★ Billy Bragg ★ Rokia Traoré ★ First Aid Kit ★ Haim ★ Jupiter & Okwess International ★ Bassekou Kouyaté

OTHER STAGE Portishead ★ Chase & Status ★ The xx ★ Foals ★ Example ★ The Smashing Pumpkins ★ Alt-J ★ Two Door Cinema Club ★ Public Image Ltd ★ Tame Impala ★ Alabama Shakes ★ Editors ★ Azealia Banks ★ Of Monsters and Men ★ The Lumineers ★ Enter Shikari ★ I Am Kloot ★ The Hives ★ Amanda Palmer & The Grand Theft Orchestra ★ Dry the River ★ The 1975 ★ The Heavy

WEST HOLTS STAGE Chic ft. Nile Rodgers ★ Public Enemy ★ Bobby Womack ★ Seasick Steve ★ Major Lazer ★ Tom Tom Club ★ Maverick Sabre ★ Lianne La Havas ★ Toro Y Moi ★ Ondatrópica ★ Sergio Mendes ★ Dub Colossus ★ The Orb ft. Kakatsitsi ★ Alice Russell ★ Goat ★ BadBadNotGood ★ The Bombay Royale ★ Fatoumata Diawara ★ Zun Zun Egui ★ Matthew E. White ★ Riot Jazz ★ The Congos ★ Classica Orchestra Afrobeat ★ Troker

THE PARK STAGE Cat Power ★ The Horrors ★ Fuck Buttons ★ Django Django ★ Rodriguez ★ Dinosaur Jr. ★ Calexico ★ Steve Mason ★ Palma Violets ★ Devendra Banhart ★ Michael Kiwanuka ★ Solange ★ King Krule ★ Stealing Sheep ★ Tim Burgess ★ Melody's Echo Chamber ★ Ed Harcourt ★ Half Moon Run ★ Josephine ★ Teleman ★ Pictish Trail ★ Rozi Plain ★ Rachel Zeffira ★ Nick Mulvey

JOHN PEEL STAGE Crystal Castles ★ Hurts ★ Phoenix ★ Bastille ★ Everything Everything ★ James Blake ★ Johnny Marr ★ The Courteeners ★ Jessie Ware ★ Tyler, The Creator & Earl Sweatshirt ★ Frightened Rabbit ★ Miles Kane ★ Local Natives ★ The Strypes ★ Savages ★ Tom Odell ★ Peace ★ Daughter ★ Villagers ★ Toy ★ Deap Vally ★ Jagwar Ma

SILVER HAYES Nas ★ Hot Natured ★ Disclosure ★ Rudimental ★ The Family Stone ★ Skream & Benga ★ Sub Focus ★ Charles Bradley ★ SBTRKT ★ Netsky ★ Dog Blood ★ The Congos ★ The 2 Bears ★ AlunaGeorge ★ Julio Bashmore ★ Wiley ★ TEED ★ Gold Panda ★ David Rodigan

ACOUSTIC STAGE Steve Winwood ★ Sinead O'Connor ★ Lucinda Williams ★ Glen Hansard ★ Bill Wyman's Rhythm Kings ★ The Bootleg Beatles ★ Gabrielle Aplin ★ The Proclaimers ★ Martha Wainwright ★ Seth Lakeman ★ KT Tunstall ★ Zac Brown Band ★ Gretchen Peters ★ Martin Stephenson & The Daintees ★ The Gypsy Queens ★ Steve Forbert ★ Bridie Jackson & The Arbour

AVALON STAGE Ben Caplan ★ Beverley Knight ★ Crowns ★ Evan Dando ★ Gary Clark Jr. ★ JJ Grey & Mofro ★ Josh Doyle ★ Lucy Rose ★ Mad Dog Mcrea ★ Molotov Jukebox ★ Newton Faulkner ★ Oysterband ★ Penguin Café ★ Shooglenifty ★ Sir Bruce Forsyth ★ Stornoway ★ The Destroyers ★ The Staves ★ The Urban Voodoo Machine ★ Vintage Trouble ★ Xavier Rudd

THEATRE & CIRCUS The Infinite Monkey Cage ★ Lost Locos ★ Roy Hutchins ★ The Monsters of Schlock ★ Chris Bull ★ Pirates of the Carabina ★ Marcus Brigstocke ★ Abandoman ★ Josie Long ★ The Demon Barbers ★ Maia ★ Olivier Grossetête ★ Twister

BLOCK9 Gene Hunt ★ Tyree Cooper ★ Maurice Fulton ★ Greg Wilson ★ Mosca ★ Bill Brewster ★ Grant Nelson ★ Youngsta ★ Digital & Spirit ★ MC Chickaboo ★ Randall ★ Flight ★ Kerri Chandler ★ Horse Meat Disco ★ Brawther ★ Robert Owens ★ Underground Paris

SPIRIT OF '71 Robyn Hitchcock and the Venus 3 ★ Slim Chance ★ Simian Mobile Disco ★ Terakaft ★ System 7 vs Eat Static ★ Don Letts ★ DJ James Monro ★ Gypsy Hill ★ Electric Swing Circus ★ DJ Tristan ★ Mixhell

ARCADIA ★ THE COMMON ★ CROISSANT-NEUF ★ THE FIELD OF AVALON GREEN FIELDS ★ GREEN FUTURES ★ GREENPEACE ★ THE HEALING FIELD ★ KIDZFIELD ★ LEFTFIELD THE PILTON PALAIS ★ SHANGRI-LA: THE AFTERLIFE ★ STRUMMERVILLE ★ THE UNFAIRGROUND

Introducing: THE ARCTIC DOME ★ BLUES ★ GENOSYS ★ GLASTO LATINO THE GLASTONBURY FREE PRESS ★ GULLY ★ SONIC ★ THE SUMMERHOUSE ★ WILLIAM'S GREEN

AND STILL MORE ACTS & ATTRACTIONS TO BE ANNOUNCED ACROSS OVER 100 STAGES!

2013

CAPACITY: 177,500
TICKET PRICE: £205

After a year off, and with tickets selling out in record time the previous October, The Rolling Stones finally confirmed on 27 March. When The Stones took to the Pyramid Stage in front of a record crowd, its crown was adorned with a giant fire-breathing phoenix created by Joe Rush. The wings rose on cue for The Stones' intro to 'Sympathy for the Devil'. Two hours later, the very first edition of the *Glastonbury Free Press*, printed on a vintage eight-ton Heidelberg cylinder in the Theatre and Circus area, was distributed across the site. Worthy View, the Festival's newest suburb, housed over ten thousand happy campers in pre-erected British-made ridge tents purchased by the Festival.

Skrillex played twenty different sets across twenty different stages, and the Gully and the Sonic stages were launched at Silver Hayes. At the end of the weekend the BBC announced its highest-ever viewing figures since coverage began in 1997, and a container of Glastonbury memorabilia was donated to the Rock and Roll Hall of Fame in Cleveland, Ohio.

Previous page: Mick Jagger on the Pyramid with The Rolling Stones (top) and the phoenix which came to life during their show (bottom left). Beth Gibbons of Portishead on The Other Stage (centre), and Mumford & Sons on the Pyramid (bottom right). This page, clockwise from top left: The Blues in Silver Hayes; Arcadia's Spider; Nick Cave and fan; and a long-standing meeting point in The Common.

Dolly Parton
Musician

One of the greatest thrills and achievements of my entire career was doing a concert at Glastonbury Festival. I was so nervous, thinking that I might not fit in with the types of shows and artists who had performed there in the past. But I was humbled and so appreciative that the fans welcomed me with open arms. I still remember the exact feelings I had during and after the show ... and I'm still glowing. Thank you, Glastonbury, for making me part of your wonderful history.

Right: Dolly Parton on the Pyramid Stage, 2014.
Opposite: Glastonbury Festival's long-serving sign creator Dan Stuart (centre, top) and artist Mo (centre, left) with a selection of their work.

GLASTONBURY FESTIVAL 27-28-29 June 2014

PYRAMID STAGE Arcade Fire★Metallica★Kasabian★Dolly Parton★Jack White★Elbow
The Black Keys★Robert Plant★Lily Allen★Ed Sheeran★Lana Del Rey★Rudimental★De La Soul
Kelis★Rodrigo Y Gabriela★The 1975★Angel Haze★Toumani & Sidiki Diabaté★The War On Drugs
Nitin Sawhney★Nick Mulvey★Caro Emerald★Turtle Island★English National Ballet

OTHER STAGE Skrillex★Jake Bugg★Massive Attack★Paolo Nutini★Pixies★Manic Street Preachers
Interpol★Ellie Goulding★HAIM★Bombay Bicycle Club★Foster The People★Imagine Dragons
Blondie★White Lies★Kodaline★Warpaint★The Horrors★John Newman★Midlake★Sam Smith
Band of Skulls★Lucy Rose★The Subways★Circa Waves★Jake Isaac★Bajofondo

WEST HOLTS STAGE M.I.A.★Bryan Ferry★Disclosure★Jurassic 5★Goldfrapp★Bonobo★tUnE-yArDs
Seun Kuti & Egypt 80★The Wailers★The Daptone Super Soul Revue★Sun Ra Arkestra★Vintage Trouble
The London Sinfonietta & Jonny Greenwood★Deltron 3030★Public Service Broadcasting★The Internet
The Stepkids★The Lee Thompson Ska Orchestra★John Wizards★Troker★Melt Yourself Down

THE PARK STAGE Metronomy★Mogwai★James Blake★Four Tet★John Grant★St Vincent
Yoko Ono Plastic Ono Band★ESG★Danny Brown★Anna Calvi★Parquet Courts★Phosphorescent★2 Bears
Jagwar Ma★Connan Mockasin★Jimi Goodwin★Courtney Barnett★Nina Persson★Juana Molina
Cate Le Bon★Thunderbirds Are Go★Don Cavalli★Lau★Young Fathers★Bipolar Sunshine★Vance Joy

JOHN PEEL STAGE Kaiser Chiefs★MGMT★London Grammar★Lykke Li★Chvrches★Wild Beasts
Chromeo★Crystal Fighters★Little Dragon★Chance The Rapper★Clean Bandit★Royal Blood
King Charles★Poliça★Temples★Jungle★Wolf Alice★Fat White Family★Hozier★Drenge
The Brian Jonestown Massacre★Bleachers★Dry The River★George Ezra

ACOUSTIC STAGE Dexys★Suzanne Vega★Tinariwen★Nick Lowe★Paul Heaton & Jacqui Abbott
Alison Moyet★Kacey Musgraves★Fisherman's Friends★Rainy Boy Sleep
John Illsley (Dire Straits) & Band★Clannad★Thea Gilmore

SILVER HAYES Fatboy Slim★Richie Hawtin★Annie Mac★Above & Beyond★Ella Eyre★Toddla T★Ben Klock
Marcel Dettmann★Maya Jane Coles★Loco Dice★Maxi Priest★Go Chic★Skip&Die★Jamie Jones★Seth Troxler
TOK!MONSTA★Stromae★Parov Stelar Band★Bomba Estéreo★Kiesza★Bernhoft★The Beat★Myron & E★Congo Natty

AVALON STAGE Beth Orton★Dervish★Emiliana Torrini★Gabrielle Aplin★Hazel O'Connor★Hudson Taylor
Johnny Flynn & the Sussex Wit★Jonny Lang★Michael Kiwanuka★Newton Faulkner★North Mississippi Allstars
Peatbog Faeries★Skinny Lister★Sophie Ellis-Bextor★The Bad Shepherds★The Selecter

THEATRE & CIRCUS Briefs★The Monster Sideshow★Circus Kathmandu★Leo & Yam★Le Navet Bête
Dot Comedy – The Chain★John Hegley★The Fugitives★Marcus Brigstocke★Josh Widdicombe★Robin Ince
Josie Long★Michael Rosen★Lee Nelson★Phill Jupitus★Cuban Brothers★Stephen Frost Improv Allstars

THE GLADE Pretty Lights★System7vGong★Alabama 3★Stanton Warriors★Dub Pistols★Dreadzone★Jon Hopkins
Dinos Chapman★Drumsound & Bassline Smith★Mad Prof ft General Levy★Alexis Taylor★Machinedrum★Nihal

LEFT FIELD Billy Bragg★Dan Le Sac V's Scroobius Pip★Anti-Flag★Tribute to Tony Benn

KIDZ FIELD What The Ladybird Heard★Dr Seuss's Cat In The Hat★CBeebies Stage Extravaganza
Chicken Licken★Billy's Birthday Bash★Mr Yipadee★Rhyming Rockets★Panic Circus

ARCADIA Glastonbury Landing Show★Finale★The Mechanical Playground
BLOCK9 Genosys★The London Underground★NYC Downlow★The Downlow Radio
THE COMMON The Rum Shack★The Cave★The Temple★The Totem Gardens★Paint Fight★Tomato Fight
SHANGRI-LA The CPU★The Dept. of Future Selfies★Hell Mary's★Plutos PR Dept.★Temple of Oil
THE UNFAIRGROUND Acid Lounge★Bez's Acid House★Salon Carousel

A Kiss on the Apocalypse★Babylon Uprising★The Bandstand★Birdsong Symphony
Croissant Neuf★Field Of Avalon★Free University of Glastonbury★Glasto Latino
Glastonbury Free Press★Green Fields★Green Futures★Greenpeace★Healing Field
Pilton Palais★The Spike★Strummerville★William's Green

AND STILL MORE ACTS & ATTRACTIONS TO BE ANNOUNCED ACROSS OVER 100 STAGES!

2014

CAPACITY: 177,500
TICKET PRICE: £205

Work continued on the Festival-supported Pilton village social-housing project, with over twenty houses completed by May.

Metallica were confirmed as surprise Saturday headliners, with Arcade Fire (Friday) and Kasabian (Sunday) making it a trio of debut Pyramid headliners. Art installations were unfurled across the site, Banksy's 'factory farming' installation parading noisily through the market areas and gaining global interest. Arcadia moved to their new home next to The Park and introduced the Bug.

The main stages got off to a stormy start on the Friday afternoon, when Rudimental's Pyramid performance – complete with special guest appearance from Ed Sheeran – was cut short after lightning struck the stage. Happily, the weather improved from there, with Yoko Ono and the Plastic Ono Band gracing The Park Stage and Dolly Parton appearing on the front page of every UK broadsheet the morning after she played to an enormous Sunday afternoon Pyramid crowd.

The success of the event helped the Festival to be able to give around £2 million to Oxfam, Greenpeace, WaterAid and hundreds of other worthy causes, both local and international.

This page: Blazes of glory, 2014 — fire show in the Circus Field (top), open-all-hours markets (centre), and Joe Rush's mechanical horse (left).
Overleaf: Photographer Mary McCartney's contact sheet from a backstage shoot with Arcade Fire (left), and (right, from top) a Theatre and Circus duo; the Mutoid Waste Company's Hand of God; and the Metallica show on the Pyramid.

Lars Ulrich
Metallica

For a music-obsessed kid growing up in Denmark, Glastonbury was the stuff of legend. I didn't get to attend back then, but I knew all about it. And then with Metallica we were fortunate to play at the biggest festivals in so many different countries, including some great years at Donington, which is the centre of the UK's hard-rock world. But Glastonbury was the one that had eluded us. I think I'd wanted us to play there for at least a decade before we eventually did, in 2014.

I guess it could have been an anticlimax when I finally made it to Worthy Farm, but in fact it was even better than I could've imagined. We flew in by helicopter and it just looked so magical from the air. Seeing how a quarter of a million people had all got together on this farm in England was mind-blowing. Then, when we landed and got in the thick of it, the buzz and the energy were overwhelming.

On that first night, Nick Dewey — Emily's husband — sort of took me under his wing. He led me and my crew around for hours, showing us all the different stages and the sacred sites, until about 6 a.m. After that tour I was completely converted. You just surrender to Glastonbury. It swallows you whole in its safe embrace. Every single day that the Festival's been on since Nick took me on that walk, I've been there.

Previous page:
The NYC Downlow in Block9.
Opposite: Lars Ulrich on the Pyramid
Stage with Metallica in 2014.

The unbelievable thing about Glastonbury is that they've managed to extend the world-view of Michael and Emily. They've kept the big corporate entities at bay. It feels like you're at a giant garden party.

That's because the Eavises are such warm, welcoming, caring people. Whatever is happening at the very top of any organisation is the flavour that permeates down. With Glastonbury, Michael and Emily are directing everyone to be courteous, respectful and embracing. That flavour runs through every single person who's working there.

I also love the fact that Emily, Michael and Nick make unexpected choices with their bookings and then stand up for them. The English media can occasionally overdramatise these things, but the Eavises stood up for booking JAY-Z. They stood up for booking Dolly Parton. They stood up for booking Metallica. And they always get it right.

A lot of people wound themselves up about our appearance. There was controversy about a metal act headlining, and about James from the band being on a TV show about hunting. When you've been around for as long as we have, it's not often that you're put in a position to still feel like the underdogs, with something to prove. But we love that. It makes us step up a level.

As soon as we broke the ice with our little self-deprecating fox-hunting intro video on the big screens – which climaxed with us dressed as bears shooting some fox hunters – it felt like everybody knew it was going to be okay. When we walked out onstage, it was like all the negativity had dissipated. We were just another rock band. And, dare I say, we're quite good at making everybody feel very welcome, warm and fuzzy at a festival. Plus, we had 500 fans up behind us onstage, waving the flags and jumping around. It felt like we were in this Glastonbury circle of love.

Being on the Pyramid Stage was an incredible high. As a musician, it's one of the most hallowed and sacred places you can play, and it felt right to be there. It was a magical night.

We ended up spending the whole weekend at the Festival. We wandered the site with Nick on Friday, we played on Saturday and then we experienced Glastonbury on Sunday in all its glory, with no obstacles, until eight in the morning. My wife and I and a couple of friends made a pact there and then, that this was too precious a weekend not to try to repeat. Since then, we've booked off the fourth week of June every year to be there.

There are so many different things I love about being at Glastonbury: seeing old friends and sharing memories from the years past, alongside all the new possibilities and the anticipation of what's going to happen.

We usually do the night shift. We'll go and check out who's playing on the Pyramid and see if there are friends to say hello to, and then we'll start trekking. We don't overthink it; we just see where we end up and it falls into place. I think what makes Glastonbury so different from any other festival is that it goes twenty-four hours. There are so many nooks and crannies. All the areas are like different neighbourhoods. There is diversity and different experiences everywhere you look.

The only thing we'll always try to do is be up by the Ribbon Tower in The Park on the Monday morning as the sun rises. We'll sit and reminisce and look at 200,000 people all coming to the end of their own experiences.

That's what's so great about Glastonbury. Everybody's got a different version of what Glastonbury means to them. There'll be 200,000 different stories to tell, and mine's just one of them. I love the paradox of it being an incredible place to get lost while also knowing that you're always with all these other similar souls.

And even if you're a musician who's played the Pyramid Stage or someone from the film or art world, you really can get lost there. You might occasionally get recognised, but it never feels intrusive or inconvenient. It always just feels like we're sharing an experience together before passing on to our next place.

I love it there. I plan to keep going as long as I can keep going.

GLASTONBURY 2015
Festival of Contemporary Performing Arts
24–28 June

"Though a good deal is too strange to be believed...
...nothing is too strange to have happened" –Thomas Hardy

PYRAMID STAGE Florence & The Machine_Kanye West_The Who_Pharrell Williams Paul Weller_Motörhead_Paloma Faith_Alt-J_Mary J. Blige_Lionel Richie_Alabama Shakes Patti Smith_Burt Bacharach_George Ezra_The Waterboys_Hozier_Courtney Barnett_James Bay Chronixx_Songhoy Blues_Michael Clark Company_The Unthanks_Burtle Silver Band

OTHER STAGE Rudimental_Deadmau5_The Chemical Brothers_Mark Ronson_Ben Howard_Jamie T Courteeners_The Maccabees_Belle and Sebastian_The Vaccines_Clean Bandit_Future Islands_Jungle Ella Eyre_Twin Atlantic_Catfish & the Bottlemen_Everything Everything_Young Fathers_The Cribs Palma Violets_Azealia Banks_Adam Cohen_Frank Turner_Soak_Swim Deep_Rival Sons

WEST HOLTS STAGE Hot Chip_The Mothership Returns: George Clinton, Parliament, Funkadelic & the Family Stone_Flying Lotus_Caribou_Todd Terje & The Olsens_FKA twigs_Run The Jewels_Vintage Trouble Roy Ayers_The Gaslamp Killer Experience_Gregory Porter_Steel Pulse_Kasai Allstars Soil & Pimp Sessions_Cumbia All Stars_Marcos Valle_Sinkane_Hiatus Kaiyote_Dorian Concept Jane Weaver_Ibibio Sound Machine_Cambodian Space Project_K.O.G & the Zongo Brigade_Flamingods

THE PARK STAGE Super Furry Animals_Jon Hopkins_Ryan Adams_Jamie xx_Spiritualized_Goat Mavis Staples_The Fall_Sharon Van Etten_Father John Misty_Perfume Genius_Wolf Alice_Kate Tempest Fat White Family_Benjamin Booker_Gaz Coombes_The Staves_Glass Animals_Giant Sand_Rae Morris Pussy Riot_Shlomo_Ibeyi_Jack Garratt_King Gizzard_Eaves_Rhodes_Flo Morrissey_Denai Moore

JOHN PEEL STAGE Enter Shikari_Suede_FFS (Franz Ferdinand & Sparks)_Modestep_La Roux Deathcab For Cutie_Sbtrkt_Death From Above 1979_Lianne Le Havas_Circa Waves_Jessie Ware_Charli XCX Peace_Years and Years_Django Django_Chet Faker_The Pop Group_Alvvays_The Districts_Sleaford Mods Prides_Leon Bridges_Slaves_Saint Raymond_Rainy Boy Sleep_Coasts_Mini Mansions

ACOUSTIC STAGE Christy Moore_The Moody Blues_The Proclaimers_Nick Lowe, Paul Carrack & Andy Fairweather Low_Wilko Johnson_Texas_Donovan_Tommy Emmanuel_Jack Savoretti_Eric Bibb

SILVER HAYES Circo Loco_Fatboy Slim_Flight Facilities_Four Tet_Fuse ODG_Gorgon City Herbert Live_Idris Elba_Jess Glynne_JESuS_Leftfield_Sigma_Skepta_Tourist_Tricky_Alo Wala Andreye_Batida_Bunji Garlin_Krept & Konan_Hannah Wants_Milky Chance_Rag'n'Bone Man_Roni Size

AVALON STAGE Bear's Den_Cara Dillon_Dreadzone_I Am Kloot_Idlewild_King Creosote_Lamb Lulu_Molotov Jukebox_Moulettes_Neville Staple Band_Raghu Dixit_Seth Lakeman_The Zombies

THEATRE & CIRCUS La Soirée_Svalbard_Eric McGill_Michael Clark Company_Frisky & Mannish Los Excentricos_Palo Volador_John Hegley_VIP Puppets_Dr John Cooper Clarke_Lords of Strut_Les Bubb The Insect Circus Show_Murray Lachlan Young_Professor Elemental_Shappi Khorsandi_Demon Barbers

THE GLADE Public Service Broadcasting_Alabama 3_Slamboree_Nic Fanciulli_Annie Nightingale Dub Pistols_Paul Woolford_Don Letts_Way Out West_Eat Static

LEFT FIELD Billy Bragg_Thea Gilmore_Buzzcocks_Sam Duckworth & (The Brackets)_Akala

KIDZ FIELD Professor Stephen Hawking_Coreo_Cbeebies Alex & Katie's Roadshow_Re-Play Music Panic Circus_Rhubarb Theatre_Dynamo_Milkshake Live_DNA_The Flying Seagull Project_Mr Yipadee

ARCADIA New show – "Metamorphosis"_Adam Beyer_Groove Armada_Spor_Maceo Plex Booka Shade_Pan-Pot_Skream_The Bug_Foreign Beggars

BLOCK9 Cerrone_Phuture (Live)_Joe Claussell_Awesome Tapes From Africa_Jah Shaka Robert Hood_Mr G_Point G_Honey Dijon_Prosumer_Four Tet

THE COMMON Fast Eddie_CASPA_Mickey Finn_Jackmaster B2B Joy Orbison

SHANGRI-LA Skints_Zion Train_Hospital Records_Norman Jay_Babyhead

FAIRGROUND Bez_Dillinja_808 State_Primal Scream DJ Set

GLASTO LATINO Mercadonegro_Ricardo Lemvo_Angel Y La Mecanica Loca

AND MANY MORE ACTS ACROSS OVER 100 STAGES!

Plus: Bimble Inn▲HMS Sweet Charity▲Groovy Movie Picture House▲Stonebridge Bar▲The Spaceport▲The Spike Speakers Forum▲The Beat Hotel▲Ancient Futures▲Pilton Palais▲Healing Field Music Space▲The Engine Room The Totem Gardens▲Babylon Uprising▲Tor View Theatre▲Free University of Glastonbury▲The House of Come Ons▲Toad Hall Mavericks▲Croissant Neuf▲Mustoid Waste Company▲The Temple▲The Crows Nest▲Small World Stage▲The Rabbit Hole Strummerville at the Spinney▲Peace Garden▲Glastonbury Free Press▲The People's Front Room▲Poetry&Words Outside Circus Stage▲Croissant Neuf Bandstand▲Battle of the Beanfield▲Wango Riley's Stage▲Memories of a Free Festival

His Holiness the Dalai Lama visited Glastonbury for the first time with appearances in The Green Fields and on the Pyramid Stage alongside Patti Smith. The Pyramid also played host to Lionel Richie in the legend slot, resulting in his first number one album for twenty-five years the following week.

The plan had been for the Foo Fighters to headline on Friday, but two weeks before the show Dave Grohl broke his leg jumping offstage in Sweden and the Foos were forced to withdraw. Florence + the Machine were promoted up the billing to take their place, with Kanye West headlining on the Saturday night.

Arcadia introduced the Metamorphosis live show; Strummerville moved up into the woods above the Tipi Field; Pussy Riot were on The Park Stage, introduced by Charlotte Church; Greenpeace launched their silent disco in Silver Hayes; and the Michael Clark Company entertained in The Astrolabe Theatre.

The Festival asked everyone attending to take the initiative to use the toilets, not the hedges, and to refill water containers rather than buy plastic bottles. The BBC distributed footage of the weekend to more than thirty countries, and it was another record year for donations to the Festival's charities and worthy causes.

2015

CAPACITY: 203,000
TICKET PRICE: £220

Below, clockwise from top left: Florence + the Machine, Kanye West and Motorhead's Lemmy on the Pyramid.

2015

This page: Night-time above The Park (top); the Tony Benn Tower and William's Green (bottom left); Shangri-La (bottom right). Overleaf, clockwise from top left: All together in 2015 — the Dalai Lama on the Pyramid with Patti Smith; Pharrell Williams; Burt Bacharach; Lionel Richie.

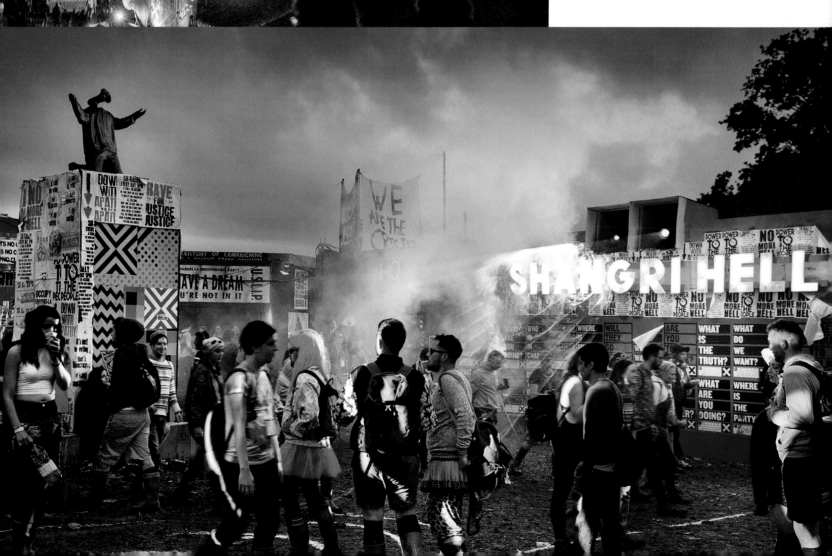

Daisy Jones
Writer

For me, there are two versions of Glastonbury. There's the Glastonbury of *then*, in which I was flung over the fence by family members, made to eat lentils in the Peace Garden and usually sitting on someone's shoulders in a bucket hat while a nineties indie band like Travis whined in the distance. And then there's the Glastonbury of *now*, which is something else entirely. Today, when I think of the Festival, I think of candy-pink lights and being drenched in sweat. I think of huddling behind a toilet cubicle at 4 a.m. taking bumps of ket with a drag queen called Barbarella who tells me my skin is glowing. I think of how weird it is that the best queer club in the UK right now exists for just a few nights, once a year, in a field in Somerset, like a lucid dream you can't fully grasp with both hands afterwards.

These divisions of 'then' and 'now' aren't entirely based around my own perceptions — in which I experienced Glastonbury as a child, in the late nineties and early noughties, and then later as an adult. Other people observe these divisions too. Because for a long time Glastonbury wasn't necessarily intertwined with club culture. Instead, it was where travellers, anarchists and music fans came together to watch their favourite bands and do tarot cards and fling their bodies in the mud. And after midnight, once the music was over, the revelry would turn inwards, to people's campsites or makeshift dance tents.

Right: Daisy Jones riding a Glastonbury zebra.
Overleaf: Inside NYC Downlow in Block9 (left) and Glastonbury's
legendary oil-drum bins, individually hand-painted by Hank's
team of on-site artists before the Festival.

I was too young to remember this era fully, but if I close my eyes I can just about recall the atmosphere: boomboxes blasting out of vans and bodies around campfires, adults on mushrooms leaning in closely to whisper nonsensical truisms, and chaos, literal feverish chaos, back when a hundred thousand-plus people could gate-crash over the fence.

But then, at the turn of the millennium, everything changed. Most people pin this sudden shift to the birth of Lost Vagueness, the Festival's first-ever after-hours 'party' – brought in by a guy called Roy Gurvitz to alter the trajectory of where Glastonbury was headed. Carved out of a space in the south-east corner of Worthy Farm, suddenly there was somewhere you could go after midnight. In this new place – which was loosely supposed to be an absurd, psychedelic version of Vegas, and comprised of a series of temporary venues – you could go ballroom dancing, attend cabaret shows, take part in burlesque casinos and dance to DJs all night. Lost Vagueness came to an end ten years later, but the area – nicknamed 'the naughty corner' – continued to bloom and multiply. In its place sprang what we now know as The Unfairground, The Common, Arcadia, Shangri-La, NYC Downlow and Block9, and from then on Glastonbury's naughty corner became the place to be once the sun had set.

To truly understand the naughty corner's place in the world, we need to first zoom out and look at club culture back then as a whole. In the mid- to late 2000s, when I was a teenager, queer nightlife in the UK was thriving – or at least it felt that way. In London, especially, clubs like the Joiners Arms, Nelson's Head, the George and Dragon, Candy Bar and the Black Cap were spaces where LGBTQ people could dance and dress up, offering a much-needed place where you could escape straight culture for the night and do what you wanted. If you'd swung open the doors of the Joiners on a Tuesday night in 2007, for instance, you'd have walked straight into a room of wrinkled old men in fishnets, lesbians in leather chokers and fashion kids in creepers and hi-top fades, all dancing to Yazoo deep cuts and *Island Life*-era Grace Jones until getting kicked out at 4 a.m. In other words, there was nothing else like it.

And then, one by one, these clubs began to disappear, as if eradicated by a virus in the middle of the night. There are a multitude of reasons for these mass closures – and we don't have time to go into them here – but LGBTQ spaces became this rare and precious thing. There were no longer so many places to escape from reality or in which to lose your shit. In some ways it felt as if queer culture had turned inwards – existing online, in other people's flats, on our phones – and while some of that reflects the natural evolution of our times, I think there was definitely a sense of loss during those years, and maybe ever since.

NYC Downlow, Glastonbury's first-ever LGBTQ club – situated in the farthest reaches of the naughty corner – arrived in 2007, just as club culture in the rest of the country was beginning to falter. Launched by creative partners Stephen Gallagher and Gideon Berger, it was intended to be a campy, X-rated, 'homocentric' disco in a festival that was, until then, largely known for rock bands and rave music. The pair of them are set designers, so the first NYC Downlow was a film-set replica of a crumbling Lower East Side tenement block, meant to reflect the gay club 'golden era' of 1970s New York. In later years, the venue became an authentic reproduction of a warehouse in the Meatpacking District circa 1982, with fake pig carcasses hanging from the walls and butch men with hairy chests and moustaches pumping their biceps to throwback house music.

My first time at NYC Downlow – in the summer of 2015 – was a complete blur. At the time I was working for *Dazed & Confused* and had arranged to meet Stephen and

Gideon in a campervan to discuss their vision. We ended up getting deep into how gay culture had become pinkwashed in recent years and how Downlow was in some ways a response to gentrification, with all the most chaotic, alternative gay clubs in the city replaced by luxury flats, bank chains and branches of Pret a Manger. In essence, they wanted to create a space where people could have the freedom to do what they like – and be whoever they want – even if just for the weekend.

Later that night, I must have spent twelve hours straight in Downlow alone. What had begun with watching a troupe of drag queens in PVC bikinis lip-synching their way through a half-choreographed dance routine beneath purple strobes and dry ice (they do this every year) ended with me punching Florence Welch in the tit while flinging my arms around her too vigorously onstage during her secret set (they have one of these every year too; I always think it's going to be Grace Jones). By the time the sun had risen, I was slumped outside, cross-legged in the mud, marinating in warm Red Stripe, music still pumping inside, thinking to myself that this must be the best queer club in the country. I would say 'in the world', but I've not been to all the others yet – so other people can confirm that claim.

Sometime around 2010, NYC Downlow gave birth to Block9 – comprised of two other venues – which is what Stephen and Gideon have referred to as its 'older, straighter, butcher big brother'. First came the London Underground, a fifty-foot-tall warehouse space with a life-size tube train that genuinely looks like it's on fire bursting out of the side, intense dance music bouncing from within its walls. And three years later came Genosys, which is an outside venue that resembles a futuristic laser show, techno music blasting outside, geometric glass structures towering above you. I often think that those who are drawn to Genosys clearly party the hardest, because for some reason they're always still there, all hours of the day and night, stomping on the mud like zombies.

Each of these venues pushes the boundaries of what art and club culture can be, but NYC Downlow will always be my personal favourite.

Glastonbury is the most well-known and iconic festival in the world. After fifty years, it has become an institution. There have been films made about it. T-shirts. Books. It's on the news. On our TV screens. It's embedded into the fabric of British culture, like

football or sunburn or going, 'Wheeyyy!' when someone drops something. It is unusual, then, that Glastonbury has retained such a fierce political streak. We are used to mainstream events distancing themselves from the issues that affect us – maybe so as not to alienate attendees or piss off brands – but Glastonbury has only got louder and more outspoken as each year passes. This makes sense when we consider the counter cultural roots of the Festival alongside the trajectory of politics in the UK. If Glastonbury wasn't political, it wouldn't really be Glastonbury.

One of the clearest examples of this is Shangri-La, which is the first area you come across in the naughty corner. If you've never been to Shangri-La, it can best be described as this: a kind of nightmarish outdoor village full of twisting alleyways, dystopian installations, immersive theatre and men riding unicycles while handing out glowsticks. Vibes-wise, it's a mixture between 'Fright Night' at Thorpe Park and what Brexit coverage might be like if the BBC was overtaken by hackers and the whole thing glitched. The walls are smeared with anti-fascist messages and tongue-in-cheek slogans, coupled with a kind of 'glued this together at a dumpster' aesthetic that completely comes alive at night. In other words, it's the last place you want to end up if you're on hallucinogens or very anxious (aside from The Unfairground), but it's also one of the most beloved and interesting parts of the naughty corner.

That said, some of my most relaxing nights at Glastonbury have been connected to Shangri-La. In 2016 – at a time when festivals were only just beginning to address the problem of sexual assault, and male-dominated line-ups continued to persist – Shangri-La opened the first-ever women-only venue at Glastonbury, named The Sisterhood. Tucked inside what looked like a nail salon from the outside, you could knock on the door and pretend you had a nail appointment, before being invited into this womblike tent full of women dancing to J Hus, rolling around on velvet cushions and drinking mugs of gin below a huge disco ball. Crucially, The Sisterhood was an intersectional queer-, trans- and disability-inclusive space, open to all female-identifying people. And at a time when second-wave feminists were – and still are – often refusing to make room for all these facets of womanhood, it felt important that Glastonbury was leading by example.

So much of the naughty corner is like this. Small, imaginative venues buried within areas that are hard to find, or else huge, absurdly creative art constructions that respond to the outside world in unpredictable ways. In essence, though, it's the place you end up getting lost in after trekking down the railway tracks at night – which took you two hours because one of your friends got into an in-depth conversation about her asthma with an old woman called Karen who was dressed as an oak tree – and where you don't leave until the sky changes colour and you realise you need to eat a veggie hot dog, like, right now. The central identity of Shangri-La is political, perhaps, but mostly, like the rest of Glastonbury, you just go there to escape and have fun.

In 2017 my friend wrote an article about the two different sides of Glastonbury. First, he hung out with some of the wealthiest people in attendance, drinking champagne and glamping in their peaceful yurts. Next, he spent some time with those who clean the compost loos and urinals, driving trucks and downing instant coffee. None of this is relevant, other than the fact that, before his tour of the toilets, he waved goodbye at 6 p.m. and said he would return to his tent in a few hours. A few hours went by. Then some more. And some more. He didn't return until a day later, his clothes crumpled, his face and body completely splattered in multi-coloured paint, his eyes wide. When I asked him where he'd been, he just shook his head, perplexed, and mouthed something under his breath: 'The Unfairground'.

Obviously not everybody who ends up at The Unfairground accidentally gets spiked with acid by a toilet attendant taking them on a tour of the compost loos. But this particular image – of him bleary-eyed, breath-taken, face like a haunted plate – is what comes to mind when I think about some of the weirder sections of the naughty corner. The Unfairground – and Arcadia and The Common, which are directly across from it – are where you end up when you do not want to even slightly chill. They're places to dance, sure, but they're also places to lose your sense of time and phone and friends – but have fun anyway – and emerge victorious.

Apparently, these areas are comprised of over thirty venues, each playing everything from acid house to jungle and techno, but when I think about the times I've ended up there I can't really remember the music. I can just about recall seeing Mike Skinner in a purple tent spitting 'Fit But You Know It' in 2017, but mainly I recall giant spiders that spit fire (Arcadia) or mutant baby heads swaying in the wind (The Unfairground) or an actual neon-lit waterfall (The Common). These are absurd, bewildering spaces custom-built by set designers to make you think you have entered a new dimension, when in fact you've just walked across some rainy fields in Somerset in your wellies.

Everybody's experience of the naughty corner will be different. It's been around for nearly two decades, and in that time we've seen it go from a few circus-style dance tents to what now feels like a very small, weird town that only exists at night-time. It's a place where queer culture, nightlife, feminism, art, music and activism have come together over the years in ways that have no parallels in the outside world, let alone in festivals in general, and that's something to be celebrated.

Whenever I return from Glastonbury – despite having spent five days sleeping in a fabric house, living off crushed cereal bars and tinned peaches, and probably having touched another person's actual human shit at least once – I always feel peaceful, calmer and a little bit kinder to those around me. Glastonbury is chaotic and filthy and ridiculous, but it is also good-natured, easy-going and safe, and it reminds you of all the things that are important, like wearing a disposable poncho and drinking warm cider while Cyndi Lauper screams in the distance, or standing on a bin in a string vest while chanting, 'Bin! Bin! Bin!' to a confused crowd of onlookers, or kissing someone you've fancied for ages, or having your first pill, or getting lost in the naughty corner, high on mud and emotion, dancing in the dark.

GLASTONBURY FESTIVAL
of Contemporary Performing Arts

22-26 June 2016

'Oh, to capture just one drop of all the
ecstasy that swept that afternoon,
To paint that love upon a white balloon'
—D. Bowie

PYRAMID STAGE Muse ❀ Adele ❀ Coldplay ❀ Foals ❀ Tame Impala ❀ Beck ❀ Jeff Lynne's ELO ❀ ZZ Top ❀ Ellie Goulding
The Last Shadow Puppets ❀ Jess Glynne ❀ Madness ❀ Skepta ❀ Two Door Cinema Club ❀ Wolf Alice ❀ Laura Mvula ❀ Baaba Maal
Gregory Porter ❀ Rokia Traoré ❀ Squeeze ❀ Caravan Palace ❀ The Orchestra of Syrian Musicians with Damon Albarn & Guests
Lewisham and Greenwich NHS Choir ❀ Burnham and Highbridge Band

OTHER STAGE Disclosure ❀ New Order ❀ LCD Soundsystem ❀ PJ Harvey ❀ Bastille ❀ Chvrches ❀ Bring Me the Horizon
The 1975 ❀ Catfish and the Bottlemen ❀ James ❀ Editors ❀ Tom Odell ❀ Years & Years ❀ The Lumineers ❀ Band of Skulls
Jamie Lawson ❀ Frightened Rabbit ❀ Hurts ❀ Paul Heaton+Jacqui Abbott ❀ Christine and the Queens
St. Paul and the Broken Bones ❀ Bear's Den ❀ Blossoms ❀ Shura ❀ Newton Faulkner ❀ Haelos ❀ Anteros

WEST HOLTS STAGE Underworld ❀ James Blake ❀ Earth, Wind and Fire ❀ Róisín Murphy ❀ Santigold ❀ Gary Clark Jr
White Denim ❀ The Very Best ❀ Quantic All Stars ❀ Protoje ❀ Shibusashirazu Orchestra ❀ Anoushka Shankar ❀ Vince Staples
Mbongwana Star ❀ Michael Kiwanuka ❀ Dakhabrakha ❀ Little Simz ❀ Kamasi Washington ❀ Bixiga 70 ❀ Oddisee & Good Compny
Paradise Bangkok Molam International Band ❀ Anna Meredith ❀ Eska ❀ Human Pyramids

THE PARK STAGE Richard Hawley ❀ Philip Glass' Heroes Symphony ❀ Grimes ❀ Savages ❀ Mercury Rev ❀ Ronnie Spector
Floating Points (Live) ❀ Guy Garvey ❀ Daughter ❀ Ernest Ranglin & Friends ❀ Saint Etienne ❀ Ezra Furman ❀ Kurt Vile ❀ Kwabs
Unknown Mortal Orchestra ❀ Jagwar Ma ❀ Nathaniel Rateliff & the Night Sweats ❀ NAO ❀ Lady Leshurr ❀ Hinds ❀ Night Beats
Izzy Bizu ❀ C Duncan ❀ Declan McKenna ❀ Cat's Eyes ❀ Holly Macve ❀ Gwenno ❀ Car Seat Headrest ❀ Khruangbin

JOHN PEEL STAGE Sigur Ros ❀ M83 ❀ Jake Bugg ❀ AlunaGeorge ❀ Fatboy Slim ❀ Mac DeMarco ❀ Explosions in the Sky
Example ❀ Of Monsters and Men ❀ Jack Garratt ❀ John Grant ❀ Band of Horses ❀ Half Moon Run ❀ Mø ❀ Bat for Lashes ❀ Aurora
Lapsley ❀ Mystery Jets ❀ Rat Boy ❀ Alessia Cara ❀ Matt Corby ❀ Elle King ❀ Dua Lipa ❀ Tired Lion ❀ X Ambassadors
Nothing But Thieves ❀ Dan Stuart with Twin Tones ❀ Palace ❀ She Drew the Gun

ACOUSTIC STAGE Art Garfunkel ❀ Paul Carrack ❀ John Lees' Barclay James Harvest ❀ Cyndi Lauper ❀ Hothouse Flowers
Ralph McTell ❀ The Bootleg Beatles ❀ Fisherman's Friends ❀ Sharon Shannon ❀ Patty Griffin

SILVER HAYES Bicep ❀ Blackalicious ❀ Charlie Sloth ❀ Craig David's TS5 ❀ Dele Sosimi ❀ DJ Premier ❀ DJ Yoda ❀ Four Tet
Idris Elba ❀ Jungle by Night ❀ Kano ❀ Kovacs ❀ Lee Scratch Perry ❀ Levelz ❀ Mabel ❀ Mr Vegas ❀ Mura Masa ❀ Nadia Rose
Netsky Live ❀ Oliver Heldens ❀ Palms Trax ❀ Stormzy ❀ Tensnake

WILLIAMS GREEN Reef ❀ The View ❀ Beak> ❀ Syd Arthur ❀ The Temperance Movement ❀ Black Peaches
Meilyr Jones ❀ Georgia ❀ Pixx

AVALON STAGE Blackberry Smoke ❀ Corinne Bailey Rae ❀ KT Tunstall ❀ Newton Faulkner ❀ Show of Hands ❀ The Feeling
This Is The Kit ❀ Treacherous Orchestra ❀ Turin Brakes ❀ Will Young

THEATRE & CIRCUS Gravity and Other Myths ❀ The Infinite Monkey Cage, featuring: Prof. Brian Cox, Robin Ince & Ross Noble
Vou Dance Fiji ❀ Shappi Khorsandi ❀ The Demon Barbers ❀ Mik Artistik's Ego Trip ❀ Josh Widdicombe ❀ Umami Dancetheatre
The Natural Theatre Company ❀ Marcus Brigstocke ❀ Pirates of the Carabina: Flown ❀ John Hegley ❀ Murray Lachlan Young

THE GLADE Carl Cox ❀ Dubfire: Live Hybrid ❀ Example & DJ Wire ❀ Roni Size & DJ Krust ft Dynamite ❀ Stereo MCs
Funktion One Experimental Soundfield ❀ Plaid ❀ Danny Howells ❀ Ozric Tentacles ❀ Tristan ❀ Dub Pistols

LEFT FIELD Billy Bragg ❀ Tom Robinson ❀ The Selecter ❀ Rhoda Dakar ❀ The King Blues ❀ The Membranes
Man & the Echo ❀ Ferocious Dog ❀ Stick in the Wheel ❀ Jeremy Corbyn

KIDZ FIELD Basil Brush ❀ Dynamo ❀ Milkshake Live! ❀ Andy, Alex & Katy Cbeebies Odd Sox ❀ Art Ninja ❀ Professor Panic
Dynamic New Animation ❀ Rhubarb Theatre ❀ John Row ❀ Flying Seagull Project

ARCADIA Carl Cox ❀ Craig Charles ❀ Andy C ❀ Basement Jaxx ❀ DJ Hype ❀ Todd Terry ❀ Eats Everything ❀ Stanton Warriors

BLOCK9 Roger Sanchez ❀ The Black Madonna ❀ Mike Dunn ❀ Chez Damier ❀ Fast Eddie ❀ Joey Beltram ❀ DJ Deeon

THE COMMON Kate Tempest (Spoken Word) ❀ Delta Heavy ❀ The Upbeats ❀ Sub Focus ❀ Ben UFO + B2B + Job Jobse

SHANGRI-LA Caravan Palace ❀ Shy FX's Party on the Moon ❀ Nortec Collective (Mexico) ❀ Symphonica and Mr Switch

UNFAIRGROUND 808 State ❀ Plump DJs ❀ Jagz Kooner ❀ DJ Stivs ❀ Eddie Temple Morris ❀ Carl Cox

GLASTO LATINO Maykel Blanco Y Su Salsa Mayor ❀ Edwin Sanz All Stars ❀ Rumba Caliente ❀ Son Yambu

AND MANY MORE ACTS ACROSS OVER 100 STAGES!

Ancient Futures ❀ Babylon Uprising ❀ Bez'z Flying Bus ❀ The Beat Hotel ❀ Bimble Inn ❀ Croissant Neuf ❀ The Crows Nest ❀ Free University
of Glastonbury ❀ Glastonbury Free Press ❀ The Greencrafts Village ❀ Green Futures ❀ Greenpeace Field ❀ Groovy Movie Picture House ❀ The
Healing Field ❀ HMS Sweet Charity ❀ The House of Come Ons ❀ Mavericks ❀ Mutoid Waste Company ❀ Opening Night Wall of Fire (Weds)
The Outside Circus Stage ❀ The Peace Garden ❀ Pilton Palais ❀ Poetry&Words ❀ The Rabbit Hole ❀ Spaceport ❀ Speakers Forum ❀ The Spike
❀ Stonebridge Bar ❀ Strummerville at the Spinney ❀ The Temple ❀ Tor View Theatre ❀ The Totem Gardens ❀ Wall of Heaven ❀ The Wood

supporting GREENPEACE ❀ WaterAid ❀ Oxfam and other worthwhile causes

2016

CAPACITY: 203,500
TICKET PRICE: £228

The date of the historic EU referendum was confirmed in February, with voting set for the Thursday of the Festival; a stall was set up in Goose Hall crew catering to enable site workers to register to vote.

Multi-Grammy Award winner Adele – who'd joined Emily to watch Kanye West perform in 2015 and confirmed that she would headline the following year during his set – finally appeared. Meanwhile Muse headlined on Friday and on the Sunday night Coldplay became the first act to top the Glastonbury bill four times. Elsewhere, Disclosure, Shibusashirazu Orchestra, Grimes, Sigur Rós, Art Garfunkel, Explosions in the Sky, Craig David's TS5, Blackberry Smoke, Beck, ELO, ZZ Top and The 1975 were just some of the acts playing across the site.

The John Peel Stage moved up the hill to a new location and a new area was created in the adjacent woodland nature reserve: The Wood. The site continued to see new focal points erected by the Mutoid Waste Company, the Croissant Neuf solar-powered tent celebrated its thirtieth birthday and Block9 opened a new venue, Genosys.

This page: Coldplay on the Pyramid in 2016 (top) and Muse (left) in the same year.
Overleaf, clockwise from top left: After the referendum — Christine and the Queens on The Other Stage in 2016; ZZ Top prepare to take the Pyramid; the Kidzfield; Green Futures; The Healing Field; and Stormzy on the Sonic Stage in Silver Hayes.

Adele
Musician

Glastonbury for me — like many other people, I'm sure — isn't just a festival. Some of the most defining moments of my life have happened there, on every level. My happiest, wildest, fondest, weirdest, saddest, never-felt-better, lonely and enlightening moments. But one thing that I've never- ever felt there, is lost!

Plus, on top of all that range of emotions and the genuinely pivotal experiences that I've had there, there's the music. The smallest discoveries that you never hear of again; the squeezed and sweaty sets; the moment when you're one of a hundred thousand people just belting out a song at the top of your lungs; the perfect gentle serenade to the biggest hangover in a tiny, quiet field while you're stinking of bonfire, but it's the most comforting smell in the world. I feel like I've seen everyone I love or have ended up loving play Glastonbury at some point.

It's like the minute I set foot onto Worthy Farm I feel this mad energy and connection to the place and everyone there. I definitely don't have the ability or stamina to handle going annually any more. But when I do, I still feel it. I feel like I could be a kid again, wandering around and constantly looking for people but not caring.

I felt it when I headlined too, the buzz and calmness of knowing I was somewhere I knew. It made me feel safe and in good hands to face my biggest musical fear. The idea of headlining festivals freaks me out. So. Many. People. As nervous as I was, there was no other place I could have done it. There's no place like Glastonbury. It was the absolute highlight of my career and one of the greatest moments of my life!

GLAST☉NBURY 2017 FESTIVAL

21st JUNE - 25th JUNE

OF CONTEMPORARY PERFORMING ARTS
WORTHY FARM, PILTON, SOMERSET

RADIOHEAD   FOO FIGHTERS   ED SHEERAN

THE XX   THE NATIONAL   BIFFY CLYRO   KATY PERRY

BARRY GIBB   ROYAL BLOOD   STORMZY   CHIC

MAJOR LAZER   ALT-J   BOY BETTER KNOW   LORDE

SOLANGE   RUN THE JEWELS   LAURA MARLING   KRIS KRISTOFFERSON

THE JACKSONS   EMELI SANDÉ   PHOENIX   FIRST AID KIT

JUSTICE   ANDERSON .PAAK & THE FREE NATIONALS   HAIM

TOOTS & THE MAYTALS   FATHER JOHN MISTY   THE FLAMING LIPS

DIZZEE RASCAL   WARPAINT   BADBADNOTGOOD   METRONOMY

ANNIE MAC   KANO   GOLDFRAPP   SLEAFORD MODS   KATE TEMPEST

WILEY   HALSEY   THE CAN PROJECT   THUNDERCAT   THE AVALANCHES

CLEAN BANDIT   GEORGE EZRA   GLASS ANIMALS   COURTEENERS   SAMPHA

DJ SHADOW   LONDON GRAMMAR   RIDE   SONGHOY BLUES   LITTLE DRAGON

KAISER CHIEFS   WILD BEASTS   ANGEL OLSEN   THE LEMON TWIGS

NINES   MODERAT   RAG'N'BONE MAN   CRAIG DAVID   CIRCA WAVES

FUTURE ISLANDS   ANI DIFRANCO   NADIA ROSE   SHAGGY   TOVE LO

BRITISH SEA POWER   MARK LANEGAN   THE MOONLANDINGZ

GIRL RAY   FRANK CARTER & THE RATTLESNAKES   TEMPLES   DYNAMO

THE CINEMATIC ORCHESTRA   ALL WE ARE   SASHA & JOHN DIGWEED

JOE GODDARD   BOYS NOIZE   KURUPT FM   NOISIA   DECLAN MCKENNA

LOYLE CARNER   LISA HANNIGAN   BIRDY   MARTHA WAINWRIGHT

PLUS MANY MORE ACTS AND ATTRACTIONS TO BE ANNOUNCED ACROSS MORE THAN ONE HUNDRED STAGES!
SUPPORTING **OXFAM, WATERAID, GREENPEACE** AND OTHER WORTHY CAUSES

2017

CAPACITY: 203,500
TICKET PRICE: £238

Announcing their return with a surprise gig at the 850-capacity Cheese and Grain in Frome in January, the Foo Fighters finally headlined the Pyramid on the Saturday night. Meanwhile, Radiohead announced their Friday headline slot by painting a giant version of their logo on the grass in front of the Pyramid, which was spotted by viewers of the Festival's year-round site webcam. The year's other headliner was Ed Sheeran, who closed proceedings on the Pyramid on the Sunday night.

The Park celebrated its tenth birthday. It was joined by the newly created Cineramageddon, a drive-in movie space with over 200 vintage cars reimagined by the Mutoid Waste Company in the fields beyond The Park.

Bradley Cooper also recorded a scene for his upcoming blockbuster, *A Star is Born,* on the Pyramid, directly before Kris Kristofferson's Friday set.

Following the Festival, Glastonbury was able to distribute more than £3 million to good causes for the first time.

This page: Sunday headliner Ed Sheeran (top) and the Foo Fighters' Dave Grohl (left) on the Pyramid on the Saturday; a customised car in Cineramageddon (below).
Overleaf, clockwise from top left: The Flaming Lips onstage in The Park; Nile Rodgers on the Pyramid with Chic; The Unfairground by night; Barry Gibb; and Katy Perry.

THE KILLERS THE CURE STORMZY KYLIE JANET JACKSON

GEORGE EZRA LIAM GALLAGHER MILEY CYRUS TAME IMPALA

THE CHEMICAL BROTHERS VAMPIRE WEEKEND MS LAURYN HILL JANELLE MONAE

CHRISTINE AND THE QUEENS HOZIER TWO DOOR CINEMA CLUB JORJA SMITH

BASTILLE BILLIE EILISH SNOW PATROL SIGRID CAT POWER WU-TANG CLAN

ANNE-MARIE YEARS & YEARS SHERYL CROW THE GOOD, THE BAD & THE QUEEN

HOT CHIP STEFFLON DON JON HOPKINS THE STREETS TOM ODELL COURTEENERS

LIZZO KAMASI WASHINGTON IDLES ROSALIA JOHNNY MARR MAGGIE ROGERS

DIPLO MAVIS STAPLES REX ORANGE COUNTY BCUC LITTLE SIMZ LEWIS CAPALDI

MICHAEL KIWANUKA KATE TEMPEST LOYLE CARNER KING PRINCESS SLAVES

JUNGLE NENEH CHERRY KURT VILE & THE VIOLATORS THE COMET IS COMING FREYA RIDINGS

INTERPOL PALE WAVES FRIENDLY FIRES SHARON VAN ETTEN POND OCTAVIAN

BRING ME THE HORIZON THE LUMINEERS ROY AYERS MAC DEMARCO DAVE AURORA

SONS OF KEMET FAT WHITE FAMILY THIS IS THE KIT MARIBOU STATE TANK AND THE BANGAS

FATOUMATA DIAWARA BUGZY MALONE LOW SAM FENDER SHURA SLOWTHAI M8 BABYMETAL

PLUS MANY MORE ACTS AND ATTRACTIONS TO BE ANNOUNCED ACROSS MORE THAN ONE HUNDRED STAGES!
SUPPORTING **OXFAM, WATERAID, GREENPEACE** AND OTHER WORTHY CAUSES

GLASTONBURY
FESTIVAL 2019
26TH - 30TH JUNE

2019

CAPACITY: 203,500
TICKET PRICE: £248

With a new permanent licence approved by Mendip District Council in July 2018, the Festival spent the fallow year preparing for its return in 2019.

Following another fast ticket sale, the first news to emerge was a ban on single-use plastic drinks bottles on site (after more than a million were sold in 2017). Festival-goers were asked to bring (or buy) reusable water bottles to refill at the thirty-seven WaterAid kiosks and hundreds of drinking-water taps on site. The second announcement was that Stormzy would headline the Pyramid Stage. Other highlights included Kylie's long-awaited fulfilment of her Glastonbury dream in the Sunday legend slot; huge crowds for Billie Eilish, Lizzo and Miley Cyrus (who also persuaded her dad to join her for one song); plus The Killers (Saturday) and The Cure (Sunday) headlining the Pyramid.

Sir David Attenborough reinforced his commitment to climate-change action from the Pyramid Stage, three days after Extinction Rebellion and Greenpeace had joined Glastonbury's procession from The Park to The Green Fields. Festival-goers also welcomed 2019's new installations: Arcadia's Pangea; Glastonbury-on-Sea; and Block9's stunning IICON.

This page: The human-formed Extinction Rebellion logo in the King's Meadow calling for action on climate change (top), and broadcaster Sir David Attenborough makes an appearance on the Pyramid Stage on Sunday afternoon.
Overleaf: Arcadia's Pangea lights up the south-west corner in its debut year.

Clockwise from top left: Stormzy on the Pyramid; Block9's IICON; Kylie Minogue; The Killers' Brandon Flowers; The Cure's Robert Smith; and Billie Eilish on The Other Stage, Glastonbury 2019.
Overleaf: The greatest show on earth — Glastonbury 2017 captured from space.

Thank you to all the crews that create this show – there are so many of you who aren't named in this book but who have been such an integral part of the Festival for so many years.

Thanks also to the hundreds of thousands of people who come along and make Glastonbury what it is, giving us endless support through the highs and lows. You are the best audience in the world!

Thank you to Anna Valentine, Lucie Stericker, Natalie Dawkins, Julyan Bayes, Cathy Dunn and all at Orion for your enthusiasm, support and patience in bringing this mammoth project together.

For the endless days and nights ploughing through fifty years of photographs – and for remaining patient and calm throughout! – huge thanks to our devoted picture editor Rachael Hunt.

Big thanks also to George Webb, who helped hugely just when we needed it, and to Dave Henderson for all his work on the yearly entries.

Extra thanks to John Shearlaw for the yearly pieces, editing, captions, cuttings and archive. Also for his spirit and coffee/ reggae vibes.

And to Chris Salmon for the mountain of interviews, writing, editing, deadline-keeping, steer and after-hours work bringing this whole thing together.

To Aoife Dick for keeping the project afloat, fact checking and editing pieces with an eagle eye.

And also to the many artists who have contributed over the years including Kurt Jackson, Stanley Donwood and Alister Sieghart.

And last but not least, to Nick Dewey for all the written contributions, art direction, music timeline, endless guidance, love and support.

Left: A view of the Pyramid field by longstanding Glastonbury Festival artist Kurt Jackson.

This edition first published in Great Britain in 2019 by
Trapeze • an imprint of the Orion Publishing Group Ltd • Carmelite House • 50 Victoria Embankment • London EC4Y 0DZ
An Hachette UK Company

1 3 5 7 9 10 8 6 4 2

The author and publishers would like to thank the following for permission to reproduce their photographs:

Andrew Allcock pp215, 234, 249, 254, 259, 260, 261, 267, 274, 285, 300, 301; Stephen Angell pp209, 231; Anna Barclay pp243, 297, 300, 301; Alamy/Adam Beeson p77; Alamy/MARKA pp29, 150, Alamy/Pictorial Press Ltd p92, Alamy/Edd Westmacott p200; Paul Assinder Photography pp97, 102, 103, 119, 123, 164, 165; Architects Journal p50; Liam Bailey pp116-117, 133, 135, 143, 153, 159, 164, 165, 170, 210, 222-223; Photos courtesy of Banksy/Pest Control Office pp188, 189; Bauer Media p181; Steve Bayfield pp6, 37, 38, 39; Brendan Bell p227; Polly Birkbeck pp130, 131; Andi Blake Via rockarchive.com p289; Jason Bryant pp164, 169, 173, 177,183, 188, 197, 189, 213, 214, 220, 237, 273, 276, 230, 231, 255, 263, 267, 273, 281, 285, 290, 300, 301; Bleddyn Butcher p156; Camera Press/David Dagley p27, Camera Press/Steve Double pp114, 128, 136, 137, 139, 144-145, 146, 187, 226, Camera Press/Scarlet Page p149, Camera Press/Ron Reid pp15, 24-25, 34, Camera Press/Adrian Sherrat p245, Camera Press/Mark Shenley p245, Camera Press/Paul Slattery pp38, 77, 78-79,144-145; Matt Cardy pp175, 189, 199, 201, 213, 219, 289, 297, 300, 301; Stuart Roy Clarke pp100-101, 211, 227, 231, 300; Ann Cook pp151, 161, 162, 191, 202, 203, 230; Tony Cordy p103; 'Record image taken from the triple album set, "Revelations" 1973. Produced by John Coleman and Barry Everitt pp6-7; Daily Mail p50; Simon Davies p61; Clive Farndon pp128, 133, 164, 165, 231, 301; Grant Fleming pp124, 125, 162; Allan Gregorio p280; © Jill Furmanovsky via rockarchive.com pp113, 127, 141, 142, 154-155, 165, 192, 219, 230, 231, 244, 248, 254, 259, 273, 277, 291, 296, 300; Lucinda Garland p193; Adam Gasson pp178-197, 217, 262; Jo Gedrych courtesy Ian Anderson p23; Charles Gervais pp265, 267, 300; Getty/Matt Cardy pp200, 211, 227; Getty/David Corio pp65, 66, Getty/DigitalGlobe p299, Getty/Jim Dyson pp171, 228-229, 257, 263, 300, 301; Getty/Shirlaine Forrest pp271, 284, 296, Getty/GAB Archive p33, 120-121, 136, 137, 141, 149, 150, 158,161 Getty Images/Ian Gavan p286, Getty/Martin Godwin p214, Getty/Rune Hellestad pp231, 290, Getty/Samir Hussein pp241, 277, 283, 297 Getty/Mick Hutson p244, Getty/Hayley Madden p214, Getty/Naki p214, Getty/Leon Neal pp247, 296, Getty/Martin Philbey p195, Getty/Photofusion p195, Getty/Michael Putland p87, Getty/Brian Raisic p253, Getty/Oli Scarff pp273,301, Getty/Pete Still p184, Getty/Jon Super p183,184, 187, 191, 197, 209, Getty/Gary Wolstenholme p259; Glastonbury Festival pp6, 7, 8, 9, 10, 11, 14, 16, 20, 36, 44, 45, 47, 48, 50, 51, 53, 54, 55, 56-57, 58, 64, 70, 73, 76, 80, 82, 84, 86, 87, 88, 89, 90, 94-95, 96, 102, 108, 114, 118, 122, 123, 127, 126, 131, 134, 140, 147, 148, 152, 160, 164,165, 172, 174, 176, 182, 190, 196, 200, 204, 208, 212, 218, 230, 231, 235 238, 239, 240, 246, 252, 258, 264, 272, 281, 282, 285, 288, 292, 300, 301, Glastonbury Festival/BBC p225; Glastonbury Festival/Martin Elbourne p300, Glastonbury Festival/Clare Elsan p300, Glastonbury Festival/Beth Greenwood p300,Glastonbury Festival/Chloe Gamble p301; Glastonbury Festival/Jaz House p300, Glastonbury Festival/Luke Piper p301, Glastonbury Festival/Emma Reynolds p241, Glastonbury Festival/Solstice Capers p30, Glastonbury Festival/Hannah Walker p301; Roddy Glasse p97, 99, 164, 165, 255, 285; Mike Goldwater pp72, 111, 198, 199, 206; David Green of Fosse Studios pp12, 21, 22, 23; Judy Green p60; © Greenpeace pp230, 151; Alan Gregorio p280; Koichi Hanafusa pp46, 67, 69, 71, 72, 73, 82, 83, 91,102, 103, 128, 136, 156, 164, 165, 191, 231; Bill Harkin p15; Marcus Haney pp253, 259, 283; Bill de la Hey p163; Mark Hughs (Taff) pp121, 128, 165, Daisy Jones p279; Richard Paul Jones p231; Ramona Carraro p291; Kenji Kubo courtesy of Koichi Hanafusa p69; Stefan Lange pp59, 60, 93, 115; Lauren Laverne p225; David Lavene p293, 300, 301; Jane Lee p12; Barry Lewis pp202, 203, 206, 207, 230, 231, 248, 250-251, 265, 27 5; Jacob Love p254; Lukonic p294; Mary McCartney pp266, 284, 300, 301; Stella McCartney pp300, 301; Mirrorpix pp50, 51, 115, Mirrorpix/Bristol Post p65, Mirror Pix/Central Somerset Gazette p14, Mirror Pix/Shepton Mallet Journal pp14, 16; NME pp50,114, 115, 180. 181; News Group p110; News UK/News Licencing p221; Orion/Glastonbury Festival pp44, 45, 48, 52, 71, 104,105; NME/Len Brown p50; NME/Getty/Kevin Cummings p115; Oxfam/Jillian Edelstein p237; Oxfam/Zed Nelson p177; PA Images/James Arnold p184, PA Images/Anthony Devlin p205, PA Images/Jonny Green p236, PA Images/Yui Mok p247; Peter Podworski p268; Paul Misso pp32, 41, 42, 43,86; Royston 'Stone' Naylor p127; Gabi Pape p31; Andre Pattenden p293; Iwona Pinkowitz pp287, 301; Mervyn Rands p42; Derek Ridgers p114; Reuters p99; SWNS p300; Chris Salmon p230, 231, 256, 276; David Scott 1944-2001 pp38, 39, 42, 43, 60, 73, 164, 256; Shutterstock pp50, 91, 300; Brennan Simpson- for Daily Mail p300; Jackie Slade pp107, 164, 165; Matthew Smith pp47, 97, 98, 102, 164, 165, 168, 192, 193, 185, 205, 213, 223, 230, 231, 263, 281; Ian Sumner p74-75, 77, 81, 143; The Sun/News Licensing p17; Diana Temperley p4-5, Matilda Temperley p120; The Times p181; Brian Walker pp2-3, 13, 16, 17, 18-19, 34, 35, 37, 55, 60, 66, 82, 83, 91, 109, 119, 123; Conde Nast/Tim Walker p157; Andy Willsher pp205, 211; Ray Yates pp91,164, 209, 230; YOUTH CLUB/Peter Anderson p63; Cassette courtesy of Crispin Aubrey and family p89.

Reproduction of Scorcher, Femi Kuti on the Pyramid stage, Glastonbury 2010 © Kurt Jackson, contemporary environmental artist and Glastonbury Festival artist in residence since 1999 p302-303

Endpapers illustrated by Stanley Donwood

A CIP catalogue record for this book is available from the British Library.

Hardback ISBN: 978 1 4091 8393 8 • Ebook ISBN: 978 1 4091 8394 5

Printed in Italy

FSC
www.fsc.org

MIX
Paper from responsible sources
FSC® C104740

www.orionbooks.co.uk